FASHIONING INDIE

Dress cultures

Series Editors: Reina Lewis & Elizabeth Wilson

Advisory Board: Christopher Breward, Hazel Clark, Joanne Entwistle, Caroline Evans, Susan Kaiser, Angela McRobbie, Hiroshi Narumi, Peter McNeil, Özlem Sandikci, Simona Segre Reinach

Dress Cultures aims to foster innovative theoretical and methodological frameworks to understand how and why we dress, exploring the connections between clothing, commerce and creativity in global contexts.

Published

Delft Blue to Denim Blue:
Contemporary Dutch Fashion
edited by Anneke Smelik

Dressing for Austerity: Aspiration,
Leisure and Fashion in Post War Britain
by Geraldine Biddle-Perry

Experimental Fashion: Performance
Art, Carnival and the Grotesque Body
by Francesca Granata

Fashion in European Art: Dress and
Identity, Politics and the Body,
1775–1925
edited by Justine De Young

Fashion in Multiple Chinas: Chinese
Styles in the Transglobal Landscape
edited by Wessie Ling and Simona
Segre Reinach

Modest Fashion: Styling Bodies,
Mediating Faith
edited by Reina Lewis

Styling South Asian Youth Cultures:
Fashion, Media and Society
edited by Lipi Begum, Rohit K.
Dasgupta and Reina Lewis

Thinking Through Fashion: A Guide to
Key Theorists
edited by Agnès Rocamora and
Anneke Smelik

Veiling in Fashion: Space and the
Hijab in Minority Communities
by Anna-Mari Almila

Wearing the Cheongsam: Dress and
Culture in a Chinese Diaspora
By Cheryl Sim

Reina Lewis: reina.lewis@fashion.arts.ac.uk
Elizabeth Wilson: elizabethwilson.auth@gmail.com

FASHIONING INDIE

POPULAR FASHION, MUSIC AND GENDER

Rachel Lifter

BLOOMSBURY VISUAL ARTS
LONDON • NEW YORK • OXFORD • NEW DELHI • SYDNEY

BLOOMSBURY VISUAL ARTS
Bloomsbury Publishing Plc
50 Bedford Square, London, WC1B 3DP, UK
1385 Broadway, New York, NY 10018, USA
29 Earlsfort Terrace, Dublin 2, Ireland

BLOOMSBURY, BLOOMSBURY VISUAL ARTS and the Diana logo are
trademarks of Bloomsbury Publishing Plc

First published in Great Britain 2020
This paperback edition published in 2021

Copyright © Rachel Lifter, 2020

Rachel Lifter has asserted her right under the Copyright, Designs
and Patents Act, 1988, to be identified as Author of this work.

For legal purposes the Acknowledgments on pp. xi–xii constitute an
extension of this copyright page

Series design by BRILL
Cover image: SolStock/Getty Images

A catalogue record for this book is available from the British Library.

A catalog record for this book is available from the Library of Congress.

ISBN: HB: 978-1-3501-2632-9
PB: 978-1-3502-3807-7
ePDF: 978-1-3501-2633-6
eBook: 978-1-3501-2634-3

Series: Dress Cultures

Typeset by RefineCatch Limited, Bungay, Suffolk

To find out more about our authors and books visit www.bloomsbury.com
and sign up for our newsletters.

To my parents

CONTENTS

Contents

LIST OF ILLUSTRATIONS

Acknowledgments

Fashioning Indie is the product of two stages of research and writing, two stages of my life. The project began as a PhD thesis at London College of Fashion, University of the Arts London, where I worked under the supervision of Reina Lewis, Agnès Rocamora and Joanne Entwistle. As I wrote in my thesis acknowledgments, their work sets standards for scholarship on fashion, and I am thrilled to have had the privilege of studying with them. At LCF, I was part of a growing community of fashion research students. I am very lucky to have shared ideas with Serkan Delice, Morna Laing, Ane Lynge-Jorlén, Felice McDowell, Marco Pecorari, Mario Roman and Monica Titton. At this time, I also was working in the Department of Cultural Studies at London College of Fashion, and I am grateful for the academic companionship from my colleagues there. In particular, I want to thank my teaching mentor, Janice Miller, my mentor and guide in all things pop culture, Sina Shamsavari, and Neil Kirkham, who traveled with me to many of my research sites.

The project became a book while I was working in the School of Art and Design History and Theory at Parsons School of Design, The New School. I am indebted to Dean Sarah Lawrence, who supported my research and paved a way for my early career development. I am honored to have worked alongside the faculty of the MA Fashion Studies program at Parsons – Hazel Clark, Heike Jenss, Francesca Granata, Christina Moon and Charlene Lau – who helped me see myself as a scholar, colleague and mentor to aspiring fashion thinkers. I met Victoria Pass at a conference in 2013 and, since then, have benefited from her fashion knowledge and thoughtful editing. I also have had the opportunity to work in the Fashion Department at Pratt Institute and the School of Fashion at Parsons. I am grateful to Jennifer Minniti and Emily Mader at Pratt and Neil Gilks, Brendan McCarthy and Markus Huemer at Parsons for giving me the chance to emerge from the dark corners of the library and into light-filled design studios, as this project came to its conclusion.

I could not have risen to the challenge of writing this book without help. I am indebted to Reina Lewis and Elizabeth Wilson, the Dress Cultures series editors, for supporting my work. From the beginning of my PhD through the completion of this book, Reina has been a *sublime* mentor and guide through the obstacle course of research and writing. I greatly appreciate the patience of Philippa Brewster, the commissioning editor from I.B. Tauris, and the support of Frances Arnold, Yvonne Thouroude and the production team at Bloomsbury.

This book is enriched by the thoughtful and generous insights of my interviewees and the beautiful work of the photographers, who let me reproduce their images. Thank you to Diane Allford, Steven Bethell, Doug Brod, Amber Butchart, Simbarashe Cha, Michelle Egiziano, Adham Faramawy, Rob Flowers, Christian Joy, Jenna Rossi-Camus, Driely S., Dean Sidaway, and Don Stahl, as well as the many people, who kindly spoke to me about their dress practices and the photographers I met at Afropunk Fest, who shared with me their views on the festival.

I am very lucky to have a wonderful network of friends and family, who have offered me in equal parts interest in my work and distraction from it. In particular, I would like to thank Helen Kim, who is the very best of editors and friends; my sister and brother-in-law, Abby and Eric Hochberg, and my dear nieces; and Don Stahl, who has shown me love and life in New York these past few years. Finally, I want to thank my parents, John and Karin Lifter, for their unwavering support for me and my fashionable interests. I dedicate this book to them, with love, admiration and gratitude.

INTRODUCTION

This book is about how indie transformed from a niche British music scene into a twenty-first-century international fashion phenomenon, informing the sartorial aesthetics and fashionable identities of a generation of young people in Britain, North America, and beyond. It explores how the indie look was commodified, sold in designer collections, high street stores, and second-hand shops. It examines how the indie look was embraced by the fashion media, mobilized to articulate emerging ideals of masculinity and femininity. And it shows how—amid these market and representational shifts—what it means to do and be indie also changed. In the twenty-first century, indie is about making and listening to music, going to gigs and summer music festivals; it is also about dressing up at those festivals and getting one's picture taken by friends, amateur street style bloggers and even professional photographers working for the fashion media. That the practices of listening to music and dressing up in photo-ready ensembles are gendered male and female, respectively, reveals that indie's transformation from British music scene to international fashion phenomenon is also a gendered transformation.

Fashioning Indie is best read as a cultural history, spanning from the early 1980s until 2018 with the greater part of the analysis focused on the period after 2005. It tracks the indie look from its origins in the dingy venues and independent record shops of 1980s Britain; through indie rocker Pete Doherty and supermodel Kate Moss' appearance at the Glastonbury festival in 2005; to high street festival fashion collections and proliferating media coverage of California's Coachella festival and Brooklyn's Afropunk Fest in the 2010s. I identify 2005 as the point when the figure of the indie rocker was thrust to the center of popular fashion; however, it actually marked the end point of a gradual process by which the indie music scene, the indie look, and the slender male bodies, on which this look was articulated, had been gaining visibility within popular fashion culture (Chapter 1). The remainder of the book explores how twenty-first-century indie is produced through the market and representational practices of contemporary neoliberal consumer culture. I take my cue here from Dick Hebidge's discussion of what he calls the commercial and ideological forms of subcultural incorporation.[1] By the commercial form he means "the conversion of subcultural signs (dress, music, etc.) into mass-produced objects," and with the ideological form he speaks of "the 'labelling' and re-definition of deviant behavior by dominant groups—the police, the media, the judiciary."[2] Hebdige thus offers methodological directions through which to explore the intersection of a subculture and the commercial fashion industry: to focus on, first, the "real network or infrastructure of new kinds of commercial and economic institutions" that make money from the sale of subcultural signifiers[3] and, second, the institutions of meaning-making that shape how such signifiers work, how they carry and create cultural knowledge. Taking up this methodological prompt, across the chapters I examine how the twenty-first-century indie look is materialized through the merchandizing strategies of designer collections, high street stores and second-hand clothing shops and how it is narrated in popular music and fashion magazines. I also explore how this post-incorporated indie is performed through dress practice. Whereas Hebdige was concerned with "the subversive implications of style"[4] and how those modes of stylistic subversion could be recuperated by dominant culture, he was less concerned with what such acts of recuperation produce in turn. In this book, I am keen to explore, first, how the representational and market practices that transform indie also produce new forms of subjectivity and, second, whether and how young men and women take up these new subjectivities. Here, I am drawing on the work of Michel Foucault, who offers frameworks for thinking about the subject as produced through discursive and institutional practices,[5] on the one hand, and the subject as actively productive of itself, on the other.[6] I consider dress as a Foucauldian "practice of the self," a means of inventing the self: in this instance, through decisions about what clothes to buy, where to buy them, and how to wear them. This dialogue between the commercial market and young people's dress practices—specifically: an exploration of how the former offers models for practice that are taken up by the latter—stands at the center of analysis in the remaining chapters.[7] Chapter 2 focuses on the male indie rocker as a new figure of fashion and the discomfort this status created for some male participants in indie; Chapters 3 and 4 examine the phenomenon of festival fashion and the stylizations of femininity it both idealizes and demands from its participants; and Chapter 5 considers transformations in both second-hand retail and alternative consumption practices that parallel to and intersect with the story of indie.

No longer subcultural in form, twenty-first-century indie continues to signify in and through the tropes of authenticity and individuality. The slender, male indie silhouette that came to fashionable prominence in the mid-2000s is read as a challenge to prevailing fashion ideals of masculinity; the summer music festival is framed as an opportunity for young women to buck fashion convention and display their individual style; and second-hand garments continue to be valued as authentic and unique, even when they are mass-reproduced and reconsumed. The complexity of twenty-first-century indie's "alternative" status lies in the fact that it is manufactured, produced, and given meaning within the global, commercial fashion market. How should one understand this contradiction? By contextualizing it within broader economic and cultural shifts in the fashion industry and its relationship to subcultural practice. Angela McRobbie recently identified "the immense commercial value emerging out of 'subcultural theory,'" noting that, in the 2010s, students, freelance designers and even multinational brands use subcultural languages to articulate their professional identities and to position themselves within the fashion market.[8] "What [is] needed," she continues, is "a meta-critique, one that ... could show how capitalism replenishes itself by conceding ground and admonishing itself under the impact of the ... pop or subcultural critique."[9] This book offers this meta-critique as a context for understanding twenty-first-century indie and the fashionable identities that form within it. It shows how the fashion system has incorporated subcultural language into its own meaning-making systems and now offers spaces within the market through which alternative cultural objects and identities can form. Specifically, it shows how "style," once theorized as a practice of subcultural identity-making and resistance-staging, has become a historically specific fashionable ideal, pervasive throughout the twenty-first-century market, shaping identities within indie and beyond. Although this account might read like a dim prognosis, the final incorporation of subcultural language and practice into capitalism, *Fashioning Indie* illuminates new forms of popular cultural politics that can emerge from and within a commercial fashion industry obsessed with all things "subcultural."

How this book works

The term "indie" is an abbreviation of the word "independent," originally coined to refer to the independent music scene that emerged in the wake of punk in the United Kingdom during the late 1970s and early 1980s.[10] Since the early 1980s, however, indie music culture has transformed several times over. In Chapter 1, I chart this evolution, winding through various stages of indie's international development: the independent music scene of the 1980s; the Britpop revolution of the 1990s; and the downtown rock scene in early 2000s New York City. To an extent, this history has been covered already in various music cultural histories and pop star memoirs.[11] What Chapter 1 adds is a focus on fashion. Looking at music, style, and fashion media, I track changes in both who was representing indie music culture and how indie music culture was represented. Whereas in the 1980s only the music press would discuss indie, in the 1990s and 2000s first the alternative style press and later the high fashion and broadsheet presses began to produce discourse on indie musicians and the indie look. Contingent on such representational shifts, the male indie musician, who was cast in the 1980s as an almost-comically childish figure, was reimagined in the 1990s as a rock 'n' roll sex god and in the 2000s as a fashion icon. Throughout the chapter, I am keen to emphasize the processes of exclusion by which the indie figure was imagined and reimagined: for example, by delimiting popular music references to only those bands that were part of a white, British rock tradition. In addition to whiteness, I also address the varying forms of visibility that were afforded to female musicians at different moments in indie music culture's history as well as how a rivalry between the middle-class members of Blur and the working-class members of Oasis underpinned the formation of rock 'n' roll masculinity in Britpop. In short, I contextualize indie music culture's rejection of the sounds and styles of the mainstream within the processes of gender-, ethnic-, and class-based exclusions, through which this rejection was articulated. As such, Chapter 1 offers a historical backdrop for the remainder of the book. In the twenty-first century, some of the exclusions through which the indie figure was idealized in the 1980s and 1990s ceased to exercise their constitutive power, as fashion—and festival fashion in particular—transformed indie into a market-driven cultural space, within which both white and black women were recognized as ideal subjects.

Chapters 2, 3, and 4 examine how indie identities were fashionably reimagined through fashion discourses and market practices post-2005. Chapter 2 focuses on the newly fashionable indie rocker. Central within my discussion is French fashion designer and fine art photographer Hedi Slimane, for it was he who translated the indie rocker's look into successful collections for Dior Homme, which then informed the visual imagery of both fashion and music throughout the following decade. Slimane's photographs of British indie musicians, taken between the years 2003 and 2007, offer a vantage point into the processes of how he commodified the indie look.[12] As Nick Rees-Roberts argues, Slimane's photography functions "to focus his design work by accentuating its tonal qualities and distinct visual identity."[13] From Slimane's photographs of the London indie music scene, an idealized indie figure emerges—the focus of Chapter 2. The incarnation of the bohemian spirit of Britain's earliest white rock 'n' roll stars, Slimane's indie figure was imbued with an authenticity seemingly stemming from his ability to reveal his true persona within performance and through his appearance. And yet, Slimane's indie figure was, in fact, the commercial product of a savvy designer with a keen eye for marketing and merchandizing. Drawing on textual analysis and interviews with nineteen young, male participants in indie music culture, whom I interviewed in 2009, I go on to examine the varying strategies by which musicians and fans responded to this ambivalent recoding of indie masculinity. Taking my cue from Simon Frith and Howard Horne's discussion of rock and pop sensibilities, I coin the term fashion sensibility to account for those strategies that successfully negotiated the authenticity–fashion tension.[14] For musicians, demonstrating a fashion sensibility involved an elaborate media game of being styled in the "right" designer garments for press coverage. To make this argument, I conducted interviews with two former editors at the American music magazine *Spin* concerning how the magazine visualized indie musicians through editorial spreads. Their interviews reveal, moreover, that not only musicians and fans, but also magazines were attempting to capitalize on indie's newfound fashion status. From 2006 to 2011, by clothing musicians in designer garments, *Spin* attempted to reposition itself within the magazine market and attract fashion advertisers. As a result, indie musicians' decisions about how to represent themselves within media were informed by Slimane's intervention *and* magazine market practices. For fans, exhibiting a fashion sensibility meant mobilizing what Agnès Rocamora calls "fashion capital": specifically, an ability to fashion oneself in a Slimane-inspired look in such a way that it seemed second nature, *not* like one was simply following a trend.[15] Very few of my male respondents were able to do this. Indeed, negotiating the conflicting demands of authenticity and fashion proved a tall order.

In contrast, the art of balancing the conflicting demands of alternative style and popular fashion cultures is central to festival fashion, both as a site-specific dress practice and as a globe-circulating, commercially manufactured, popular fashion trend. According to fashion media lore, festival fashion was born in 2005, when British supermodel Kate Moss attended Glastonbury with bad boy indie rocker Pete Doherty, who was then her boyfriend, their looks documented by numerous paparazzi. Of particular interest to the fashion presses of the period was Moss' pairing of rain boots (i.e. "wellies")—necessary footwear to protect oneself against Glastonbury's notoriously muddy fields—with hotpants on one day and a vintage, gold micro-dress on another. The combination of rain boots and butt-skimming garments became a formula for festival dressing in the years following, often even when there was no threat of inclement weather. From 2010, the festival look evolved. With the rise in visibility of the Coachella Festival, held in the desert of Indio Valley, California since 1999, the look shifted away from the wet weather-inspired Glastonbury aesthetic to a desert-oriented "boho chic," sun-goddess look, characterized by bangle bracelets and leather-fringed bags, waistcoats, shorts, and booties. This shift in aesthetic foretells an internationalization of British indie music culture, and the widespread visibility of Coachella's fashionable female attendees played a role in this internationalization. British indie music culture had been made visible in certain ways before the exponential rise in popularity of its summer music festivals: through music media images of Britpop, for example. Festival fashion imagery circulates differently and more widely than music media, however, not least because of a broadening of the mediascape in the twenty-first century to include digital platforms, such as magazine websites, personal style blogs, and Instagram. As a result of this new visibility, new processes of identity formation have emerged within indie, which have less to do with music and more with fashion. That division between music and fashion is and historically has been gendered. Women have limited recognition within music culture. As Janice Miller writes, popular music is produced by an "industry which largely values female musicians as visual images rather than producers of music." She continues, "the patterns of female behavior that are sanctioned by the music industry echo the roles and behaviors stereotypically legitimated for women in Western society generally."[16] The meaning-shaping worlds of music journalism, production, and A&R have also been dominated by men,[17] although Simon Frith counters that there are other influential roles within the music industry—his example is rock photographers—that are played by women.[18] I take up Frith's point in Chapter 2, when I consider the critical influence of the female photo editor of *Spin* over the look of twenty-first-century male indie musicians. In contrast, fashion stands as a feminized cultural form, the association of women and fashion going back to some of the earliest writings on it.[19] So, whereas music creates limited visibilities for women, fashion offers a bigger space for the representation and performance of femininities. Of course, the modes of femininity promoted through fashion are conflicting and conflicted, and the fashion and beauty industries are routinely identified as wrongdoers within discussions of female body discipline and lack of diverse representation.[20] Those critiques can be leveraged at festival fashion, too, and I take them up in Chapters 3 and 4. But what I want to argue is that, through the proliferation of British summer music festivals and, as a result, the expansion of festival fashion as a set of visual images, material objects, and performative practices, new spaces have opened up for women to become visible within indie music culture.

In the first part of Chapter 3, I analyze media images and store collections to chart the emergence and growth of festival fashion as a trend, highlighting how it has become a marketing trope used to sell goods. Over this same period, individual style emerged as a new form of fashion doxa. Here, is where the story of indie's incorporation intersects with a broader narrative on the commodification of "style." The period 2005–15 witnessed the proliferation of street style imagery and the emergence of personal style blogging. Street style has been around since 1980, when *i-D* magazine was established and made this particular photographic style its "visual signature."[21] Nonetheless, with the rise of fashion's digitalscape in the twenty-first century, street style images have proliferated, both on independently owned and operated blogs and on established magazines' digital platforms. As Rocamora astutely notes, "blogs … have given [street style] a new visibility, to the point that it has become tightly associated with the fashion blogosphere as if no other media before it had represented it."[22] This period of fashion's digitization also saw the rise of personal style blogging. Underpinning these ascendant forms of digital fashionable representation is the ideal of individual style. Individual style is a pernicious ideal. It demands that women meet the criteria set out by the fashion industry, and yet it purports to be an expression of personal taste. Why does this broader story of the rise of the ideal of individual style matter to the story of indie? The ideal subject of festival fashion is—alongside the street style subject and the personal style blogger—an ideal subject of the fashion discourse on individual style, artfully combining first- and second-hand garments into looks that are both "unique" and festival-ready. Drawing from interviews with twenty-seven young women, which I collected in 2009, I consider how and to what extent living women inhabited this ideal subject position. Only those women who possessed what I call alternative fashion capital were able to take up the truths of festival fashion and inhabit the ideal of individual style. Thus, far from representing the fashion of "real" people, the ideal of individual style is just that: an ideal that worships certain bodies and identities over others: i.e. white, fashionable ones.

Although the term gender is prioritized in the book's subtitle, *Fashioning Indie* takes an intersectional approach to the analysis of identity. Like most youth and popular cultural research, youth is assumed across the chapters. Class and ethnicity are addressed in my discussion of Britpop in Chapter 1. Analyzed across all the chapters, moreover, are racialized gender identities. Chapters 2 and 3 reveal that the overwhelming whiteness of indie music culture, identified in Chapter 1, persists in the indie rocker of Slimane's imagination and the idealized female figures of Glastonbury and Coachella. In the early 2010s, however, a discursive space opened up within festival fashion media representations to acknowledge the black festival attendee. To explore this process, Chapter 4 turns attention to Afropunk Fest and the stylish bodies who represent the festival throughout the fashion media at the end of August each year since 2013. Afropunk Fest is a two-day music event that has been held in Brooklyn's Commodore Barry Park since 2005. Due to the recent popularity of the festival, Afropunk Fests have been established in Paris, Atlanta, London, and Johannesburg, as well. The festival features only those musicians and groups with black singers, and the crowd of attendees is also predominantly African-American. In recent years, attendees' ensembles have received media recognition; their looks are understood as decidedly unique takes on what are by now the well-worn tropes of the festival look. In the first part of this chapter, I identify and examine the contemporary Afropunk Fest look as a historically specific articulation of black style. Here, I follow Stuart Hall, Kobena Mercer, and Monica Miller, who have in different ways explored black style as a hybrid form, combining both "authentically" black features with aspects from dominant white culture—a syncretism that is at the heart of diasporic cultural production.[23] Drawing from textual data and interviews with sixteen attendees at Afropunk Fest 2015, I explore how the Afropunk look worn by many attendees is a syncretic product, combining dashikis and natural hairstyles with flower headbands and crop-tops. In the second part of the chapter, I consider to what extent representation of these syncretic looks in the mainstream fashion media—American *Vogue*, *W*, and *Vogue Italia*, among other titles—offers a platform for the idealization of a complex and cosmopolitan form of black fashionability, which contradicts and combats the limited tropes through which black bodies are routinely represented within fashion. I base my discussion here on textual analysis of fashion media and interviews with photographers, who covered Afropunk for independent blogs and major magazines. Like the preceding chapter, Chapter 4 locates the analysis of festival fashion within broader shifts in media representation. To attract a younger market, mainstream American magazines incorporated the discourse on individual style into their own meaning-making frameworks. In so doing, they also embraced a form of fashion representation – street style – unbound by the strict racial codings of traditional fashion editorial imagery. That Afropunk Fest has been identified as a key site for the display of individual style has, in turn, opened up one pathway through which Afro-diasporic blackness has found its way into the twenty-first-century popular fashion imagination and into twenty-first-century indie. Thus, in 2018, when African-American pop star Beyoncé headlined Coachella—a performance heralded as the radical insertion of black imagery into indie music culture—she was in fact drawing on the political work already being done on the grounds of and in images of Afropunk Fest.

This book thus makes the claim that the material and discursive tools of commercial popular fashion took indie from the UK and across the globe. In the process, the ideal figure of the indie rocker was transformed and new spaces for identification and recognition within indie emerged. By charting these new spaces for recognition, Chapters 3 and 4 are concerned with a series of destabilizations, specifically having to do with indie's masculinity, whiteness, Britishness, and coherence around music. These chapters also highlight new forms of exclusion within indie, having to do with the regulation of the fashionable female body. The idealized figure of festival fashion must first meet the demands of "individual style," proving that she understands, but then can move beyond, set festival trends. Her subjectivity is formed also through exclusions around body size and hair. For example, the Coachella star continues to be idealized through a slender physical frame. And, although the star of Afropunk Fest is represented through a range of body shapes, hair hierarchies emerge, wherein those black women with naturally styled hair are foregrounded within festival documentation and those with processed styles—or natural hair that cannot conform to current ideals—are not made visible in the same way. Together, the destabilizations of what indie music culture once was, on the one hand, and these new forms of visibility and bodily exclusion, on the other, shape how the ideal indie subject is produced in the twenty-first century, how we understand who this person might be.

The evolving indie look offers a framework for imagining and performing identity. It is also for sale: in designer collections, on the high street and in second-hand shops. Chapter 2 examined the designer collections of Hedi Slimane, and Chapter 3 explored the merchandizing and marketing techniques of several high street stores. Chapter 5 focuses analysis on one of the many second-hand retailers involved in the business of commodifying the indie look: Beyond Retro. I draw on observational research as well as interviews with Beyond Retro's owner—Steven Bethell—and several of its original staff members, who have all gone on to other jobs in the creative industries. Beyond Retro's warehouse-sized flagship store on Cheshire Street in East London cultivates a sensation of shopping at the edge of the acceptable consumption-scape, and its product is organized in a haphazard manner, prompting shoppers to search for "unique" pieces from the massive amount of stock on offer. In this regard, the shop seems typical of second-hand retail, falling into a category that Nicky Gregson and Louise Crewe call "retro retailers."[24] Beyond Retro distinguishes itself from other retro retailers, however, in that it operates within the global commercial fashion industry, thus competing with major first-hand retailers. Owned by the second-hand textile trader Bank & Vogue, Beyond Retro selects its product from the millions of tonnes of waste produced within the first-hand production cycle and aligns that product to compete aesthetically with contemporaneous first-hand trends. Beyond Retro thus offers a second-hand product that other retro retailers cannot—one that is on trend, produced *en masse*, and made widely available for purchase, in Beyond Retro's brick-and-mortar stores in Britain and Sweden and internationally via its website. As such, Beyond Retro represents a new type of second-hand retail: what I call, the pop ragtrade. I include this chapter within *Fashioning Indie* as Beyond Retro and other second-hand stores inform the evolving indie look, by offering garments for sale and mobilizing staff members' fashion knowledges to shape this offering. What's more, this case study of Beyond Retro contextualizes through analysis of production and consumption a trend that I charted in the preceding chapters through discursive representations. That is, I argued across Chapters 3 and 4 that "individual style" has gone from subcultural language to mainstream fashion doxa. So too alternative consumption and what McRobbie calls "subcultural entrepreneurship" have become mainstream fashion practices, no doubt incited by the increasing hegemony of the doxa of "individual style."[25] This new fashion environment, with its emphases on authenticity and individuality, provides a context from which, first, second-hand garments are made central to the fashionable wardrobe and, second, second-hand retailers can enter the mass-fashion market and attempt to compete with first-hand retail on a global scale. In the twenty-first century, the indie look is constituted within neoliberal consumer culture; so too independent entrepreneurship and alternative consumption can now take shape within a capitalist fashionscape.

At the time of writing this introduction in 2018, indie was but one cultural form that took subcultural shape in the 1980s, but then was reimagined in and through the commercial fashion market in the late 2010s. Some other examples include: a Dapper Dan–Gucci collaboration, the sensational visibility of drag balls within contemporary media and fashion, and the rise of skatewear brand Supreme, whose designer James Jebbia won the coveted "Designer Menswear Brand of the Year" at the 2018 Council of Fashion Designers of America (CFDA) Awards. To explain: in the 1980s the hip-hop designer Dapper Dan worked, as he says, "to blackanize fashion,"[26] by making extraordinary garments with knock-off designer monogram fabrics. The labels would not sell to his Harlem shop, so he took matters into his own hands. He now collaborates with Gucci. The Italian label came under scrutiny, when creative director Alessandro Michele sent a model down its 2017 cruise collection runway, wearing a look inspired by one of Dan's designs for athlete Diane Dixon. In response, Gucci offered to go into business with Dan, a collaboration that includes an updated version of his Harlem boutique, where he now produces custom pieces using materials supplied by Gucci.[27] My second example: although queer subcultures have a centuries-long history in New York, Jennie Livingston's 1989 film *Paris is Burning* brought mainstream attention to drag ball culture.[28] That subcultural world is now regularly referenced on VH1's hit show *Ru Paul's Drag Race*, which is in turn referenced by other television shows, across social media and in fashion.[29] Hip New York-based label Opening Ceremony, for example, staged its S/S 2019 presentation like a drag ball, its looks walked by top drag performers. Here, the subcultural art of walking the ball, which is a send-up of a model's catwalk strut, often involving well-rehearsed hand gestures and signature strides and typically performed afterhours in uptown nightclubs, is used to display high fashion goods in spectacular fashion at New York Fashion Week. Finally, skater brand Supreme has spent the last several years building collaborations with top fashion houses, including Louis Vuitton, all the while building its own brand identity by making its (very expensive) skater- and hip-hop-inspired products available only through limited drops. At the 2018 CFDA awards, Jebbia noted, "Never considered Supreme to be a fashion company or myself a designer," suggesting he saw the company as "outside" fashion, even as he stood on one of its biggest stages.[30] Indie is one part of this bigger story about the presence of subculture *within* the fashion market. While I have remained critical of the mechanisms of global capitalism that shape these new iterations of a once subcultural form, I also have made sure not to ignore the shifting relationship between "youth and the youth market industry"[31] that indie's evolution illuminates, for these shifts speak to historical change and the new forms of identification and cultural politics that take shape within and through such change.

CHAPTER I
FROM SUBCULTURE TO HOT LOOK: THE EVOLUTION OF INDIE

This chapter charts the evolution of indie music culture: from the inception of the British independent music scene in the wake of punk in the late 1970s and early 1980s, through the rise of Britpop in the mid-1990s, to indie rocker and tabloid star Pete Doherty's now infamous romp across the muddy fields of Glastonbury with his then-girlfriend Kate Moss in 2005. Guiding the chapter's narrative is the question: How did the term "indie" go from signifying a space of music production and distribution functioning outside of the control of the commercial music industry to signifying a fashionable masculine type, characterized by his slender physical frame and seemingly effortless style of dress? The chapter argues that this skinny indie man was first seen in the independent music scene of the 1980s, but was mocked for his childish stature and too short trousers. However, the widespread visibility in the 1990s of both Britpop and its American counterpart grunge created a popular cultural environment within which the skinny indie man was reimagined, first as a rock 'n' roll sex god and, in the early 2000s, as a fashion icon. The chapter explores, moreover, the processes of race-, gender-, and class-based exclusions through which this figure was imagined and reimagined anew.

1980s: Subculture and awkward youth

As indie historian Sam Knee puts it, the independent scene was "punk's last gasp, if you like."[1] Indeed, the scene was also called post-punk.[2] This legacy was complicated, however, by the scene's obsession with pop music and the childlike and thus non-threatening identities that such an obsession inspired.

Punk's heir

Punk's influence was multifold. As David Cavanagh details in his lengthy record of the British independent scene, both musicians and label owners sometimes took on the in-your-face presentation styles characteristic of punk and its leading faces: the Sex Pistols. Cavanagh details, for example, interviews that Edwyn Collins of the band Orange Juice and Postcard Records founder Alan Horne gave in which they "poured scorn" on their interviewers.[3] The altercations recall the Sex Pistols' 1976 interview with television presenter Bill Grundy—an interview, in which Pistol Steve Jones called Grundy a "dirty bastard" after the latter made a sexually suggestive remark toward Siouxie Sioux, who stood behind the group during the live evening television interview. Similarly, Cavanagh continues, Creation Records founder Alan McGee took his band the Jesus and Mary Chain on a tour of the UK in 1985 that was, in McGee's own words, "so bad it was good. Complete and utter anarchy."[4] Two of the four scheduled concerts were canceled by either the police or the local council because of the band's reputation for inciting violence. "It was, McGee reminded everyone, just like the Sex Pistols 'Anarchy' tour in December 1976: an outlaw spree around the country. A game of tag with the establishment."[5]

In addition to a pro-forma in-your-face snarl, punk bequeathed to the British independent music scene its organizational structure: the independent labels and distribution networks, from which "indie"—an abbreviation of the word independent—would take its name. As David Hesmondhalgh explains, "No music genre had ever before taken its name from the form of industrial organization behind it."[6] Of course, independent labels existed well before the punk period. Simon Reynolds gives the examples of Virgin, Island and Chrysalis;[7] however, "[t]he people who started Virgin and Island, were enterprising, sure, and 'independent' in terms of what they did creatively. But they had the support of major record-company distribution, finance and marketing."[8] In contrast, the labels that emerged during the punk period were to "go it alone" … at least to a certain extent. In the place of major label distribution, Geoff Travis, the unassuming founder of the record shop and label Rough Trade, established the Cartel— an independent distribution network that supplied independent record shops across the UK with new independent music.[9] Reynolds explains, "Unglamorous but absolutely crucial, the Cartel network provided the infrastructure for a genuinely alternative culture."[10]

This "hard-headed network of post-punk companies"[11] underpinned the musical output of a range of acts in the UK throughout the 1980s: fledgling musicians who would go on to sign major record deals, such as The Smiths and The Cure; mediocre musicians who would never be offered major record deals; and musicians who wanted to produce music without the commercial restraints that would be placed on them if they were to sign a major record deal. As Geoff Travis noted to Cavanagh, "We were a new generation of people and we wanted to do things our own way. And we also wanted to deal with music whose reason to exist was nothing to do with its commerciality. All that mattered was whether or not the record gave you a thrill."[12] Such sentiments were shared by bands and label employees as well as by writers for the weekly music press. As Roger Holland wrote in the July 5, 1986 issue of *Sounds*, "The concept of an independent record label, *properly defined*, is of a body run without undue regard for market forces. One which is unwilling to compromise its integrity simply to make a few quick bucks."[13] Indeed, it was by linking the themes of "independence" and "integrity" that the indie scene marked its own worth. As Hesmondhalgh explains, "indie proclaimed itself to be superior to other genres not only because it was more relevant or authentic to the youth who produced and consumed it (which was what rock had claimed) but also because it was based on new relationships between creativity and commerce."[14] Daniel Miller, founder of the Mute label, recounted to Simon Reynolds, "none of us knew what we were doing! We were huge music enthusiasts, though, with a strong idea of what we liked and what we wanted. I had no business grounding whatsoever. But all of a sudden you realized you could have access to this industry that had always seemed very mysterious."[15] He continued, "The record industry went from being pretty closed, which it was even during the first wave of punk, to totally open. And that encouraged a lot of people like me and Tony Wilson [founder of Factory Records]—not obvious record-company people by any means—to get involved and make our dreams come true."[16] The ideology of "anti-commerciality" also fuels contemporary accounts of the British independent scene of the 1980s. For example, writing in the mid-2000s, former *NME* journalist John Harris remembers, "In the scratchy, shambolic guitar music that defined the 80s left field, there was a clear sense of the rejection of all kinds of dominant cultural norms: the slick commerciality of the 80s mainstream, ambition as defined by sales figures and chart positions, and the swaggering masculinity that united the likes of Simon Le Bon, Spandau Ballet's Tony Hadley and—ironically—Wham!'s George Michael."[17]

There is a slippage within Harris' words, however. He does not root indie's rejection of the mainstream in the institutional structures provided by independent production and distribution networks organized and run by music industry outsiders, but rather in "scratchy, shambolic guitar music" and forms of alternative masculinity. His words reveal—to borrow from

Hesmondhalgh—the slippage between "institutional" and "political-aesthetic" definitions of indie,[18] wherein the former refers to networks of production and distribution and the latter refers to what Matthew Bannister has characterized as "mainly white, male groups playing mainly electric guitars, bass and drums."[19] Reynolds explains, "In the mid-eighties most chart pop was glossy, guitar-free, black-influenced, soulfully strong-voiced, dance-oriented, hi-tech, ultra-modern." In contrast, "Indie made a fetish of the opposite characteristics: scruffy guitars, white-only sources, weak or 'pale' folk-based vocals, undanceable rhythms, lo-fi or Luddite production, and a retro (usually sixties) slant."[20] Hesmondhalgh explains: "While many musicians, fans and journalists had increasingly turned to pop and black musical traditions, such as electro and hip-hop, as fresh sources of inspiration in the early 1980s, indie was constructing a canon of white, underground rock references."[21] Both Reynolds and Cavanagh identify the *NME*'s compilation *C86* as solidifying these sonic borders around this new definition of "indie." The mail-order cassette featured twenty-two bands signed to independent record labels. Cavanagh writes, however, "As the *NME*'s advertisements for *C86* mentioned no particular genre, 'C86' became the genre,"[22] and, because the cassette heavily featured boy groups with guitar-based music, the term "indie" came to signify "a helter-skelter, jangly racket performed by four or more pale boys with hurt feelings."[23] As early as 1988, music journalist Keith Cameron addressed this inconsistency between independent production and what Reynolds calls indie's "distinct sensibility."[24] Discussing for *Sounds* the contradiction of Australian soap-opera-actress-cum-pop-star Kylie Minogue's success on an independent label, he wrote, "So, just in case you're confused: [...] Kylie Minogue isn't an indie band but she's on an indie, err, independent label and doesn't need to go to a major, although if she did, things might just become a lot less complicated."[25]

Indie pop

Despite the "anti-commercial" ethos that infused the British independent scene of the 1980s, much of the music coming out of it was identified with the same term as indie's commercial counterpart: "pop." For example, after listing several independent bands, *Sounds* contributor Ron Rom declared, "All these groups, and plenty more, showed that the three minute pop single was alive in Britain in 1986."[26] Similarly, Dave from the indie band The Mighty Lemon Drops admitted in an interview with journalist Mr. Spencer,

"My mother ... finds it ridiculous that I can make a living out of being in a pop group."[27] As Bannister explains, it was only in the UK that indie music was characterized as pop; other scenes—in the United States and New Zealand, for example—leaned harder, toward a rock aesthetic.[28] "Of course," Bannister continues, "what was meant by 'pop' was complex: for some it meant an idealization of 1960s pop naivety—a style; for others it meant an actual desire to be commercially successful."[29] There is plentiful evidence of the latter. As Lawrence from Felt remembered for the Saatchi Gallery magazine *Art & Music* in 2009,

> I didn't think we were in an underground scene; I thought we were overlooked but one day we would be in [the style magazine] *The Face* and it wouldn't be a big deal. [...] I wanted to be part of the whole pop scene at the time but I just wanted to do it with guitar music. I thought it could happen in the '80s and Felt would sit next to Duran Duran and Boy George and could have given them a run for their money.[30]

Similarly, Phil Wilson from The June Brides recalled for the same publication, "I thought the bands I was listening to were totally pop. It didn't feel like any of it was hard music ... it was the music that should have been popular."[31] There is also evidence of Bannister's first definition of indie pop: as an indication of a certain naivety or childishness. Reynolds argues, the indie scene of the mid-1980s "espoused an ideal of 'perfect pop'" that drew on 1960s referents and the music of the post-punk period (1978–84). "But it was post-punk with the most radical elements (the politics, the black/white fusion, the studio experimentation) purged. [They] left out Orange Juice's disco-funk influence but kept the sparkly guitar jangle and 'worldliness must keep apart from me' naivety."[32] Not only in the sound of British indie music of the mid-1980s, this naïveté also manifested in its look.

In the earliest academic account of the indie look, Reynolds writes, whereas most young people in the 1980s were interested in adulthood and, correspondingly, overt displays of sexuality within their bodies and dress, indie kids were trying to "liberat[e themselves] from sexuality."[33] Cavanagh explains further, "Within the scene itself, words such as 'cutie' and 'charming' were used to underline the infantilism of the songs and personalities. Turned off by the invasion of Smiths concerts by macho hordes, the cuties were delicate flowers, pacific and childishly attired."[34] Both authors identify the anorak—in Reynolds' words, "the kind of short anorak, in bright optimistic patterns that remind you of curtain material"[35]—as the staple element of indie kids' wardrobes. Stephen Pastel of indie band the Pastels recounted to Cavanagh, "The anorak was a style statement. [...] It was saying: 'Everything else is fucked up and we've got to get back closer to the start of things. Being children.'"[36] The 1980s indie look was also inspired by the 1960s—an aesthetic inspiration that demanded young indie enthusiasts rifle through second-hand markets. As Pete Momtchiloff from indie group Heavenly remembered, his look was "a sort of beat-up '60s look." He continued, "you couldn't really buy these clothes in the high street so charity shops were a godsend."[37] Similarly, Paul Kelly, who directed the film *Finisterre* for the indie group St. Etienne, recalled,

> It's difficult now to imagine how hard it was to find good clothes back then. Nothing was quite what you were after or even the right size and as a result any attempt at replicating the '60s dandy could have you looking like a cross between a geography teacher and a tramp. Our suede jackets, cord trousers and winkle-picker boots were at odds with the '80s high street chic.[38]

And yet, many indie musicians of the 1980s did, in fact, incorporate 1980s high street garments into their ensembles. Crucially, however, such garments were from unfashionable shops. Stephen Pastel relayed to Sam Knee,

> I liked new clothes that were intrinsically good but unfashionable; Marks & Spencer's V-neck sweaters, Clarks shoes, brown cords. If it was raining, an anorak was okay, and in winter, a dufflecoat. You could really put a good look together from all these things and with odd bits of second hand too.[39]

Similarly, Amelia Fletcher of Talulah Gosh explained to Knee, "Most of my clothes were second hand from charity shops, apart from shoes, pants, bra and turtle neck jumpers from British Home Stores."[40] Indeed, it seems that the "cross between a geography teacher and a tramp," of which Paul Kelly spoke, was exactly what some indie musicians were, in fact, looking to achieve.

Sam Knee's *A Scene In Between: Tripping Through the Fashions of UK Indie Music 1980–1988* provides a photographic account of the sartorial landscape of the British independent scene of the 1980s. Archival images reveal overgrown bowl-cut hairstyles; anoraks; cardigans, roll neck sweaters, turtlenecks, and corduroy trousers sourced from staple department stores of the British high street; Doc Marten and Chelsea boots; and skinny black jeans worn on extremely skinny legs. Indeed, as Bannister notes, the British independent scene nurtured a "soft" masculinity,[41] wherein "Middle-class white men flirted with pop androgyny partly as a way of defining themselves against heavy metal machismo."[42] Perhaps surprising then is that the images presented in Knee's archive also reveal, firstly, an abundance of leather—a material associated with rock 'n' roll—and, secondly, many young women, who participated in the indie scene as both musicians and fans. Champions of the leather look were the Creation Records band Jesus and Mary Chain— the band that, as noted above, were feared to be the second coming of the Sex Pistols by city councils up and down the UK. Although the group embraced such a categorization, their wearing of leather was perhaps more playful than sincere. Instead of wearing motorcycle jackets with metal studs, as their predecessors did, the members of the Jesus and Mary Chain coupled leather trousers with woolly jumpers. As Michael Kerr of the band Meat Whiplash noted, the Jesus and Mary Chain's Jim Reid and Douglas Hart wore black jumpers knitted by Kerr's mother for their 1985 performance on the television show *The Old Grey Whistle Test*.[43] Referring to the Jesus and Mary Chain's drummer Bobby Gillespie's aesthetic, Amelia Fletcher explained, it was about mixing childish anoraks and rock-inspired leather trousers—a look that says "ha ha not really."[44]

According to cultural theorist Angela McRobbie, irony is one of the modes through which second-hand style functions as a subcultural practice.[45] She writes, second-hand style "is marked out rather by a knowingness, a willful anarchy and an irrepressible optimism, as indicated by colour, exaggeration, humour and disavowal of the conventions of adult dress."[46] Crucially, McRobbie identifies second-hand style as a feminine practice and notes that, in addition to the knowing and optimistic look, young women in the 1980s also used second-hand garments to produce an androgynous look that was later mimicked by high street retailers. Although McRobbie does not mention the British independent music scene by name, she could easily be speaking about the young women who populated it. For example, Jill Bryson of Strawberry Switchblade appears in photographs wearing dresses in floral and other "optimistic" patterns. Her chest-length brown hair is styled into a look typical of the 1980s: crimped, brushed out to a great volume, and accessorized with a large bow and ribbons.[47] McRobbie's description of television presenter Paula Yates's wardrobe resonates, as Bryson too looks like she "salvaged [her outfit] from a late 1950s children's birthday party."[48] Other photographs from Knee's archive reveal gender

Figure 1 Talulah Gosh. Amelia Fletcher (third from left) sports a bowl-cut hairstyle. Elizabeth Price (front) wears her chin-length hair in a playful, punky style. The male members of the group wear leather jackets, anoraks, T-shirts, and woolly sweaters. © Steve Double/Camera Press.

ambiguities. Photographs of The Shop Assistants, for example, show the band's four female members in cropped trousers and dark, boxy jackets of denim, trench, and anorak varieties. Their hair is shorter than Bryson's, also teased and sprayed to create maximum volume.[49] Photos of Amelia Fletcher of Talulah Gosh have her switching between girlish and androgynous ensembles, all the while sporting a hairstyle that volleyed between a bowl-cut and a buzz-cut, natural brown, and bleached blond.[50] McRobbie argues that such looks "pla[y] with the norms, conventions and expectations of femininity, post feminism."[51] Indeed, the British independent scene of the 1980s nurtured such challenges to gender expectations: crucially, for both young men and women (see Figure 1).

Unfashionable (white, middle-class) youth

Despite its potential to subvert the norms and expectations of both femininity and masculinity, the indie look of the 1980s was largely ignored by the style press and the fashion media of the period. In 1986 and 1987, for example, *The Face*'s coverage of indie consisted of an article about the greasiness of the band Pop Will Eat Itself. It identified the band as "The ultimate expression of Grebo Power (a grebo being an oily yob you wouldn't scrape off your Honda saddle with a shoehorn)" and closed with the snobbish warning "Catch them on tour now, that's when the dandruff really hits the fan."[52] i-D's coverage of indie during this same period consisted of an article by William Leith that read,

> What it comes down to is that today's "Indie Scene" ... are not "anti-style". They're just not stylish. For the most part, they don't wear anoraks and national health specs as some kind of showbiz rejection number. They wear them because they can't afford anything else, or because it's not important enough to them to wear anything else, or because once they'd got started on kitting themselves out, they wouldn't know where to stop. So they just don't bother ... They can't be bothered with all the fashion sophistication and they're wondering whether it's possible to just ... opt out.[53]

Taking note of the classed and raced underpinnings of the 1980s indie scene might shed some light on the style press's distaste for it. As Reynolds explains about the scene, "This is a white middle-class bohemianism that's cleansed of the fast-living and self-destruction of earlier forms of rebellion."[54] Indeed, not a single non-white face appears in Knee's photographic archive of the scene. In contrast, The Face and i-D were developing a fashionable aesthetic that had as its centerpiece what Frank Mort calls "a visual philosophy of social and sexual plurality."[55] Stylist Ray Petri was foremost amongst the producers of this aesthetic. Petri began his styling career at The Face in 1983 and continued to work throughout the 1980s at a range of style publications, including its competitor i-D and The Face's founder Nick Logan's menswear title Arena.[56] As Mort notes, Petri's "bias was for young men who were Latinate, Afro-Caribbean, chicano, or of mixed-race origins."[57] His images, Mort continues, refused to rely on racial tropes, however. "The images moved rapidly from one type of masculinity to another. The effect was to promote the idea of cultural diversity as part of a diaspora of style."[58] Speaking about Petri's first editorial for Arena, entitled "Ragamuffin" (March/April 1987), Sean Nixon adds that the models pictured embodied "a 'tough', stylish masculinity—men who carried their maleness with a self-contained poise."[59] In contrast, the anorak- and national health spec-wearing indie kids of the 1980s were popularly understood as far from poised, as far from fashionable. In retrospect, even the NME—the British independent music scene's biggest cheerleader—recalled the indie look of the 1980s with disdain. As one contributor wrote in 1998, "In 1987 […] 'indie' had become a generic straitjacket for dull, skinny men with fringes strumming guitars and pretending not to be able to sing."[60] In the 1990s, however, that (somewhat pathetic) indie male figure would be reimagined as a rock god.

1990s: Britpop and rock swagger

At the beginning of the 1990s, the stereotype of the indie musician as an unfashionable youth playing guitar was all but fully solidified within the weekly music press. For example, in a review of a Strangelove gig, music journalist Johnny Cigarettes wrote, "they immediately nail their colours … proudly to the suburban lamppost of indie guitar mediocrity, with no fewer than three unreconstructed fringes, two Rickenbacker guitars and a lovingly uncultivated crappy dread mop assaulting our finer aesthetic sensibilities."[61] This stereotype was relevant not only to indie musicians, but also to fans of indie music. Descriptions of indie fans—or indie kids—included "white, spotty, middle class boys,"[62] "pubescent and college kids,"[63] "the mimsy, Keats-reading, middle-class undergrad mummy's boy called Quentin with spots, a blue-and-white hoped [sic] tee-shirt,"[64] and simply "the T-shirted kids."[65] This awkward, boyish young man is immortalized in Nick Hornby's *High Fidelity*—a first-person narrative about a frustrated man who works at a record shop in North London. In one passage, Hornby paints a scene in which the narrator and his coworkers—a trio of music-loving record shop employees, who each in his own way is socially and sexually inept—attend the gig of an attractive American singer: "Marie takes a break after an hour or so. She sits on the stage and swigs from a bottle of Budweiser, and some guy comes out with a box of cassettes and puts them on the stage beside her. […] We all buy one from her, and to our horror she speaks to us."[66]

That the stereotypical "indie kid" was male should not surprise, despite the number of young women who participated in the scene throughout the 1980s. Although the "indie kid" was a category rooted in lived subjectivities, it was also a discursive construction, produced within an overtly masculinist body of writing: music criticism. As Helen Davies explains about the weekly magazines *NME* and *Melody Maker* as well as their glossier counterparts, *Q* and *Vox*, music journalists are overwhelmingly male and they assume that their readership is also male.[67] As such, "the discourses employed in music journalism exclude women from serious discussion both as musicians and fans."[68] The masculinist orientation of music journalism is mirrored within academic discourse, specifically that focused on youth subcultures. As McRobbie explains, "Youth sociologists have looked mainly at the activities of adolescent boys and young men and their attention has been directed to those areas of experience which have a strongly masculine image."[69] McRobbie has gone some way toward rewriting the history of youth cultural studies, by inserting young women and their activities into focus.[70] However, until the publishing of Knee's visual account of the 1980s British independent scene, which, as already noted, sheds light on the number of young women who participated in the scene, the story of indie has been an overtly male one.[71] For example, within Bannister's account of the 1980s indie scenes in the UK and New Zealand, he focuses solely on how masculinities were performed in the scene, making the rather uncomfortable concession that the young women who did participate in the scene "did not have recourse to the type of group solidarity available to men, and this would tend to make them, for want of a better word, 'stroppy.'"[72] This emphasis on young men— as well as a corresponding assumption of whiteness—would serve as a foundation from which the indie figure would be reimagined in the image of the rock 'n' roll sex god during the 1990s.

From pop to rock

Similar to the indie musicians of the 1980s, those of the early 1990s expressed a desire to achieve widespread popularity. For example, in an interview with *NME*, Brett Anderson—the lead singer of Suede—criticized the limited amount of success achievable within the independent scene, arguing, "That's slightly pointless, isn't it?" He wanted instead "to appeal to people who aren't utterly obsessed with music; because it tends to mean that you're writing good tunes."[73] Anderson's claims resonate with those made by indie musicians in the pages of the weekly music press throughout the 1980s. The difference between Brett Anderson and indie musicians from the 1980s, however, lies in the fact that Brett Anderson's band Suede did, in fact, become the most popular band in the United Kingdom in 1993—a success that would alter the group's fortunes and also the cultural significance of the label "indie."

Suede did not resemble many of its indie predecessors. At the center of the early 1990s indie scene stood an indie sub-genre called shoegazing—so called for the tendency of band members and audience members to stare at their shoes while playing/appreciating live music. The indie shoegazer was, in a sense, an extreme caricature of the previously described indie figure; he was the embodiment of awkward youth. In contrast, Brett Anderson's stage presence was electric, resembling David Bowie's more than that of an insecure student. As Noel McLaughlin argues, Anderson's clothing and movements indicate a blurring of gender and sexual boundaries.[74] That is, the clothes Anderson wears in performance are neither straightforwardly masculine nor feminine. He wears simply a pair of jeans and a black shirt. However, the latter is "tight-sleeved" and has "a low-cut circular neck" that, McLaughlin notes, "has feminine connotations."[75] Moreover, McLaughlin explains, Anderson turns his back to the audience and, "utilizing the low-cut top, he pushes his shoulder-blades together to form 'breasts', creating the image of a cleavage."[76] According to McLaughlin, his performance style works to subvert gender expectations precisely because it is presented within "a 'naturalized' masculine rock space."[77] On the one hand, "rock space" refers to Suede guitarist Bernard Butler's swirling solos, which served as the musical lynchpin for the band's first album. On the other, the term indicates the broader context of indie music in the 1990s: in McLaughlin's words, "a period marked by the rise to prominence of 'the lad' and a new type of 'old' masculinity […] personified in the rock group Oasis."[78] John Harris cites a journalist for *The Guardian*, who wrote in 1996 that "this was 'the wrong era to be anything but a red-blooded geezer playing unambiguous geez-rock.'"[79]

This shift from pop to rock—and the attendant rise of Oasis' Beatles-inspired guitars and rock star personas as the dominant sound and image in indie music—is underpinned by institutional shifts within the structure of the independent music scene. Attempting to stave off bankruptcy resulting from broad economic recession in the late 1980s and early 1990s, many independent labels signed what are called P&D—pressing and distribution—deals with major record labels.[80] Suede, for example, released their first record, *Suede* (1993), on the independently owned Nude Records, which was distributed internationally by Sony. Why did so many independent labels sign P&D deals with major record labels during the early 1990s? And why did such collaborations herald a shift in indie's sound and image from pop to rock? Hesmondhalgh explains that, within popular music discourse, such P&D deals were framed as one of two options: "sell-out" or "burn-out."[81] The reality, he continues, is more complex, especially when one examines how each label balances the "institutional" and "political-aesthetic" aspects of independent music-making.[82] Creation Records founder Alan McGee, for example, never demonstrated a commitment to the ideal of corporate independence, which circulated within the independent scene of the 1980s. Instead, Hesmondhalgh explains, McGee was—and always had been—committed to the goal of "develop[ing] a new generation of classic pop stars."[83] Here, he defines "classic" as "adher[ing] to a traditional rock notion of what constituted quality and success."[84] Accordingly, Hesmondhalgh argues, "[a]cts on the label have generally been in the mold established by rock and roll in the late 1950s."[85] Such a reading of Creation Records' "political-aesthetic" characteristics provides a space for rethinking the politics of style by the label's preeminent band from the 1980s, the Jesus and Mary Chain. Indeed, perhaps their leather trousers were not worn ironically, but rather—or also—sincerely, in an attempt to perform a version of rock masculinity that was easily recognizable within the twentieth-century pop canon. And yet, whereas the Jesus and Mary Chain's legacy is known only to independent music fans, label founder Alan McGee's later discovery—Oasis—looms large in the popular imagination. Seeing the band play an intimate gig in 1993, McGee quickly signed the Northerners, charmed by the dynamic of Noel and Liam Gallagher, the band's song-writing guitarist and singer, respectively. Cavanagh writes, "Attempting to describe Oasis to people, McGee would sometimes mention the Kinks, the Stone Roses and the Who, and declare that Oasis were a perfect blend of the three. At other times he would speak of the Beatles, the Sex Pistols, the Jam, and T. Rex, and claim that Oasis were as good as all four."[86] Mining—and miming—those earlier white, British rock sounds, Oasis' album would go ten times platinum. Moreover, Oasis did what most British bands, with the exception of the Beatles and the Rolling Stones, only dream of doing: take America. Such a triumph was facilitated by the fact that in 1992 McGee sold 49 percent of the label to Sony.[87] Such a triumph was accompanied by a new attitude: in Hesmondhalgh's words, "a rockist self-indulgence [and] a flamboyant display of arrogance and wealth."[88]

Oasis and Suede were not the only indie-in-origin groups to achieve global success on pseudo-indie labels and subsequently engage in the sex-and-drug-excesses of rock 'n' roll. Also, Damon Albarn from Blur, Justine Frischmann from Elastica, and Jarvis Cocker from Pulp led their bands out of the "indie ghetto" and into the international spotlight in the 1990s, offering up both their musical talents and social lives for mass consumption. This movement, known as Britpop, would remain at the center of British popular music for the next several years. Writing for *NME* on January 7, 1995, John Harris pointed to "the way [Britpop]'s binned the sad accoutrements of indie, moved away from being drab, underachieving and ever-so-slightly apologetic—and turned itself into a wagering, conceited creature with its own sparkling aristocracy."[89] Britpop consisted of some of the biggest bands in the country—Suede, Elastica, Blur, Oasis, and Pulp—and some of the bands, whose successes followed in the wake of these big five; Harris mentions Supergrass, Sleeper, Menswear, and Shed Seven, amongst others.[90] As Blur bass player Alex James explains in his memoir, "Britpop was never a scene. It was a lot of not very brilliant bands copying two or three good ones, and the good bands never really saw eye to eye."[91] Indeed, the story of Britpop is rife with competition. For example, when Justine Frischmann ended her sexual relationship with Brett Anderson to begin one with Damon Albarn, a testosterone-driven feud began between the two men and played out on the popular charts. Similarly, when Blur and Oasis's labels set to release the bands' new singles on the same day in 1995, any seeming cordiality between the two groups quickly dissolved, and in its place the media constructed an epic battle-of-the-bands narrative.[92] What tied Britpop's aristocracy together was their shared desire for success. As Alex James recounts, "The very first flush of success was the most enjoyable, the initial paradigm shift from wanting something to actually getting it, but by then it was already too late. Success is the most addictive commodity in the cosmos."[93] Reflecting upon the scene almost a decade later, former *NME* journalist John Harris concluded, "Britpop seemed to have replaced the imperative for innovation and iconoclasm with the worship of wealth and success."[94]

Gender, class, race, and Britpop

Britpop's new attitude was best exemplified in the figures of—and tension between—Damon Albarn of Blur and Liam Gallagher of Oasis. Each of the two musicians saw himself as the savior of British rock music, and each articulated distaste for grunge—the Seattle-in-origin rock sub-genre that swept into the UK in 1993 via Nirvana's second studio album *Nevermind*. To play this central role within the historical narrative of British music, both musicians performed versions of masculine "rock 'n' roll abandon."[95] As *The Face* contributor Danny Scott noted in 1995,

> The argument runs that Blur and Oasis somehow articulated a growing male frustration at having to pretend to have politically correct opinions and feelings. Suddenly the bathetic I'm-sensitive-me standpoint [...] looked very boring indeed, and not even Brett [Anderson of Suede]'s foppish *frissons* could save it.[96]

Scholars have explored this sense of "growing male frustration" within analyses of the figure of the "new lad" and the men's magazine title *loaded*. As

Rosalind Gill explains, the "new lad" emerged in the 1990s in response to the central masculine figure of the 1980s—the "new man." Whereas the latter "is generally characterized as sensitive, emotionally aware, respectful of women, and egalitarian in outlook," its successor "is depicted as hedonistic, post- (if not anti) feminist, and pre-eminently concerned with beer, football and 'shagging' women."[97] Whereas the "new man" was produced discursively within media titles such as *The Face* and *Arena*,[98] the representational home of the "new lad" was *loaded*—a magazine title, launched in April 1994, that was publicized as the voice of "the working-class male public."[99] *loaded*'s classed identity was far from straightforward, however. As Ben Crewe explains, the magazine's editors—James Brown and Tim Southwell—each oscillated within their own self-identification between middle- and working-class, having come from the former but strategically aligning themselves with the latter. As Crewe notes, they positioned themselves in opposition to "the Oxbridge-educated, liberal journalists who [they thought] monopolized the men's lifestyle press,"[100] instead producing a magazine that was "unapologetic about men's instincts and imperfections. The point was to celebrate, rather than challenge or channel, the condition of masculine enjoyment."[101]

Such class ambivalences could be mapped onto the laddish bodies of Albarn and Gallagher. Whereas the Blur frontman was a former drama school student, whose father lectured at an art school, the Oasis frontman was a working-class Northerner, raised in Manchester by an overworked mother and a mostly absent father. Albarn's bandmate Alex James implicitly refers to the difference in the two bands' class backgrounds in his memoir, noting,

> I suppose if I was trying to explain to a very old lady what I did for a living, which I do have to from time to time, I would have said, "I'm a musician, I make records and behave appallingly. It's great." If the old lady said, "Do you mean like Oasis?" I would have to say, "Yes, exactly." There wasn't that much different between the two bands and, when viewed from a little old lady's point of view, they were pretty much the same thing. That said, I think on the whole old ladies prefer Blur to Oasis. Oasis probably had the edge with "geezers" and "lads."[102]

That Albarn's laddishness was a working-class identity that he put on was obvious to those who knew him. His girlfriend at the time, Justine Frischmann, relayed to Harris, "All of a sudden, he was getting really macho.

The swing from super-PCness to *loaded* magazine—which in theory I was in favour of—went too far." She continued, "I like the idea of no self-censorship, but it seemed to be all about football and being an idiot."[103] Of course, the working-class Gallagher was also "putting it on." As Danny Scott keenly noted, "lad rock does not articulate real emotions so much as sell an aspiration. It sells the *idea* of rock 'n' roll abandon."[104] Throughout the mid-1990s, Gallagher personified that idea. On the March 1997 cover of the American magazine *Vanity Fair*, for example, he is pictured in bed with his then-partner Patsy Kensit—a British singer/actress who, by the time she met and began a relationship with Gallagher, had already been married to musicians Dan Donovan and Simple Minds' Jim Kerr. In the image, Gallagher's bare torso is wrapped in a Union Jack duvet cover, and Kensit lies on top of the covers, wearing black leggings, black ankle-boots and a sheer black brassiere. The image reads in tropes of rock 'n' roll: the male star with the glamorous, blond groupie-cum-girlfriend. Citing *Time* magazine's famous April 1967 cover, the caption to the image reads, "London swings, again!"—a statement that pronounces Britain's dominance within global popular culture. As one *Melody Maker* writer remarked,

> In 1994, Oasis were a phenomenon. In 1995, a religion. In 1996, they were the context. They ceased to be an object with a location or a presence and turned into the atmosphere we moved in, a fact as inescapable as the weather. They weren't just the dominant force in pop, but the milieu where much of the rest of British cultural life took place.

The author concluded with a challenge: "Think that's an exaggeration? It's simply a sober assessment."[105]

Within the "context" of Oasis, several non-white, non-male musicians attempted to make their mark. For example, the Britpop bands Cornershop and Echobelly were fronted by British Asians. As Sonya Aurora-Madan of Echobelly explained to Avril Mair of *i-D*, "I wanted to get involved in music precisely because it's so white, masculine and middle-class."[106] Such criticisms were also leveled at the Blair government's "Cool Britannia" project, of which Britpop was a central feature. Youth cultural theorist Rupa Huq argues, "Although the post-1997 Blair government's 'Cool Britannia' project which aimed to update outmoded images of the UK acknowledged British Asians, the term turned out to be short-lived."[107] Indeed, Britpop's ethnic insularity is marked by comparison with the other 1990s youth cultural formations that

Huq examines. For example, she identifies Bhangra as the diasporic product of migration from the Indian subcontinent to the UK and she explores hip-hip as a black American-in-origin sound that took hold in Finland and France, amongst other international sites. Like Bannister's book on the 1980s independent music scene, she entitles her chapter on grunge and Britpop "White Noise." What's more, Aurora-Madan and the other female stars of Britpop were routinely sexualized within the music press. Davies explains about the music press, female musicians are usually ignored, and when they are addressed, they are "always represented primarily *as* women, rather than as musicians."[108] Further, the type of questions they are asked tend to emphasize "their appearance and sexuality."[109] Louise Wener—frontwoman of Britpop band Sleeper—recounts such experiences in her memoir.

> How does it feel to be a sex symbol? How does it feel to know boys are masturbating over your photography? Hmmm. These aren't questions I ask myself all that much. They are questions male music journalists ask me. *All* the time. […] I don't think they're asking Liam [Gallagher] and Damon [Albarn] this kind of question. And I'm pretty sure people are masturbating over their pictures, too.[110]

She continues by noting that it might feel good if she were not asked about it so frequently, if she could just be let alone to enjoy it.[111] To counter sexual objectification, members of Britpop's female-fronted bands donned androgynous ensembles within performance. For example, the three female members of Elastica sported a look consisting of black jeans, bovver boots, and short haircuts. Despite their androgyny, the music and fashion presses found means to sexualize these artists, not least through styling for press photographs. While the American riot grrrls were resisting sexist representation by refusing to comply with press coverage,[112] the female stars of Britpop were routinely placed within sexualized tropes on the pages of magazines. Wener explains, "Justine [Frischmann] aping [former showgirl] Christine Keeler on the cover of *Select*, Sonya Echobelly falling out of her shirt in *i-D*, […] and how the hell did I end up being photographed in a wet-look PVC catsuit carrying a gun?"[113] She concludes, "This isn't the girl from [American rock band] L7 pulling her pants down on *The Word* to reveal her big hairy bush. This is neutered and neat. Conformist and traditional. Same as it ever was. Indie playboy."[114]

Non-white and female musicians were not alone in bucking against the seemingly omnipresent—and somewhat paradoxical—tropes of indie machismo in the 1990s. So too did Jarvis Cocker—the slender, white frontman of Pulp. Pulp was a remnant of the British independent scene of the 1980s. The Sheffield-in-origin five-piece had been together for twelve years before they began to garner fame in the early 1990s. As one music reviewer for *The Face* wrote of the band, "They've had more false starts than the Grand National, but eleven years after their wimp rock debut, Pulp romp into the final furlong with their swooping, swooning Technicolor pop. Sometimes it pays to go to art college."[115] Their look—corduroy trousers, suit jackets, leather trousers, wool jumpers and stripy shirts, all thoughtfully assembled from garments sourced in charity shops—resembled more closely the androgynously slim-cut ensembles of their 1980s peers, as opposed to the looser T-shirts and jeans preferred by Blur and Oasis. Pulp's first single to get attention, "Babies" (1992), evidenced further their difference from their Britpop contemporaries.[116] The music video features the group with their instruments in a white room. The camera focuses on Cocker, who stands amid his bandmates in a black, slim-cut suit with a flared leg. His body's characteristics—long, lean, and boyish—are accentuated by the suit's cut and style, and by the fact that he wears no shirt under the blazer. Instead, his slender, white chest, adorned only with sparse patches of hair, is on

Figure 2 Jarvis Cocker at Glastonbury in 1994. He would wear a similar look and move in a similar style the following year, as his band Pulp would take the festival's headlining slot. © Michael Putland/Getty Images.

display. As his bandmates play their instruments, Cocker dances around the center of the room, wiggling his hips, shimmying his shoulders and pointing coyly at the camera. He is, in one sense, the physical embodiment of the song's lyrics, which tell the story of a teenage boy's obsession with his virginal girlfriend's sexually precocious older sister. That is, Cocker is boyish in frame, but sexual in performance—a seeming contradiction that would define his star persona throughout the 1990s.

Cocker's celebrity would reach its peak in 1995 because of Pulp's performance at the twenty-fifth annual Glastonbury Festival in Somerset, UK (Figure 2). Since the first Isle of Wight festival in 1968—and its American counterpart, Woodstock, in 1969—summer music festivals have been held in fields throughout the British countryside each summer. In contrast to the hundreds of thousands of attendees that flooded the Isle of Wight and Woodstock, New York during the "flower child" revolution, British music festivals throughout the 1970s and 1980s were generally niche affairs, often catering to hard rock and heavy metal audiences.[117] The 1990s saw a change, however: in Blur bassist Alex James's words, "The festival transformed from a countercultural beardy bond session into a mainstream mass phenomenon, like fishing and football."[118] The Face's Danny Scott noticed a similar shift. He explained, "Today's festival is no longer a 'rock thing,'" before naming the different subcultural types that now frequent festivals: "ravers and grungers, crusties and parents, hippies and indie kids."[119] Of the many British summer music festivals, Glastonbury emerged as preeminent, perhaps because it was understood to be the festival with closest links to the music industry. When the Stone Roses backed out of their headlining spot in 1995, Pulp took the opportunity to give what is understood retrospectively as a career-changing performance.

Like Brett Anderson of Suede, Cocker's stage performance was (and still is, at the time of writing) electric. At various points during the band's hour-long Glastonbury set, he makes love to the microphone and engages in a series of Mick Jagger-esque jumps and twists, demanding the audience's attention. Unlike Anderson, however, Cocker's performance is ultimately masculine. Throughout, and despite the sweat that pours down his face, Cocker wears a charcoal, gabardine blazer over a black button-down shirt and skinny gray tie. The outfit's seeming insistence on masculine signifiers is playful and coy. Indeed, it seems that, if in the mid-1990s Oasis's rock 'n' roll machismo was the "context" of British music, this context did not obliterate oppositional performances of masculinity within indie. Instead, the newly reimagined indie of the 1990s also allowed for a typically 1980s indie figure—Cocker—to develop a sexualized rock persona. Amy Raphael's 1994 profile on the star for *The Face* addresses this possibility of Cocker's sex appeal. The article is entitled with the question "Sex on a Stick?"—"stick" playfully referring to what Raphael describes as Cocker's "long and stick insect skinny" frame.[120] One answer comes from the author's friend:

> First gig, and my immediate reaction was "yum, yum". He's scrawny but very sexual. He's quirky. He's a poseur but he gets away with it. He knows what he's doing; he's not a 19-year-old playing around with an image he doesn't understand. I like men who dress up without being effeminate.[121]

Thus, it was perhaps the dressed-up Cocker to whom *i-D*'s Susan Corrigan was referring, when she wrote in 1995, "There's never been a better time to be a pretty boy in a band. Indie's gone glam, and that three-button suit is more important than the three-chord song."[122]

Stylish teenage outsiders

In great contrast to the way they received the indie music scene of the 1980s, the monthly and bi-monthly alternative style magazines greeted the stars of Britpop with excited wonder, framing these new rock 'n' roll sex gods as style icons. Eager to detail precisely what the bands were wearing at a gig or during a magazine interview, *The Face*, *i-D*, and *Dazed & Confused* presented glowing characterizations of the visual qualities of the Britpop bands. For example, in the March 1993 issue of *The Face*, Suede's "jumble sale chic" is noted; the author writes about the group, "They had dubious shoes but a nice line in fake fur jackets and your mum's shirts with fuck-off collars, and, to boot, a swaggering singer who was pale, gaunt and a bit camp. They were touted as 'the new Smiths.'"[123] In the December 1993 issue of *i-D*, Tony Marcus describes Pulp as "the ultimate Oxfam band." The article celebrates the band's sartorial ragpicking: "'Pulp keep using everybody's cast-offs, the things other people have rejected,' says Jarvis. He's wearing an old LCD wristwatch, the kind that tells the time in flashing electric red when you press the button." Marcus continues his admiring description: "Jarvis is a glamour queen drawn to the flared collars, crooners, lipgloss and razzmatazz that are easily dismissed as kitsch."[124] It is in a May 1994 issue of *The Face* that Graham Coxon from Blur receive praise. Cliff Jones writes, "From his Ben Sherman through to his pristine desert boots, he's every inch the stylish mod Face about town."[125] He continues by stating that the band is undergoing a "transformation from gangly indie wastrels to would-be Britpop saviours" and, in doing so, is leading the way into a new Britain, "where dressing well and having a good haircut matter."[126] Finally, in an article detailing the multiple reincarnations of black drainpipe jeans, soon-to-be fashion designer Luella Bartley writes that "This time around they are once again appearing on the most fashionable lower halves in the pop business. Elastica are the '90s patron saints of all that is fashionably black and drainpipe."[127] Such praises mark a drastic change in the alternative style media's representation of indie musicians. For example, in the October 1994 issue of *i-D*, journalist Tony Marcus writes, "There might be 100,000 different reasons to like Suede, but the most immediate revolve around how deeply the idea of this teenage outsider works its way into Brett: body, voice, sexual identity, songs."[128] In no uncertain terms, Marcus calls the Suede frontman an outsider. His words are not critical, however. Marcus does not use the term "outsider" negatively to relegate Anderson to the edge of popular culture, but rather he regards Anderson's outsider status as an asset: in his opinion, the most poignant reason to like Suede. By the 1990s, it seems, indie outsiderism had evolved from being a badge of "uncool" to being a badge of "hipness."

Omitted from the style press' praises was Oasis. Perhaps the band was too "mainstream" to be considered; perhaps its members were too working-class. It is possible that *loaded*'s Brown and Southwell's disdain for the style press's "Oxbridge-educated, liberal journalists"[129] was reciprocated and that the Gallagher brothers' laddish personas were not condoned by the editors of *i-D*, *The Face* and *Dazed & Confused*. Indeed, in the above-cited article from *The Face* about Blur, Damon Albarn and Graham Coxon received implicit praises from the style press precisely because of their sartorial distance from the working class. The interview took place at the Walthamstow dog races, and the author gave an account of how boys wearing shell suits—a garment associated with the working class in the UK—made fun of Albarn and Coxon's clothing choices.[130] Such an account builds a positive picture of the musicians' clothing by relying upon the readers' aversion of the boys in shell suits. The account also willfully ignores the fact that Albarn and Coxon too were known to don shell suits in their attempts to perform working-class laddishness.

In an attempt to understand how the skinny indie male was being reimagined as a style icon, it is important to consider the influence of grunge on the 1990s British fashion scene. At the forefront of the grunge movement was the troubled musician Kurt Cobain—the lead singer in the band

Nirvana—and, with him, his wife Courtney Love—the lead singer in the band Hole. His look consisted of un-brushed blond hair hanging just past his ears, plaid lumberjack shirts, and filthy, old jeans. Her look consisted of un-brushed blond hair hanging just past her ears and pretty, second-hand dresses that were often in tatters. In media images from the early 1990s, the pair look disheveled, and much of the press coverage of the couple related to their drug use and marital problems. Cobain and Love's grunge look has received academic attention. Deena Weinstein, for example, "interprets the uniform of ripped jeans and lumberjack shirts as [...] standing for 'identification with the homeless and destitute.'"[131] Cobain and Love's grunge look also got the attention of several fashion designers, most notably Marc Jacobs, who in 1993 took the helm of the Perry Ellis design house. Jacobs' spring 1993 collection took direct inspiration from the grunge look. It consisted of "floaty, flowery dresses [like Love's], silk 'flannel' shirts [modeled on Cobain's], shrunken tweed jackets, and knitted caps, all tossed together in seemingly random combinations, often over satin Converse sneakers or clunky army boots."[132] The collection served as an example of Ted Polhemus's "bubble-up" diffusion: when a style emerges from the streets—in this case, the Seattle music scene—only to be emulated and co-opted by high fashion designers.[133] Jacobs's collection for Perry Ellis arguably had a large influence within high fashion in the 1990s, as British *Vogue* at times guided readers to take on the grunge look. For example, in an April 1993 issue of the magazine, fashion designer Rifat Ozbek summarized the grunge look; he said, "You get out of bed and put whatever's on the floor next to you. Isn't that what grunge is?" The article's author continued,

> He's quite right—the point is not how *much* thought goes into grunging it, but how little. "Accessorizing" may be a newly dirtied word, but if your current cache amounts to a pair of gilt earrings and a choker, you might want to line up a few extras to reach out for from under the duvet this summer, such as dainty thermal vests, crochet-knit anything—belts, bags, beanies, gloves—and workaday boots or sneakers. Ditch the earrings for a homespun thong necklace hung with a minute ornament ... and then forget that you've put any thought into it at all.[134]

The grunge look brought positive attention—and negative attention, as Marc Jacobs was fired from Perry Ellis shortly after his grunge-inspired collection—to a visual aesthetic that greatly resembled the indie look. As

Britpop took over from grunge in 1993 to be the most popular guitar-based musical movement in Britain, moreover, the indie look—and the skinny indie man, on whose body it was displayed—began to take center stage. In an end-of-the-year fashion review of 1994, *i-D*'s then-fashion editor Edward Enninful wrote, "in the UK, quintessentially English indie bands like Blur, Pulp and Elastica defined a style that could only be described as a one-step progression from grunge."[135]

Even some representatives from the music press seemed to get excited about indie's newfound fashion status. *NME* contributor John Robinson included in his commentary on Britpop group Supergrass the following description of the band's drummer: "impeccably draped in skinny jeans, desert boots and a mod-poppers mohair jacket."[136] Robinson's interest in the band's look marked an aberration within *NME*'s discourse of the time—a discourse that was framed largely around the nationalistic celebration of Britpop's avenging of grunge. Robinson's statement was prophetic, however, as *NME*'s language would change drastically in 2001, when a New York-based five-piece band called the Strokes would storm the UK and place its boyish, DIY aesthetic at the center of popular fashion.

2000s: American invasion and fashion darlings

Before they even made a name for themselves in their hometown of New York City, the Strokes achieved success in the UK. Mark Hooper wrote in the September 2001 issue of *i-D*, "In the press (and what press—from the indie inkies [i.e. the weekly music press] to the broadsheets in a matter of weeks), they've come across as a group raised in New York but aimed squarely at London."[137] Indeed, part of the band's initial success was due to their seeming resemblance to in sound and in appearance the Britpop bands of the 1990s. In the words of music journalist Rob Sheffield, for example: "I mean, it's funny, when the Strokes started and people said 'The Ramones! Television!' They don't sound like those bands at all. They sound like Elastica."[138] Former *NME* editor Conor McNicholas explained further, "Post-Britpop there was this terrible nether-land that was filled with Travis and Coldplay," and as a result British indie kids were saddled again by the stereotypes that framed them at the beginning of the 1990s. "Suddenly, when the Strokes turned up," he continued, "we were the cool kids again."[139] Indeed, in the July 2001 issue of *The Face*, Johnny Davis wrote, "Not since the good years of Britpop (Suede, Blur, Elastica) have we had style-and-content pop stars you'll want to take to your hearts and pin to your walls."[140] Unlike the Britpop bands, however, the Strokes were not celebrated for their quirky outsiderness. Instead, as Davis later described them, the band embodied "coolness itself."[141] Fifteen years later, veteran music journalist Marc Spitz would explain, "The Strokes got on a bus, and they brought 'downtown cool' to the world."[142]

The downtown scene

The Strokes' "cool" factor was inextricably tied to their New York City origins. Four of the five band members were raised in New York, weaned on the city's hustling and bustling streets. The band's breakthrough EP *The Modern Age* and album *Is This It* in 2001 are understood to have reinvigorated the downtown New York music scene, whose heyday in the 1970s with Debbie Harry, Richard Hell and the now legendary venue CBGBs seemed long gone. Lizzy Goodman's 2017 oral history *Meet Me in the Bathroom: Rebirth and Rock and Roll in New York City 2001–2011* provides an invaluable account of this scene that emerged at the turn of the millennium in the wake of the September 11 attack. Among her interviewees, there is consensus that the Strokes started the twenty-first-century rock revival. As the music critic Austin Scaggs claimed about the band, "They were writing the autobiography of the East Village."[143] Nonetheless, several other bands quickly made their mark: Interpol and the Yeah Yeah Yeahs. Although from Detroit, the White Stripes would also be included in what the music press would frame as "America striking back" or "the return of punk." Gigs, popular bars, and club nights sustained this early twenty-first-century downtown music scene, nurturing a sense of community. The club nights also worked to define the scene's identity, linking it to Britpop and the British rock music that influenced Britpop. Thomas Onorato, who worked as a doorman at several of these clubs, explained, the club night "Tiswas mattered to me because I was an Anglophile, whether it was David Bowie or whether it was Blur and Oasis and that was the music that was played there."[144] Much like Suede, Oasis, Blur, Pulp, and Elastica not even a decade earlier, the Strokes, Interpol, the White Stripes, and the Yeah Yeah Yeahs were heralded as a sort of royalty amongst their peers.

Like Elastica, the Yeah Yeah Yeahs were fronted by a woman: the dynamic Karen O. O is well known for her two personalities. Whereas she might present as a shy person on the street, she incites riot on stage, "grabbing three beers in her fist, drinking one and pouring the other two over herself and the mic stand," as music journalist Joe Levy recounted to Goodman.[145] For her part, O explained,

I always felt like because I was a woman I just had a completely different perspective. […] I was not beholden to the rules of the game, which is a big thing in the rock world. It's very dutiful. There's a legacy that is laid out. There's a cannon [sic] of rock, and a lot of men worship that and kneel at the alter [sic] of that. I didn't have to play by those rules.[146]

What's more, O created a space for other young women to do the same. The front row of each Yeah Yeah Yeahs' show was populated by young women, and they were the fans who were handing O beers to pour all over herself and them.[147] As O's costume designer Christian Joy remembered,

I feel like a lot of girls, myself included, finally felt like we had someone onstage we could relate to, someone who did not give a fuck in the same way we did and didn't mind being dirty and unsexy and was just being herself and was not a dude. I think we felt like we owned the moment. We would go to the shows and go absolutely bonkers in the front row. Karen was our fearless leader. We would come out of the shows absolutely covered in bruises, dirty, and drunk. We were totally arrogant fuckers just like boys. It was the first time I felt like I had women like myself around.[148]

Such sentiments must have been felt by the female fans of Elastica when viewing Frischmann, Donna Matthews, and Annie Holland on stage. Crucially, O was able to translate her powerful stage presence into a feminist media image as well, specifically by working closely with Joy to create a look that was both over-the-top and androgynous.

Joy's collaboration with the audacious frontwoman was well known to the band's fans. As Joy recalled to me during interview, "Karen used to get on stage and go, 'how do you like this outfit? It's by Christian Joy!'" During the early 2000s, the outfits under consideration were usually some form of deconstructed prom dresses that O would then destroy further during performance as she tore across the stage. As Joy noted, "all the really early stuff was mainly kind of like these tests and learning to sew and trying things, but it worked well because it also went with her chaotic stage presence." Joy's inspirations during the touring and press for the band's first album—*Fever to Tell* (2003)—were shrimp and film director John Waters, who is known for his camp aesthetic. Leading into the band's second album—*Show Your Bones* (2006)—Joy took inspiration from Little Lord

Fauntleroy and David Bowie. As she explained, "with Karen I've always looked more at men's fashion […] I've always found it more interesting the way that men wear clothing. I think they wield a different power than women do." A turning point in their collaboration, Joy determined, was one of the last costumes she made for the *Fever to Tell* tour: an androgynous onesie skeleton suit with a "three-dimensional heart and lungs [and] intestines that she was supposed to pull out and they were to be pulled into the audience." Joy's part-camp, part-androgynous costumes for O served as a focal point for much press attention. Indeed, reproduced across a range of music magazine covers throughout the 2000s, including *NME* and *Rolling Stone*, was a visual aesthetic that contrasted O in a flamboyant Christian Joy-ensemble with drummer Brian Chase and guitarist Nick Zinner's all black outfits. Thus, whereas the female stars of Britpop were routinely placed within sexualized tropes on the pages of music and style magazines, O (and Joy) controlled her own visual representation.

Not only the Yeah Yeah Yeahs, but all of the bands associated with the American rock renaissance of the early 2000s had unique looks. Dior Homme designer Hedi Slimane dressed Jack White of the White Stripes in Hedi S. Stagewear: skinny, black jeans and a dark, tightly fitting T-shirt with rips across the chest and sleeves.[149] Moreover, both he and his bandmate, Meg White, dressed in a palette of black, red, and white—a color scheme that was reproduced throughout the band's music video and stage sets. As Kimberly Mack explains, the White Stripes' music borrowed heavily from the blues and, she argues further, their red-black-white color scheme, inspired by Pop Art, functioned to mask the bands' association with—appropriation of—this Southern, black musical tradition.[150] The members of Interpol would dress in all-black ensembles, produced from combining elements of formalwear, such as ties and suit jackets. Bass guitarist Carlos Dengler is credited with originating the look; it was he who first went to the band's communal tailor: Craig Robinson, whose studio was located near Union Square.[151] As Chris Lombardi, cofounder of indie record label Matador, noted to Goodman, "Interpol dressed like rock stars. I mean, Carlos was this guy with a fucking armband on and hair greased in a certain way, wearing a fucking holster and smoking onstage, showing off his profile."[152]

It was the Strokes, whose look received the most attention, however. It seemed almost effortless. Their shoes—sometimes leather loafers, but more frequently Converse high-tops—were dirty and well worn. Their jeans—sometimes loose, but more frequently slim-cut—were faded and torn. Their tops—a mixture of vintage T-shirts, casual blazers and leather jackets—were

Figure 3 The Strokes, photographed for *NME*. © Dean Chalkley/Time Inc.

just a bit too short and tight. Their hair was shaggy and unwashed, and the cigarettes hanging from their lips were a reminder that they were just too cool to care about looking "put together" (Figure 3). But, of course, their look was put together quite thoughtfully. The Strokes' Nick Valensi recounted meeting his future bandmate Albert Hammond Jr., "We were all wearing jeans and T-shirts and New Balance sneakers and Albert showed up in a suit. Everyone all of a sudden was like, 'Okay, hold on a second, let's start thinking about this.'"[153] Soon, not only the five tall and slender members of the Strokes were "thinking about this." Rather, it seemed everyone interested in indie music was considering the Strokes' look. As journalist April Long so aptly put it, "The Strokes really did create the blueprint for the international hipster look of the aughts—the skinny jeans, leather jacket. You can add a mustache or a flannel shirt, but the baseline is essentially still the same, even now."[154]

NME *fashion*

In an end-of-the-year summary of 2001, one *NME* journalist declared, "It's a truth universally acknowledged that indie bands don't have a clue about fashion—and, it must be said, vice versa. But everything changed in 2001."[155] Putting forward a point that the magazine had belabored throughout the year, the author argued that the indie bands of 2001 "knew how to dress."[156] Such a statement would mark a profound change in the music magazine's discourse, moreover, as journalists began to write not only about the sound of indie, but also about its look. Crucially, it was the male indie musicians whose fashions were up for discussion. Whereas it was widely understood that Karen O was wearing a costume on stage, the male stars of the twenty-first-century indie rock revival were seen to be inventing a new style, a new way of being. As the only remaining representative of the weekly music press (*Melody Maker* having closed its doors in 2000, and *Sounds* having ended much earlier in 1991), *NME* seemed to take immense pride in indie's newfound fashion sense. As a result, much ink was devoted to describing indie bands' and musicians' outfits.

Of course, the Strokes were up first on *NME*'s hit list. The magazine interviewed Luella Bartley—by this point, one of London's hip young designers—asking her to explain the indie look. "She told *NME*: 'It's a bit New York old school, slightly punk, but it appeals to the English as well. It's slightly scruffy public school. It's that really scruffy blazer, shirt and tie—it's such a good look.'"[157] When the magazine implored her to explain to readers how to put together such a look, she complied, saying,

It's not really a high fashion thing. Just go to the East Village thrift stores in New York or Notting Hill. [Lead singer] Julian [Casablancas] wears a really old man's jacket, a grey pinstripe, which is easy to find. Combining that with a pink satin tie is genius. You maybe need some really faded black jeans, quite a skinny leg. They do that scruffy leather jacket too—it's the perfect look for really cheap.[158]

Complementing Bartley's guidance, *NME* also offered its own how-to fashion guide in an article called "Stroke of good luck."[159] The guide focused specifically on singer "Julian [Casablancas]'s 'grungy' look"—a byline that reminds readers of indie's similarity to its fashionable predecessor. It claimed, "The grunge look, like the gypsy look, is all about not looking controlled." The key elements of the grunge look include: "Converse shoes: generations of NY rockers from the Ramones to The Strokes have sworn by these canvas classics"; "Trews: distressed denim or the tight suit type—it's up to you"; "Tatty suit jackets or army fatigues: your local Shelter shop's never been such an oasis of fusty fashions"; "White shirts: note the 'peasant'-style lack of buttons on this one [indicating an accompanying photo]"; "Retro shirts; lose the beer belly, though, lads"; and "Ties: no fat knots though."[160] Although *NME* featured clothing advertisements in the back pages of its magazine throughout the 1950s, 1960s, and 1970s, such a dressing guide was unprecedented within its pages.

After the Strokes, *NME* celebrated Kings of Leon's Caleb Followill. On the magazine's "Cool List" for 2003, Followill ranked fourth. The accompany blurb read:

Caleb looks cool, he talks cool, he sings cool and he possibly found the original cool while rummaging through the vintage T-shirts in a thrift store in San Francisco's Haight-Ashbury. Of course, there's the look: velvet jackets, battered T-shirts, braces, drainpiped but ever so slightly flared torn jeans—all three sizes too small—coupled with the best tash-and-beard combination seen in the last 30 years. Caleb is the reason why all of your town's charity shops have been looted by the local fashionistas.[161]

The description "three sizes too small" was not an exaggeration. As Nathan Followill, Caleb's brother and bandmate, noted to Goodman, "We would go buy jeans and then have our mom sew them and then make 'em so tight."[162] He continued, "I can remember Jared [Followill, another brother and bandmate] having to straighten his legs out so stiff just to pull them on, and then we would lift him up and he could not bend his knees for a good thirty minutes."[163] After the Followill brothers, Razorlight's Johnny Borrell celebrated a moment in the *NME* spotlight: "Modelling his customary magpie-in-a-charity-shop fashion sense (tonight: knee-length football socks, pipecleaner jeans, Lacoste trainers and tweed coat), he cuts quite a dash."[164] Thus, by the time Pete Doherty of the Libertines rose to fashionable prominence under the guiding hand of designer Hedi Slimane, the groundwork had been firmly laid. The skinny, white, guitar-playing, male indie musician was well on his way to becoming a twenty-first-century fashion icon.

CHAPTER 2
SKINNY BOYS AND PARISIAN RUNWAYS: THE COMMODIFICATION OF INDIE AUTHENTICITY

In the mid-2000s, at the helm of Dior Homme, Hedi Slimane placed the indie musician at the center of popular fashion. His intervention would upend the menswear industry and establish a new ideal of fashionable masculinity based on the boyish indie frame. Slimane's idealized indie boy did not resemble the twee pop star-wannabe of the 1980s indie scene. Nor did he resemble the macho, nationalistic rock star of Britpop. Nor still did he resemble the twenty-first-century saviors of New York rock with their preconceived stage looks. Rather, the indie boy of Slimane's imagination personified the authentic ideals of Britain's earliest rock and roll stars. The seeming quality of rock authenticity imbued the designer's fashionable vision with phallic power, while also making his collections for Dior Homme commercially successful. From 2005 to 2007, Pete Doherty, frontman of the Libertines and later Babyshambles, served as his favorite muse. For male indie musicians and fans, however, balancing the values of rock authenticity, on the one hand, and the commercial opportunities afforded by the fashion industry, on the other, proved a challenging task. In the wake of Slimane's intervention, musicians and fans found themselves with new opportunities for self-fashioning, whether that meant dressing up in Dior Homme garments for press coverage, buying mass-marketed indie-look ensembles in Topman, or even slipping down to the women's section of Topshop for skinny jeans woven with a little spandex for that extra-tight fit. Many musicians and fans eschewed these opportunities, but others were able to find a balance between rock orthodoxy and commercial fashion. In doing so, they were also able to inhabit successfully the twenty-first-century fashionably authentic/authentically fashionable indie ideal of Slimane's imagination, performing indie identities that were both music-oriented and shaped through fashion.

Hedi Slimane's fashionable vision of masculinity

Slimane is known for altering the shape of fashionable masculinity in the 2000s. His design work was compelling for its creativity; through his androgynous suits he brought couture techniques to the ready-to-wear menswear market. His work was believable, however, because it tapped into the well-worn tropes of rock: authenticity, individual expression, and the purity of the live performance. Under Slimane's gaze, the twenty-first-century fashionable man was neither an athlete nor a financier. He was a rock 'n' roll star.

Bohemian masculinity

Slimane's collections were a hit with the fashion set well before he met Pete Doherty. Both he and fellow newcomer Raf Simons were celebrated within the press for their experimentations on the male silhouette. Slimane's first trials in a slender silhouette were in his teenage years, as he attempted to tailor suit jackets to fit his own long and lean frame.[1] He would develop this design aesthetic further, at YSL from 1997 to 2000 and at Dior Homme from 2001. Although she would famously fall out with the designer in 2012, the *New York Times'* fashion critic Cathy Horyn was an early and vocal supporter. In August 1999, she heralded his work at Yves Saint Laurent, where he helmed the label's menswear line. His "clean, elegant style," she wrote, "is so wildly at odds with the shapeless, insipid sportswear that flattened the recent New York men's shows."[2]

Slimane's experiments in shape were not merely aesthetic trials, however. As Jay McCauley Bowstead notes, "Slimane saw himself as intervening not only in the field of menswear, but in masculinity itself."[3] Charlie Porter of *The Guardian* explains, "Slimane is heralding a more sensitive interpretation of male self-image, at odds with the pumped-up stereotype that has dominated menswear for the past two decades."[4] In other words, he wanted to use fashion to create a new set of meanings concerning what it meant to be a man. The designer explained to *The Guardian*'s Craig McLean in 2005,

> There's so many connotations in muscles and virility, I find it crap. I'm not interested. I'm really interested in how masculinity is in your head. That's what I worked on. And Paul Simonon [of the Clash] and all these heroes had that strength. But it's not something they expressed through their body. I was always more interested in the psychology rather than the science of life. Like power and masculinity.[5]

Slimane's was not the first fashionable challenge to muscle-bound masculinity and the phallic power such virility conveyed. In the UK in the 1980s, the "new man"—a figure newly produced across advertisements, high street shops, and new media titles—"combined strong masculine features with elements of softness or sensuality."[6] The "new man" still exhibited a muscle-bound frame; however, his body was to be put on display "in ways which drew on codings traditionally associated with representations of femininity within consumer culture."[7] As such, Sean Nixon contends, "the 'new man' imagery in general resignified the relations between gay and straight-identified men [and] extended a space for an ambivalent masculine sexual identity which had precedents within the metropolitan contours of post-war British popular culture."[8] In contrast, Slimane's ideal man was stripped of his muscles, but neither of his heterosexuality nor his phallic power. *The Independent*'s Janet Street-Porter continued, "Slimane's clothes are slender, shrunken, designed to drape and cling to bodies which do nothing more strenuous than lift a guitar or hold a cigarette."[9] The guitar—a phallic symbol, wielded by male rockers and the few female rockers, who were able to "play with the boys"—assures viewers of the virility of Slimane's idealized men, of their masculinity. Slimane's work during this period thus drew on the well-worn and highly recognizable tropes of rock authenticity.

In their cultural historical account of British pop from the 1960s to the 1980s, *Art Into Pop*, Simon Frith and Howard Horne contextualize the formation of these tropes of rock authenticity. The 1960s, they contend, witnessed the emergence of rock 'n' roll in the UK. It was then that art school students bearing "bohemian dreams and Romantic fancies"[10] saw in popular music a potential outlet for their creative practice. Rock 'n' roll's earliest British participants worshiped the American blues, and their R&B sounds were thus laced with tributes to "a black original."[11] And yet, this "new generation of art school musicians"[12] also found within their music "a way of expressing individual needs, displaying individual, artistic control."[13] That is, in rock these young white British men found a way of claiming authenticity; when they had no claim on the authenticity of the "black original," they could claim authenticity through individual expression. And their music was interpreted as just that: authentic, *individual* expression. "Entertainers were, by their nature, transparent; honest simply meant giving their audiences all they'd got."[14] This transparency was to distinguish rock from its counterpart, pop. They write, as a genre, "Rock, […] unlike pop, was to be serious, progressive, truthful, and individual."[15] There is a gendered dimension to such authenticity. As the authors explain, "To make music 'seriously' [...] was to be a man; to giggle and scream and sigh was to be a woman."[16] Frith had made a similar point a decade preceding, when he and Angela McRobbie boldly claimed that "rock is a male form."[17]

In Pete Doherty, Slimane saw the personification of this masculinized rock ideal. "It's almost as if he invented the checklist," [the designer] quipped" in 2005 to Miles Socha of *WWD*.[18] And to American journalist Hadley Freeman: "I just felt an immediate connection with [the Libertines], particularly Pete," he said. "That sense of performance, that connection with the fans, none of that celebrity stuff [...] there is something very special about Pete."[19] As a result, Slimane's designs for Dior Homme were inspired by Doherty's skinny, indie look. In *The Guardian* Freeman describes, "Suits were sharp as pins, yet cut extra skinny to look more cool than a City boy, and capes, pussy bows and hats were flamboyantly Libertine-esque."[20] Reciprocally, Slimane had immense influence over Doherty's image. Photos taken at the Libertines' gigs before Slimane's intervention reveal a young man dressed in loose jeans and football shirts. After their union, however, Slimane gifted Doherty slim suits, trilby hats, skinny jeans, and narrow, black ties. As a result, most, if not all, of the images of Doherty appearing in the British press during the mid-2000s were of a man fully clad in Dior Homme. What Doherty brought to the look was his shambolic lifestyle. After the end of a gig, his tie would be loosened; after a weekend at Glastonbury, his suit trousers would be muddied. As the designer explained to *Women's Wear Daily* in 2005, "you don't dress him. [...] He improvises in such an incredible way that everything becomes his clothes right away."[21] The musician was somewhat coarser in his discussion of the collaboration. "It's fucking weird," Doherty said. "One minute I'm in a prison tracksuit queueing for chicken and rice, and then next minute I'm clobbered out in Dior."[22]

Doherty was Slimane's muse both for the fashion collections he produced at Dior Homme in the mid-2000s and for his photographic practice during the period. Doherty is the central figure within two of Slimane's early photography projects: the limited-edition photo-book *London: Birth of a Cult* (2005) and the exhibition "As Tears Go By" (2006). Speaking about the former, Slimane said,

When I started [it], it was very difficult for magazines to do something about him [...] Pete was something of an outcast. For me, it was important at that moment to share that idea that he had a very rare thing. People always get trapped into the same stories and same clichés of rock. But I had the feeling they were missing the point. And they were not seeing what was poetic about him; and musically really strong. And so I thought I could help out a little bit to at least balance the impression people had.[23]

The impression of Doherty, which Slimane presents across the pages of the photo-book, is one made up of close-up shots of the musician both in performance and backstage. In many images, including the book's cover photograph, Doherty appears shirtless or in garments so tattered they reveal his hairless torso. Slimane seems to take on the role of voyeur, capturing the musician as if he were unaware of the camera's gaze. In one of the images in the book, a broken record and a ripped banknote appear pasted onto an interior wall of Doherty's Whitechapel, London apartment. Scribbled next to the items, perhaps in Doherty's own blood, read the words: "The last of the true Romantic fantastist [sic]."[24]

Doherty's indie milieu

Slimane situates his image of Doherty-as-bohemian-rock-icon within a broader tableau of the British indie scene. He visualizes this scene in *London: Birth of a Cult*; his website *Rock Diary*; and later in "Sonic," an exhibition that ran from September 18, 2014 to January 11, 2015 at the Fondation Pierre Bergé-Yves Saint Laurent in Paris. Through these images Slimane creates a world, populated by young, white men who worship at the altar of individual expression.[25]

The live performance—what Nick Rees-Roberts calls "the corporeal experience of the live gig"—is central to Slimane's imagining of the London indie scene.[26] He photographs musicians in performance, fans in the pit of a venue during a performance, and both musicians and fans backstage, before and after performances. Such photographs function as documentary evidence of concerts that have occurred, who played, who was there, and what the atmosphere was. A common feature across these photographs, moreover, is that the subjects are covered in sweat.[27] For example, separate images of Joshua Hubbard and Martin Hines, both of The Paddingtons, show the musicians post-performance: heads hanging, white T-shirts off, chests glistening. Hubbard is pictured using his T-shirt to mop his brow; Hines has wrapped his shirt around his neck like a scarf. Indeed, in many of Slimane's images of the London scene, musicians are shown on stage in various states of *deshabille*. Most notably, of course, is Pete Doherty, who appears shirtless and sweaty in a number of photographs.

Writing about the indie gig, Wendy Fonarow explains, "Indie requires the performance be imbued with the authentic spirit of the artist's experience." She continues that audiences and critics "want to believe that the musician is being himself, that the performance onstage has some truthful relationship to the world beyond."[28] Beyond indie, the live performance is central to the production of authenticity within rock cultures. As Lawrence Grossberg explains, "it is only here that one can see the actual production of the sound, and the emotional work carried in the voice."[29] Noel McLaughlin furthers Grossberg's argument, stating "that music has often been valued within rock ideology precisely for its ability to release repressed desires, to strip away the layers of 'artifice' and reveal the core personality."[30] As both authors note, however, this form of authenticity—one based around the Romantic image of the artist—is specific to white rock cultures.[31] With the exception of very few subjects—for example, the black British lead singer of Bloc Party, Kele Okereke—the great majority of Slimane's London-based subjects are white, a denotation that almost hides itself behind the connotation of rock authenticity. In his famous essay on whiteness, Richard Dyer explains, "The colourless multi-colouredness of whiteness secures white power by making it hard, especially for white people and their media, to 'see' whiteness. This, of course, also makes it hard to analyse." He concludes, "White people—not there as a category and everywhere everything as a fact—are difficult, if not impossible, to analyse *qua* white."[32] Left with blank bodies, of a sort, viewers of Slimane's photographs of the London indie scene see only the heroism of youth. Underlying such heroism, of course, albeit largely invisible, are these privileges of whiteness and masculinity.

Not only minorities, but women too play peripheral roles within Slimane's London indie scene. Indeed, women have played a secondary role in rock throughout its history. As Frith and Horne note, rock's earliest female fans were romanticized and sexualized, transformed into "artists' models, subject to particular forms of sexual power and manipulation."[33] Within Slimane's imagining of the indie scene, female fans play a similar role, their subjectivity defined through their relationship with the scene's male stars and fans. In "Sonic," within a slideshow presentation of the wider milieu of the London scene, several images show female fans on their own or with their boyfriends. The young women are pretty, with heavily made up eyes framed by heavy fringes cut into long, brown hair. They wear short skirts or baby-doll dresses and are often pictured kissing their boyfriends. Two images, both in what appear to be backstage scenes, stand out. The former shows a young man, perhaps a musician, sitting in the corner of a sofa, surrounded by three women.

The women's faces are out of camera shot, and viewers can see only the feminine accents of their dress: a sparkly scarf, a leopard-print top, and chest-length brown hair. The young woman closest to the male protagonist rests one hand on his head. Indeed, his gaze is directed toward her, as they engage in a slight flirtation. The second image shows a member of The Paddingtons sitting on a sofa backstage, gazing toward the camera. A female body blocks the rest of his torso from view. Her back is to the camera, as she nuzzles her face into his neck. She wears a black strapless top, the upper edge of which has slipped down, revealing the strap and clasp of her nude bra. By visualizing women as faceless bodies, these images reproduce the rock 'n' roll trope of "groupies": i.e. women ready and willing to dote on and to have sex with musicians before, after (and maybe even during) gigs and performances. These women play peripheral roles within the production of rock, serving largely as markers of the heterosexuality of the men involved. Even Kate Moss, who is much better known than Doherty within Slimane's own fashion circles, is submitted to this treatment within the slideshow. She appears in one of the photographs; her back is to the camera as she canoodles with Doherty. Viewers who are familiar with that time period and Doherty and Moss' relationship know that the mop of brassy, blond hair belongs to one of Britain's favorite supermodels; others might mistake her for just another nameless woman.

Two women receive different treatment under Slimane's gaze: Amy Winehouse and Alison Mosshart of the Kills. Unlike girlfriends and groupies, these two can "play with the boys." Known for her drug addiction, Amy Winehouse extended the individualistic heroism of the indie scene (and rock and roll, more generally) to a level of "live to die" excess. Slimane's portrait of her, taken at the 2007 Benicassim Festival in Spain, is cropped to show only the top half of her face. Her eyes are foregrounded, adorned with her signature cat-eye make-up and exuding a depth of sadness that was popularly understood to be feeding her creativity, ultimately underpinning her demise. Mosshart is depicted in the moment of release, in a manner not dissimilar to that used within images of Doherty. She is photographed on stage at a 2009 performance in Paris. Her upper body—clothed in a loose white T-shirt—is bathed in spotlight. She arches her back, letting her sweaty hair hang down behind her, opening her chest up to the ceiling in a pseudo-religious pose. As exceptional figures, Winehouse and Mosshart bring attention to the overarching masculinist undertones of Slimane's photographs of the London scene.

Whereas women are shown alone or with their male sexual/love interests, young men are frequently pictured together, their friendships represented as deep and true. Dyer again: "the beauty of non-sexual love between persons of the same sex needs representing, though [...] it does at times seem to depend on the exclusion of women."[34] Slimane's photographs capture the beauty of male friendship in a variety of ways. For example, in one photograph of a Dirty Pretty Things concert in Paris (October 2005), a young male fan is pictured in a sea of others. His gaze is focused on the stage, ostensibly looking up with admiration at Barât and the other male musicians who make up the band. There are photographs of the band Egyptian Hip Hop, playing together in Hampstead Heath. In one of the images, two band members sit together, both wearing psychedelic-inspired T-shirts—a sartorial closeness that perhaps mirrors their closeness as friends. Another photograph focuses on a fan, sitting on a couch (potentially backstage) at an October 2004 London show of the Holloways. The young man appears completely wasted, barely mustering the strength to hold a cigarette between two fingers. He appears ready to slip off the couch and onto the floor. The only thing keeping him in place is the arm of his friend, which is wrapped tightly around his waist.

Nowhere is this love among men as visible as in the photographs of Pete Doherty. Slimane photographs Doherty on stage. He tugs at the microphone, the cord of which is wrapped several times around his neck. Slimane also captures Doherty off stage, but still at work: writing in his diary, for example. In further images still, Slimane and Doherty appear to be collaborating within the staging of portraits. In one photograph, dated February 2007, Doherty appears "incognito"; that is, he poses for the camera in front of a gray background, wearing a fedora and a black raincoat with the collar popped up, so that it hides the bottom half of his face. The top half of his face is masked by a mop of brown hair that peeks out from under the hat. In another collaborative portrait, dated May 2007, Doherty is pictured in Kate Moss' garden. Wearing a black cardigan and skinny jeans, a fedora and a skinny scarf, he sits in the grass, half of his body inside an open guitar case. With him in the guitar case is a kitten. The image is part of a series of portraits Slimane took that day of Doherty with tiny, cuddly kittens, perhaps Doherty's own. The images are sweet, yet underpinned by irony, as this man—known for his drug-addled lifestyle—tenderly nuzzles with newborn animals. Twenty-eight years old at the time the photographs were taken, Doherty had already broken the "curse" that the tabloids had set upon him. Like Jim Morrison and Janis Joplin before him, Doherty was said to be fated to die at twenty-seven. And yet here he was, still alive. To borrow from Dyer's analysis of Papillon—the hero of Franklin Schaffner's anti-epic film/buddy movie of the same name—Doherty's "specialness is simply that he survives."[35]

"In the morning"

This tableau of a bohemian rock 'n' roll anti-hero and his homosocial milieu directly informed Slimane's Autumn/Winter 2005 collection for Dior Homme—a collection that, according to Cathy Horyn, "showed Mr. Slimane at his most confident."[36] As Yuniya Kawamura as well as Joanne Entwistle and Agnès Rocamora argue, the fashion show "is not only a trade event, but also a cultural event."[37] For his part, Slimane's Fall 2005 show transformed the runway presentation into a totally different type of cultural event: an indie rock concert. In the early 2000s, Slimane's main photographic and design influence was Berlin. The soundtracks to his early presentations for Dior Homme were electronic and atmospheric, evoking nighttime cityscapes and transporting his attendees into the cavernous halls of Berlin's legendary club Berghain, at least for the duration of his fifteen-minute-long presentations. For Spring 2005, however, the designer began to favor a lighter sound. The show's original soundtrack, written by the American musician and multi-instrumentalist Beck, lay lyrics sung by the artist and a simple guitar line over a drum loop. Using a recorded drum sound, the piece resembled the electronic music used in the years preceding. By introducing guitar and vocals by a known musician, however, the soundtrack set the stage for a transformation of the fashion presentation into a live rock 'n' roll happening.[38]

Slimane's Autumn 2005 presentation for Dior Homme begins with the sound of drumsticks clacking together, counting off the beat. The room is still dark as the drums begin. Lights turn on, illuminating the catwalk as the guitar begins and the first model emerges from backstage. The vocals follow. The show was soundtracked by British indie group Razorlight. The thirteen-minute original song—"In the Morning"—would later be shortened and released as a single, reaching the top of the British charts. The song is a paean to youth and its mischievous missteps, as lead singer Johnny Borrell belts out: "But then last night was so much fun; And now your sheets are dirty; The streets are dirty too but; You never look back over what you've done." Pre-recorded in the studio, the soundtrack takes on a live quality, the models replacing musicians as rock stars for the evening, their footsteps landing to the rhythm of the guitars and the beat of the drum. The fact that many of the models were musicians, plucked from the British indie scene, makes the substitution easy to imagine. The looks evoke the mid-1960s countercultural aesthetic of British rock music. Look 1, for example, consists of a calf-length, structured, gray cape worn over a tight black shirt, skinny black jeans, and gold Chelsea boots. It is accessorized with a six-foot white, woolen scarf, wrapped once around the model's neck, the remainder hanging to his knees in the front and back. One might imagine legendary British rocker Mick Jagger draping the scarf around his neck and torso during a performance. In fact, one did not have to imagine it! As *The Guardian*'s Craig McLean noted that year, "Those sleek jackets, teeny midriff-baring tops and bum-hugging trousers that Mick Jagger is wearing on the Rolling Stones's new tour … Hedi did those."[39] The rest of the collection follows in the lead of this bohemian first look. It includes various capes, blazers, leather jackets and trench coats, tuxedo jackets, skinny ties, pussy-bowed shirts, and cropped puffer jackets. The models' hair is long and lank, the shortest hanging just below his ears. Their skin is white—a corporeal reproduction on the catwalk of the image of rock bohemia as devoid of diversity. Look 29 stands out for its commitment to a visual aesthetic of rock 'n' roll excess. The model wears a floor-length, structure-less woolen cape over skinny black jeans and gold Chelsea boots, his slender torso completely bare, with the exception of two delicate gold chains of differing lengths. After forty-plus looks, the lights dim again. They are raised only slightly for the finale, when the models flood the runway to the beat of live drums, the drummers, and their kits on scaffolding above the fashion crowd. During the finale, it is almost impossible to see the clothing. Instead, the audience can only hear the frantic beat of multiple drum sets, playing in synchronization. Rock had taken over the runway.

Fashioning masculinity

Carried on the backs of slender indie musicians, Slimane's fashion coup was successful (Figure 4). He had transformed fashionable masculinity from a brute display of financial and physical strength into a delicate display of "bohemian dreams and Romantic fancies."[40] Journalists fell in line with the rock theme. American *Vogue*'s Tim Blanks' review reproduced the figure of the heterosexual bohemian rock icon. He wrote,

> Slimane is infatuated with the vulnerability and cockiness of those young men. He gave them a leather trench or gold Cuban-heeled boots for rock star swagger, but also shirts with big poet's bows or fragile transparent blouses for their softer side. And the long scarves and big fringed woolen capes? Clearly something a girlfriend would knit while the group was on tour.[41]

Figure 4 Dior Homme S/S 2006 runway show. Like in the A/W show that preceded it, Slimane presents an image of youthful rock 'n' roll masculinity to an adoring fashion audience. Front row includes icons from the fashion industry: Carine Roitfeld, Karl Lagerfeld and L'Wren Scott, with her partner Mick Jagger. © Michel Dufour/Getty Images.

A contributor to British *Vogue* noted, "this is a collection bound to turn Dior fans into veritable groupies."[42] Slimane's following collections for Dior Homme, all soundtracked by young British indie bands, would continue on this theme with varying degrees of success. Spring 2006 was a hit. As *Vogue*'s Tim Blanks wrote this time, "Mr. Kate Moss's style returned to haunt the Dior Homme catwalk: the angular, rail-thin silhouette, the monochrome palette, the side-slashed, sleeveless tops, the skinny suspenders, the porkpie hats, all echoed Pete."[43] Autumn 2006 favored looser shapes and was almost entirely composed of suiting, but it was almost as if this change in cut did not matter; the Slimane-effect was already in motion.

Across the fashion industry's mass market, jeans were cut slimmer and that cerebral masculinity, linked to indie music culture, seemed predominant. Topman exemplified this trend, as it soundtracked shoppers' visits with the freshest indie music blasting through in-store sound systems. On offer were multiple cuts and color-ways of skinny jeans. And those young men who were not satisfied with the jeans selection in Topman? They could simply go downstairs to Topshop to buy women's skinny jeans, which were made with a small percentage of spandex, so as to create an extra-tight fit. Responding to these changes, and giving special mention to the role Moss and Slimane played in effecting them, Hamish MacBain, a regular contributor to *NME*, concluded, "The crux of the matter is this: 'indie' may once have been a byword for people with shaggy hair who considered themselves to be living outside of the mainstream, soundtracking their self confessed awkwardness with jangling guitars, but now it's everywhere."[44]

Ambivalent fashionistos; Or, the perils of mixing music and fashion

How did male indie musicians and fans respond to this new popular fashion environment, wherein the indie look and the indie identity had become hot commodities? There was no set blueprint. The majority of musicians and fans reproduced the tropes of rock authenticity within their discourses and dress practices. For musicians, who were styled for media coverage, adhering to the values of rock meant eschewing a too obvious engagement with appearance, often considered costume. Fans were able to demonstrate their authenticity by mobilizing their "subcultural capital,"[45] distinguishing themselves from those who bought pre-made indie look garments in Topman and other high street shops. And yet, some musicians and fans were able to adhere to the tenets of rock authenticity while also engaging directly with popular fashion and, specifically, the Hedi Slimane-designed masculine aesthetic. These young men demonstrated what I identify as a historically and gender-specific fashion sensibility.

In their account of postwar British pop music, cited above, Frith and Horne argue that the late 1970s witnessed the replacement of a rock by a pop sensibility. They write, the Sex Pistols' Svengali manager Malcolm McLaren spearheaded this shift, using the tension between "bohemian ideals of authenticity and Pop ideals of artifice" to upend British popular music.[46] "McLaren's aim was to stay sharp by burrowing into the money-making core of the pop machine, to be both blatantly commercial (and thus resist the traditional labels of art and Bohemia) and deliberately troublesome (so that the usually smooth, hidden gears of commerce were always on noisy display.)"[47] McLaren's pop art project had a short lifespan, however, as Johnny Rotten's signature snarl transformed into thousands of dramatic gestures of the New Romantics in the 1980s. Frith and Horne identify this later generation as one of poseurs, who frequented the Covent Garden wine bar

Blitz so as to receive "acknowledgement of their *individual* style."[48] McLaren's attack on commercialism had thus mutated into a "display of conspicuous commercialism."[49] No longer were the "bohemian ideals of authenticity" in tension with the "Pop ideals of artifice"; rather, they had been superseded by them. And yet, writing in the late 1980s, Frith and Horne note in their conclusion that the indie scene seemed to have bucked this broader shift within British popular music. For the authors, participants within the indie scene only pay attention to those bands they think are "*resistant* to fashion, commercialism and art school 'irony.'"[50]

Twenty years later, the indie outlook had changed, at least in part. I use the term fashion sensibility to account for this new approach to the tension between authenticity and commercial culture because indie's shift cannot be explained as a replacement of a rock by a pop sensibility. Rather, in the wake of Hedi Slimane's early twenty-first-century intervention into popular fashion, whereby he injected rock authenticity into popular fashion's DNA, indie musicians and fans had at their fingertips the sartorial tools to demonstrate a rock sensibility *through* fashion and commercial culture. In other words, those male indie musicians and fans, who demonstrated a fashion sensibility, were able to harness indie's newfound fashion status for personal and financial gain, while simultaneously maintaining their rock credentials.

Musicians

In the 1980s, indie musicians were faced with the choice of, on the one hand, remaining independent and perhaps never gaining widespread popularity or, on the other hand, "selling out" to a major record label and having the potential to become famous. In the 2000s, indie musicians were faced with the choice of, on the one hand, focusing solely on their music and perhaps never gaining widespread visibility or, on the other hand, creating a look for themselves and potentially receiving press coverage that might enlarge their audience. The Strokes, the White Stripes, Franz Ferdinand, and the Yeah Yeah Yeahs, all of which had defined looks, serve as evidence of this point. As British indie musician Johnny Borrell reflected to *Noisey*, "The first thing you ever heard about The Strokes was people writing about them. Then you saw the pictures—and only then did you actually hear some music. It always felt like a package. They obviously looked really cool and photogenic."[51] And yet, in a 2003 interview with *Spin*'s Chuck Klosterman, the Strokes bassist Nikolai Fraiture explained, "we're only interested in people who are interested in the music itself. That's all that matters to us. Listen to our music. Come to our shows. I guess our image helps us, but we're not here to be in fashion magazines."[52] The Strokes' ambivalence points to the fact that how those twenty-first-century British and American indie bands were to engage with appearance—and, more specifically, fashionable appearance—was a strategy not easily conceived, involving rather a delicate negotiation between strongly held values of rock authenticity and commercial opportunities newly afforded to them.

One good place to start is with James' interview.[53] At the time of our interview, James was the lead singer of a London-based band that had been receiving attention from some small-circulation magazines and weekly music magazines. He recounted an experience in which he and his bandmates had been styled for a magazine feature—a publicity opportunity to gain a broader audience.

> *James*: We did a photo shoot for a magazine, and they wanted to dress us. Like they wanted to style us for the shoot, but I really didn't want to do it. So, we compromised, and I swapped my … I was wearing just a plaid, checked shirt … and I swapped my own shirt for one of theirs, which was like a Levi's one. And then just put my own jacket over the top of it anyway, so you couldn't see it. But that was … that was the best compromise we could come to.
>
> *Rachel Lifter (RL)*: What did the clothes look like?
>
> *James*: They were just too clean and like … they were nice clothes, I guess, but just not something that I'd wear, so I don't really want to lie to people. I guess, I like … it's a picture of me in a magazine, and I don't want it to be a picture of someone else's idea of me. I don't want to stand there and say, "James is wearing a shirt from some brand. Go and buy this shirt." I don't care if that brand sells any shirts, you know? The other guys dressed up. They put some of the clothes on, but they looked good, and they were comfortable doing it. It's not like I have a massive problem with it, but personally I wouldn't really want to do that.

Interwoven within James' discussion are the two characteristics of British rock ideology: disdain for commercialism—"I don't care if that brand sells any shirts"—and reverence for individual expression—"I don't want it to be a picture of someone else's idea of me."

The fact that James articulates rock values in and through a discussion of clothing comes as no surprise. For McLaughlin, fashion plays a crucial role in the materialization of rock ideology, specifically through the way in which it is seemingly disregarded.[54] He writes that there "is the tendency within a rock culture concerned with authenticity […] to see clothes as the 'veneer', as essentially fickle, to 'look through them', to value what is *inside.*"[55] He continues, "For rock culture, it is 'others' who wear masks, others who dress up, '"we" just are.'"[56] When these values are applied to indie culture, what results is what Helen Davies calls "the dowdy indie uniform."[57] She explains, "'The degree to which an artist's music is viewed as 'serious' is often inversely proportional to the extent to which their image is foregrounded. Male bands wishing to be taken seriously almost without exception adopt the dowdy indie uniform of jeans and T-shirts, in order to imply that their music is the most important thing to them."[58] These values of truthfulness, transparency, and the love of music as well as the corresponding disdain for fashion—present in James' language—were echoed by other twenty-first-century indie musicians. For example, in the wake of Hedi Slimane's indie-look success, American trade magazine *Women's Wear Daily* (*WWD*) published an article, in which the authors interviewed various indie musicians about their appearance.[59] Perhaps disappointing to readers, the majority of responses seemed irrelevant to the particular publication. Ben Whitesides of the Oregon-based band the Joggers explained, "We're jeans and T-shirts almost all the time. That's sort of it." Nick Harmer, bassist for Washington State-based band Death Cab for Cutie, sounded similar: "I've always thought of us as being sort of antifashion, when it comes right down to it." He continued later in the article by posing his own question, "Where do you draw the line between fashion and putting on a costume?"—a costume, assumedly, that masks a performer's true identity.

Although an anti-fashion sentiment pervaded throughout the indie scene of the early twenty-first century, some musicians displayed a different attitude, toward fashion and specific fashion brands. In the *WWD* article, for example, Boston-based band Keys to the Streets of Fear came across as more open to the possibilities that engaging with fashion might allow. Having written a song called "Hedi Slimane," the band's four members bought Dior ties to wear to its release party. The band came across as eager to follow in the lead of Pete Doherty, who seemed perfectly content to assemble outfits from the Dior Homme clothes Slimane gifted him. By 2009, moreover, Doherty had been made the face of Roberto Cavalli, appearing in the brand's Mert & Marcus-photographed advertisements as a contemporary

James Dean figure, wearing a shiny leather jacket and a trilby hat. As Janice Miller notes, musicians can benefit from sponsorship deals with fashion labels beyond the initial payout. Drawing on Will Straw, she argues that, as "a cultural commodity rather than a necessity for life [...] music is a fundamentally precarious product."[60] As a result, "creating a contemporary circuit of shared meaning and, indeed, taste-making [with the fashion industry] arguably establishes a greater sense of certainty and a greater chance of success for this product."[61] There was no consensus within the twenty-first-century indie scene as to how to respond to such opportunities, specifically sponsorship deals. Whereas the Strokes forwent a deal with Gap,[62] both the Las Vegas-in-origin indie band the Killers and the Scottish indie band Franz Ferdinand opted to sell their T-shirts in Urban Outfitters. The Killers' frontman Brandon Flowers' reasoning: "What's the difference between buying it here and buying it at a concert? [...] I wear Rolling Stones and David Bowie shirts from Hot Topic."[63] There was also no consensus within the twenty-first-century indie scene as to how to respond to being styled for the music press.

The music press follows its own set of logics, which differ from those of musicians. To borrow from Angela McRobbie's analysis of the fashion media, these are "the logics of creative and editorial reputation, circulation figures, competition from rival publications and advertising revenue."[64] And yet, developing intertwined with one another along the same postwar time period, rock and rock criticism share ideological positions: in particular, the ideal of individual expression. Gester Gudmundsson *et al.* explain that rock criticism was born in the US in the mid-1960s and then emerged in the UK in the early 1970s.[65] They write that the first rock critics found their voices "in the more hip parts of the established press and in the underground press" and they would take on the worldview of the latter.[66] According to Steve Jones and Kevin Featherly, three themes soon came to dominate the discourses of popular-music criticism: "race, authenticity, and mass culture."[67] Looking at the *Village Voice*'s Nat Hentoff's writings, Jones and Featherly explore how the critic's definition of "authenticity" changed from the 1950s to the 1960s. That is, in earlier reviews of jazz musicians, Hentoff relied upon a definition of "authenticity" as linked to origins, as "a 'return to the roots.'"[68] Within a 1967 essay on folk music, however, the critic put forth an entirely different definition of "authenticity"—one that resonated with British rock ideologies. Jones and Featherly explain that, in order to respond to the exchange of cultural influences made possible by mass culture, "Hentoff was forced to reconceive authenticity as a form of self-expression."[69] In other words, just like Britain's earliest rock and roll stars, Hentoff needed a means of authenticating the sounds and identities of those musicians, who had no connection to the original source of the music styles they were playing. Rock took on a big role within the critic's reconceptualization of authenticity. "Rock," Hentoff would come to argue, "is fundamentally a release of feelings."[70]

Following the transition from rock to pop that Frith and Horne lay out, Gudmundsson *et al.* argue that punk forced a transition in the critical languages used by music critics, pathing the way for pop journalism. The authors cite the young *NME* journalists Julie Burchill and Tony Parsons' book on the Sex Pistols—*"The Boy Looked at Johnny": The Obituary of Rock and Roll*—as a tale filled with such "scathing, vitriolic abuse" for earlier journalists and value systems that "authenticity becomes a caricature"[71]—an intervention into music writing that mimicked McLaren's assault on the bohemian ideals underpinning rock music. The authors continue, as punk transitioned into the New Romantics, so too "the *Sniffin' Glues* of punk were exchanged for glossy new magazines, designed to blur the line between editorials, text, pictures, and ads."[72] Gudmundsson *et al.* identify titles like *Smash Hits* and *The Face*, both of which placed a heavy emphasis on pop music and bold visual design, as decidedly more capable than the weekly "inkies"—*NME*, *Melody Maker*, and *Sounds*—of negotiating the 1980s popular music environment, wherein what musicians looked like seemed to matter more than how authentic they were.[73] Unlike Frith and Horne, who were writing in the late 1980s, Gudmundsson *et al.*, writing in the early 2000s, identify a third shift in British music criticism: from rock to pop to, finally, the development of titles corresponding to segmented readership groups. The authors identify the EMAP publishing group as playing a significant role in this third stage, establishing "*Select* (1990–) for young male rock fans, *Q* for more all-round pop/rock fans, [and] *Mojo* (1993–) for old rock fans," for example.[74] Like *Smash Hits* and *The Face*, these magazines were glossy-textured; and yet, at least for *Q* and *Mojo*, they reproduced traditional notions of rock authenticity—values that best framed their readers' worldviews. In the 2000s, then, one can consider music magazine logics—again, "the logics of creative and editorial reputation, circulation figures, competition from rival publications and advertising revenue"[75]—as processes of negotiating rock and pop approaches, so as best to define an audience and outline their worldviews.

On the one hand, rock ideology continues to inform how twenty-first-century indie musicians are represented in the music press, both within written profiles and in editorial images. One example is an article on the

59

London-based group the Horrors, which appeared in the September 2009 issue of *Nylon Guys*. When the band's first album—*Strange House*—came out in 2007, its five male members received much attention: however, less for their music and more for their visual appearance. All five band members were extremely skinny, their bodies giving off a fashionably deathly look—a look accentuated by their black, gothic-style ensembles. Upon the release of their second album—*Primary Colours*—in 2009, Krissi Murison (who would later go on to become the first female editor-in-chief of *NME* magazine) explained, "The Horrors, you see, love music. Snobbishly, obsessively, and compulsively. [...] music has always been the glue that bonded them. They love it more than they love dressing up." She goes on to concede, "Yes, they looked fabulous, recognizable at 50 paces with their three-foot manes, cigarette-thin legs, and expertly applied panda eyes," before arguing, "But anyone who actually bothered to listen to their 2007 debut, *Strange House*, discovered a vital attack of primal garage punk, reflected through their love affair with stylish '60s girl groups and reverb-addled surf rock."[76] Despite using a description of their appearance to develop a portrait of the band, her words explicitly devalue appearance, playing down the central role that fashion played in the band's emergence and evolution. Anti-fashion values inform how musicians are styled for editorial images, too. In June 2009, I spoke with Adham Faramawy. He was then in charge of publicity at Beyond Retro, who outlined to me his experiences dealing with stylists for the music press:

> In terms of indie publications, we deal with a lot of music magazines, like *NME* and *Spin* and *Rolling Stone*, and I find that the stylists tend to request, in terms of menswear, it's all quite conservative. There's very much a uniform—you know, the jeans and T-shirt, sneakers and plaid shirt—and it just kind of sticks to that. It varies from month to month in terms of what might be on a T-shirt or whether they want colour or not, but that's pretty much as far as it will go in terms of menswear. [...] I mean, recently, the grunge references are quite heavy, so they're changing what might be on a T-shirt and the size of the jeans: less skinny, larger jeans, often ripped. So that, you know, has not been a massive change, but that's been the most marked thing that I've noticed.[77]

In charge of pre-selecting clothes for the stylists, Faramawy contributed to the fashioning of "the dowdy indie uniform"[78] and thus the visual representation of the anti-fashion ideals of rock orthodoxy. In so speaking, however, he sheds light on the opposing pop logic of media representation: the nuanced fashion work, his and that of the stylists, through which editorial imagery of indie musicians is produced.

Interviews with two former editorial staff members of the American music magazine *Spin* offer insight into the fashion work hidden behind media imagery of musicians. As Doug Brod, the magazine's editor-in-chief from 2006 to 2011, explained to me, the underlying goal of taking photographs of musicians was to make an image that looked exciting and dynamic.[79] "Frankly, you want it to look—I don't want to say 'musical'—but you want it to look *musically*. You want it to have the energy and dynamics of music." To realize the energy of music on the two-dimensional page, Michelle Egiziano, *Spin*'s photo editor from 2006 to 2011, relied heavily on fashion. Egiziano regularly worked with fashion photographers: "There were a lot of music photographers out there that were friends with the bands and were able to do shoots that for all intents and purposes would work for the stories, but they weren't able to bring anything new to the story." In contrast, "I felt that [fashion photographers] were able to see musicians from a fresh perspective and able to approach the shoot in a non-formulaic way."[80] She also placed an emphasis on the clothes, themselves, she explained, to "[give] the viewer a story about this person that was unexpected." As photo editor, Egiziano worked to organize these shoots, and as *Spin* did not employ a fashion editor during her tenure at the magazine, she also did the work of a fashion editor. She explained, she would put together a concept and assemble a team: photographer and stylist. "I always tell people that, when you're shooting musicians, you kind of have to fall in love with them a little bit or crush on them," she explained, "because you live, breathe, eat, and sleep the shoot." Egiziano would organize the scene: picking a location, renting props, and hiring other cast members. For example, for a shoot with the Oregon-based indie band the Shins, she hired members of a female-only motorcycle club, on the back of whose Harley Davidsons the band were photographed riding. The stylist was tasked with sourcing clothes for the shoot, pulling from his/her/their own collection and borrowing from designers and brands. Egiziano explained, *Spin* never really had clothes on hand; rather, the stylist was able to source clothes for a shoot based on who the talent was and whether brands wanted to be associated with that talent. "Like when I shot Beck in Amsterdam, I had a team from London come down and the stylist was able to get Ann Demeulemeester and Yoji Yamamoto and all the brands that he loved because those brands wanted to lend to him." At another point of our interview, she noted, "Marc Jacobs was always great because he was always into musicians."

It is common practice for major music magazines to employ photo editors, fashion editors, photographers, and stylists—some full-time and some freelance—to produce original visual content. As Egiziano explained, magazines have to produce new content because an artist or band will not look the same as he/she/they did on his/her/their last release. This content has to be original, Brod explained, so that the magazine does not become just another part of the band's own promotional material. *Spin* presents a unique case study, however, because in the mid- to late 2000s the magazine was attempting to alter its market position and attract fashion brands as potential advertisers. Under Brod's predecessor—Sia Michel—the magazine employed an "Editorial Fashion Director," who styled musicians for features *and* the occasional fashion editorial featuring models. In 2006, however, the magazine was bought by a new owner, who eliminated the fashion editorials. As Egiziano noted, "We weren't allowed to have fashion models, so we had to get our fashion on talent. It was a different game. It's hard." The "game" that Egiziano played was twofold. The first part of the game was a negotiation with fashion designers. She and the stylists she worked with would leverage the talent's name to borrow garments for a specific shoot. In turn, she would include sourcing credits on the published page, as a way of indicating to fashion designers that the magazine offered a potential market. As Brod imagined, "'Oh *Spin* has a real emphasis on fashion now, and all the artists are dressing up in really cool clothes in their photo shoots. Maybe we want to attract that audience. We can place some ads there.' So that's what we're always hoping for as a business." The second part of the game involved negotiating with artists, inviting them to play along with the theme of the shoot, even if that meant dressing up in something that they might not normally wear.

In speaking about her experiences, working with musicians to put together editorial looks, Egiziano revealed that her work involved cultivating emotional knowledge in addition to mobilizing fashion knowledge. "We weren't in the business of them walking in and saying, 'Here's your head-to-toe look' because that had happened in the early 2000s with all of these boybands and a lot of these younger artists, and they felt like their identity had been taken away from them." She continued, "We were the paradigm shift away from that: 'We want to see you in your coolest light … but what about putting on a cool tapered suit instead of wearing jeans and a T-shirt.'" Underpinning Egiziano's wording are the arts of suggestion and persuasion. Before a shoot, she would send the musicians' publicist a list of six designers they had in mind for the story. "Even if we couldn't get four of them, I would bait them with names that were both recognizable and sophisticated because I wanted them to know that

I wasn't going to downmarket them if they felt that they were upmarket." Alluding to Slimane's influence over the look of indie music, she continued, "If it was menswear, I would pick Dior." On set, she could convince artists to play along for the specific editorial. "With the guys I could say, 'Listen, we love your style, but we just want to do something different, kooky, we just want to tell this story.'" Mobilizing this emotional knowledge, she was able to put together editorials that ranged from the silly—"I had this giant blow-up panda that was like a story tall, and I have them holding it up in the air inside an empty pool, just like 'let's see what happens'"—to the sincere. But Egiziano revealed that she also made missteps. When shooting one all-male indie band, she assumed they would be open to wearing the pastel-colored suits the stylist had on set; instead, the band members insisted upon wearing their own clothes. When prepping a shoot for the Strokes, for which the stylist had brought racks and racks of clothing, she reflected, it was "a failure of judgement for me, I should have said, 'Let's put all this stuff away. Let's edit down,'" as the band members, whose own personal styles were so integral to the band identity, were reluctant to take anything from the racks. Mobilizing emotional knowledge also required that she know when to push back. Egiziano noted that, on more than one occasion, a band member wanted to wear a puffy vest, and she put her foot down. "You might not think we're a fashion magazine, but we do to the extent that we want these to be stylish images." Puffy vests were not part of that stylish image. "I try not to be too pushy in general, but if I needed something to be done in a certain way, I'd talk to the publicist or talk to the artist directly if I had to." As Frith explains, "The gender nature of the pop/rock divide has often been noted, but, in material terms, it is a false distinction," as the various departments at music labels are differently gendered.[81] He continues, "performers' visual images are as significant for their star quality as the sound of their recordings [and thus] rock photographers (often women) have a place in rock history alongside studio engineers (mostly men)."[82] In the example of *Spin*, too, Egiziano's female voice contributed to the representation of twenty-first-century male indie musicians, in both their "authentic" and fashionable guises.

This discussion of the fashion work underpinning music magazine image-making, using *Spin*—and the magazine's own fashion sensibility—as a case study, provides a context from which to consider the various strategies indie bands employed in the mid-2000s to respond to and take advantage of new opportunities afforded to them within the post-Slimane popular fashion environment. On the one hand, bands could resist—and perhaps resent—working with editors and stylists to create photographs that were, to borrow from my respondent James' interview, "a picture of someone else's idea of me." On the other, bands could embrace such opportunities, and even take advantage of magazine editors' and stylists' fashion knowledges, to develop their image. Egiziano noted that several artists she worked with asked to buy the rights to the images after the magazine's ninety-day embargo period ended, thus opting to use the magazine's images within their own future promotional material. There was also a third way: cultivating a sensibility that married rock authenticity with contemporary fashion knowledges, showing up to an editorial shoot having already done the work of fashioning.

The Nashville-in-origin band Kings of Leon displayed this sensibility. As noted in the preceding chapter, lead singer Caleb Followill ranked fourth on *NME*'s "Cool List" for 2003, wherein he was celebrated for his charity shop look: "velvet jackets, battered T-shirts, braces, drainpiped but ever so slightly flared torn jeans—all three sizes too small."[83] Between 2003 and 2008, the band's look was refined: specifically, to match the reigning Slimane aesthetic. The lead single—"On Call"—off of their third studio album—*Because of the Times* (2007)—showcases this Dior-refined look. The video starts with a white background, as the Cuban-heeled, black Chelsea boots of the band's four members pass through the shot.[84] The next scene features the band members at their instruments; they appear to be in a studio setting, complete with a white backdrop. They are dressed in all black ensembles, extremely tight jeans seemingly painted onto their extremely slender legs. The remainder of the video follows a simple concept: the band plays the song in this studio, as different scenes are projected onto the white background. The musician's fashionable look is prioritized within the narrative, as viewers are introduced to the musicians through clean shots of their boots and ensembles. By focusing for the remaining three minutes on the act of playing music, rock ideologies that privilege the live performance are reiterated. Borrowing Grossberg's phrasing, viewers are confronted with "the actual production of the sound, and the emotional work carried in the voice,"[85] as the camera moves between close-up shots of the band members at their craft. Lead singer Caleb Followill is prioritized. He whines his lyrics, "If you'd call me now baby, I'd come a running," and he stares into the camera's lens, seemingly on the verge of tears. Despite acclaim in Britain, it was only with the following album—*Only by the Night*, released in September 2008—that the band would reach the Top Five in the US. The following month, for their first *Spin* cover, Kings of Leon appeared in a staged scene that resembles their video for "On Call." The band members wear ensembles of black and white, assembled using garments from Yves Saint Laurent, American Apparel, Diesel, Adriano

Goldschmied, Dior Homme, and other fashionable sources, as the caption credit reveals. Many of the clothes were the band's own, Egiziano explained. "They were dressed in head-to-toe Hedi Slimane, and they didn't need our stuff. But then they still looked at what we had brought." Credits were given, highlighting the labels on display in Spin's pages, whether or not sourced by the magazine. The photograph, taken for the magazine by Yelena Yemchuk, is staged. The band members stand or sit in a rundown room at Fort Tilden beach in Queens, New York. Delicate beach blankets are strung up to dry behind them, blocking out some of the light pouring into the room. Wooden fruit boxes are strewn about the room, so too are a branch of dead leaves and a fishing rope. Although not carrying instruments, the four band members take on a serious pose. There is nothing playful about the image; rather, it is sincere. The band members—three brothers and one cousin—seem to embody the ideal set out by Hedi Slimane. They are fashionably authentic in appearance, and their familial connection personified the love among men, which underpinned the indie world of Slimane's imagination.

Fans

When the Strokes first gained fame, they were adorned in what *Spin* contributor Marc Spitz called "miles of streetwise New York style."[86] Dressed in second-hand clothes, assumedly purchased at one of the Lower East Side's many thrift stores, they had a certain savvy cultivated during their childhoods growing up in New York City (and Los Angeles, as Albert Hammond Jr. did). These two elements—access to second-hand shops and location within alternative cities and city-places—remained as two key sources of "subcultural capital" for male indie participants throughout the mid- to late 2000s. Sarah Thornton developed the concept "subcultural capital" in the mid-1990s to provide a framework for analyzing youth cultural activity.[87] Based upon Pierre Bourdieu's "cultural capital," subcultural capital refers to skills, knowledges, and specific tastes amassed through participation in club cultures. The markers of subcultural capital are not widely shared within a given culture, but rather are unique to a specific group and space. She explains, subcultural capital can be "objectified in the form of fashionable haircuts and well-assembled record collections"[88] and "embodied in the form of being 'in the know', using (but not over-using) current slang and looking as if you were born to perform the latest dance styles."[89] In short, subcultural capital marks those who mobilize it as having hipper taste than the mainstream. By mobilizing the forms of subcultural capital mentioned above, the young indie men I interviewed at the end of the 2000s were able to translate the ideologies of rock authenticity into a discourse of individuality. For some of the interviewees, however, the lines between subcultural capital and what Agnès Rocamora calls "fashion capital"—that is, knowledge specific to the field of fashion—began to blur.[90]

One of my respondents, Adam, was an employee at a second-hand clothing shop. Within his interview, he revealed that, since he began working in the shop, he had sourced most of his clothing from there. In her seminal essay "Second-hand Dresses and the Role of the Ragmarket," McRobbie argues that "The apparent democracy of the [second-hand] market, from which nobody is excluded on the grounds of cost, is tempered by the very precise tastes and desires of the second-hand searchers."[91] In relation to McRobbie's second-hand shoppers, the markers of subcultural capital are an ability to pick and choose which items should be used a second time around—a basis of knowledge and skills that, although highly regarded within the spaces of the ragmarkets, was not widely celebrated throughout the fashion industry when McRobbie was writing in the late 1980s. Following Bourdieu's logic, Thornton explains, "Both cultural and subcultural capital put a premium on the 'second nature' of their knowledges."[92] Indeed, Adam's knowledge of second-hand clothing comes across as "second nature." He mused, "I guess the curse of working in a vintage clothing store is that you've got so much access to stuff. You're spoilt for choice, and you're a bit of a like schizophrenic in the way you dress." He continued,

> You know, kind of, when I was younger, like, I was really superficial and judged everybody by what they wore. And I don't know if it's like, I don't know if it's the times have got more relaxed or I've just got more relaxed as I've got a bit older—and hopefully a bit wiser—but I don't know how I think. Now, you can pretty much wear whatever you want, really. [...] People just flirt with different things and take what they want. Like an infinite amount of subcultures and genres and put them all together. [...] I think it's just, because there's so much choice now, and everything's so open, people just create their own looks rather than keeping to a regimented set of rules.

Adam's words resemble Ted Polhemus's account of the postmodern creation of youth cultural styles. Polhemus theorizes a "supermarket of style," writing, "we have all these different options spread out for us and it is just like choosing tins of soup. You can't really make up your mind so you think, I'll have a couple of those and a couple of these."[93] Within this "supermarket of style," moreover, "Everyone, it seems, is an 'individual.'"[94] And yet, within the twenty-first century, the notion that "you can pretty much wear whatever you want really," upon which Adam relies, is a romanticized discourse. Whereas Polhemus was working to theorize 1990s youth cultural activity by drawing on developing theories of postmodern identities and consumer culture, in the 2000s, to use Agnès Rocamora and Alistair O'Neill's term, the notion of freedom of choice is "a fashionable ideal without dissonances,"[95] which glosses over the structural constraints and underlying privileges, which similarly influence a person's clothing choices. Adam is able to draw upon the discourse of choice precisely because he possesses second-hand subcultural capital. To paraphrase Bourdieu, one's habitus shapes both how one acts and how one thinks.[96] For Adam, he buys his clothes second-hand and he reproduces the discourse of individuality, which circulates within second-hand communities in North America and Western Europe, analyzed in Chapter 5.

Another of my interviewees—Tom—was well aware that he lacked such knowledges. Tom was a student in Brighton. He was interviewed with his two friends—Arnold and Harry—at a pub during the day. The three friends had tickets to the Great Escape Festival and were just hanging out, waiting for the evening's events to start. The conversation moved to the fact that Tom's friend Arnold was in an independent band: in Arnold's words, "we're in no way a subsidiary of any major … we're completely our own island. We're essentially like Motown." I used this point as an introduction into asking the three friends if they identified as indie kids.

Tom: I don't know … I wouldn't like to, but I think I am … I'm quite … I conform quite a lot to social—I try anyway—to social trends … I think … I don't know …

RL: It's a term you try to avoid, you say?

Tom: No I do do it, but I just don't like the thought that I'm actually doing it. I do go to shops. If you weren't indie, you wouldn't go to shops like Topman and stuff because that's commercial. If you shopped in Brighton, it would be a lot easier to find actual independent stores, like indie style, do you know what I mean? But not as commercial … I don't know.

RL: You're saying that if you shop in Brighton …?

Tom: Yeah, there's got a lot of independent shops in Brighton as opposed to other towns in England that have a lot of commercial high streets and Topmans. Brighton's got a lot more independent fashion shops and vintage shops, so you can create a lot more individual look in a town like this than in a town like Reading, can't you? So that creates the sort of style that Harry has. I think a lot of the people here are actually indie, whereas people in other towns are just following the trend of trying to look like this, but shopping in commercial outlets.

The difference between Tom and Adam's discourse is immediately apparent. For Tom, individual choice was not "second nature." Instead, in identifying himself as conforming and thus identifying a difference between his own dress practices and those of people who are creating "a lot more individual look," he spelled out the links between second-hand shopping and individuality in a way that Adam does not.

For Tom, Brighton offered a space from which to be "actually indie." Since the 1960s, Brighton has been associated with youth and "alternative" cultures.[97] Like Tom, two other Brighton-based respondents—Will and Joe— characterized the city as an "indie" city.

Will: I think it's a little different depending on where you live. I would say Brighton's a very indie town.

Joe: Yeah, so I guess around here it's a bit looser. Back where I'm from, if you wear anything other than these jock clothes, you're immediately labeled as "indie." Or if you drink in this one pub, then you're immediately labeled as "indie." But in Brighton …

Will: To be called "indie" back where I used to live would be like quite a big thing, i.e. there's not a lot of people that live there and like the less amount of people there are, the more affected it is. But like, I don't think that many people actually care that much down here.

Joe: Yeah, it's a lot more relaxed in Brighton because there's such a … I guess it is/does revolve around the music scene because there is so much music going on and so many people in bands that it's generally a lot more relaxed, yeah.

In contrast to Tom, however, Will and Joe have internalized this discourse of Brighton, allowing it to frame the ways in which they speak about the self. Right before discussing Brighton, they were discussing their own self-definitions.

RL: Would you say your look is "indie"-ish?

Will: I don't know. I would hate to describe myself as anything.

Joe: Yeah, I wouldn't really want to describe it.

RL: As anything or as "indie"?

Will: As anything really. I don't know.

Joe: No one likes to be labeled, do they? Last thing you do is label yourself, as well. You'd rather define other people, and thereby define yourself. But I guess, yeah, I would imagine from some people's point of view, from an outsider's point of view, we would be called "indie." Yeah.

Will: I personally opt out.

Joe: "Alternative" is a better phrase because it doesn't get thrown about so much, and it's not such a tight label. It's a little bit more …

Unlike Tom, these young men have acquired the subcultural capital associated with Brighton, its history of subcultural activity and its plethora of second-hand and thrift shops. Like Adam, then, they do not define themselves specifically, but rather can rely upon discourses of individuality a vague notion that they are "opting out," doing their own thing.

Alongside Brighton, East London was produced within the respondents' discourses as an "alternative" city space. East London's history is largely told through its associations with the working-class white community as well as in relation to a variety of immigrant histories: Jewish, Huguenot, South Asian. Visually, East London has an industrial feel, its streets and buildings are to an extent run-down. Because of this environment, East London is understood to stand in contrast to what is seen to be the bourgeois space of West London. Throughout the early twenty-first century, many young creative laborers, who were concerned with developing "alternative" professional identities, moved to and established businesses in East London. This professional migration has engendered gentrification within the area—a social process that was compounded by the forced displacement of some low-income people as part of the city's regeneration project leading up to the 2012 Olympics. This issue of class came up in only one of my interviews. Sean and Jeremy, who were interviewed at Field Day festival in Victoria Park, came from Walthamstow. In describing his look, Sean made reference to his home borough, saying, "Because where we live is quite a chavvy area. Chavvy in like a lot of rude boys and people who think they're gangsters and who look at you and think you're an idiot. Other people might think it looks good, but other people will think it's shocking." As Jeremy explained further, their look was not "chavvy," but rather was aligned with what they understood to be the look characteristic of the Brick Lane area of East London: "it's all vintage stuff and all like retro and all our sort of music and all record shops." As a result of this difference, Sean concluded, "My mum's not too happy about my style." Within the majority of my interviews, however, class—like race—had an invisible presence. One could substitute "middle-class" for "white" into Dyer's statement, cited earlier, that "White people—not there as a category and everywhere everything as a fact—are difficult, if not impossible, to analyze *qua* white."[98] As another respondent, whom I met at the East London hotspot Broadway Market, noted, "My friend was saying the other day that there are people that aren't in Shoreditch that say there's a Shoreditch uniform, where you just gotta wear whatever you want to wear kind of thing and just be crazy. But I don't think that it's like that at all. I think everyone that's here is just being themselves." Like rock authenticity, alternative individuality masks the social privileges of race *and* class that sustain its truths.

The discourse of alternative individuality can also mask the fashion knowledges that serve as its foundation. Chapter 5 will problematize the extent to which contemporary second-hand shops can be considered subcultural shopping locations, when the stock in Beyond Retro and other contemporary second-hand shops aligns directly with current first-hand, high street trends. Here, by directly engaging with the twenty-first-century Slimane-designed (and/or inspired) aesthetic, one could gain the fashion knowledges necessary to reproduce a discourse on individuality. Take Eric, for example. Eric was a photographer, and thus when asked to describe his look, he related his discussion to photography. He said,

I think it's your general taste, isn't it really? You know, aesthetically, the photography I like, the music that I like, it's all got a kind of like simple, kinda folky feel to it, I guess, not kind of high-end glam stuff. It's really kind of real … I don't know. Yeah, I think it all combines into one, isn't it? Your taste.

His discourse of individuality was undercut at other points in his interview, however, when he and his girlfriend Abby discussed how his look has developed over the years. Originally from Wales, Eric revealed that his look changed drastically when he moved to London. Jokingly, he said that Abby "skinny-jean-ified" him when they first began dating. Abby admitted, "I bought him a few key items for his first birthday when we were together," before claiming, "and then I just think you came into your own." In short, in being "skinny-jean-ified," Eric took on the popular aesthetic for young men in the UK. His transformation should not be understood as merely becoming trendy; rather, Eric acquired knowledge about contemporary fashion. That Abby played a significant role in this process, moreover, draws attention to a heteronormativity underlying this transformation. Despite his commitment to style as an expression of his individual taste, Eric's capital comes from somewhere else: mainstream popular fashion as articulated though Slimane's indie look.

Only one of my respondents, Harry, actively demonstrated his interest in and knowledges of contemporary fashion. Harry was interviewed in Brighton at the Great Escape Festival with his friend Tom, whose interview was discussed above. Again, Tom identified Harry's look as an "individual" look, as opposed to his own commercial "indie" look. Unlike Adam, Will, and Joe, the capital Harry mobilized to produce this "individual" look is not subcultural, but rather what Rocamora calls "fashion capital."[99] For example, at the time of interview, Harry and his two friends were wearing skinny jeans. When asked when he started wearing the style, Harry responded,

Two-thousand and five, I reckon. That'd be four years [of wearing skinny jeans] as well. What year was the first Hedi Slimane collection? […] 2003 would make sense because it's the commonly perceived idea of how something happens is actually the case. That collection comes out in 2003, and it trickles down all the way to some fifteen-year-old in Stoke-on-Trent two years later—you know what I mean?—buying some jeans from Topman.

He coupled his jeans with a black leather jacket, a button-down shirt, and Chelsea boots that, he explained, were "from a man who owns a shop in Liverpool who makes Beatles replica boots." He guessed, "These are 1963." Harry's look was decidedly more polished than those of my other interviewees, including his two friends, who wore T-shirts, plimsoll trainers, and American Apparel hoodies. I ran into the trio again at a venue, where Harry's cousin was performing as part of the opening act. Harry sat on the floor of the concert hall, joking with his peers and casually posing so I could take a picture. He was ready to have a good night, enjoying the music and confidently looking the part of the twenty-first-century Slimane-designed indie man.

* * *

Hedi Slimane left Dior Homme in 2007 and moved to Los Angeles. When he returned to the fashion industry in 2012 as Creative Director of men's and women's ready-to-wear at Saint Laurent Paris, his adopted city served as his new reference point. Slimane's collections crystalized again around the rock theme. This time around, he invented a California rock chick to walk alongside his bohemian man. His rock chick walked in his first ready-to-wear presentation for Saint Laurent, Spring 2013. In *Vogue*'s Tim Blanks' words, "The women on Slimane's catwalk today looked like the witchy covens who'd surround rock groups in the sixties/seventies heyday of the [Hollywood] Strip."[100] Over the following collections, Slimane would mine the history of rock chick sartorial imagery to fashion and refashion this ideal woman. He called on the looks of several musicians: Courtney Love and Sky Ferreira, for example. He also mobilized the gendered trope of the groupie. His Spring 2016 collection for Saint Laurent, for example, cited the twenty-first-century's most famous groupie: Kate Moss. Walking down his runway were extremely slender young women, dressed in sparkly mini-dresses coupled with wellington boots. Considering where Slimane was going with the collection, *Vogue*'s Sarah Mower declared, "To Glastonbury with Courtney and Kate it was, with an entourage of throwback shaggy-headed waifs and a caravanload of ready-made vintage-y stuff."[101] Whereas Slimane had launched a revolution in menswear, by the time he referenced Moss' 2005 Glastonbury look, festival fashion was already well established as a commercial popular fashion phenomenon, altering the shape of indie and ways identities could form within it.

CHAPTER 3
WELLIES, FRINGE, AND INDIVIDUAL STYLE: THE COMMERICAL RISE OF FESTIVAL FASHION

This chapter charts the emergence and growth of festival fashion: as a site-specific dress practice; as a set of media images; and as a merchandizing tool used to sell a range of goods. It tracks the progression of festival fashion: from Britain's Glastonbury festival to California's Coachella festival, from isolated images of celebrities to mainstream fashion practice, promoted each summer season across a range of high street stores in Britain and North America as an essential part of the fashionable wardrobe. As *The Guardian*'s Jess Cartner-Morley explained in 2010, "To register on the modern fashion radar, you need a plastic beaker of vodka and tonic and an armful of coloured wristbands to wave in faux-nonchalant style at security when you saunter backstage at a music festival."[1] The chapter also examines how an idealized young woman was constituted through the performative, discursive, and material practices of festival fashion. Produced across fashion media and high street store collections, this newly fashioned subject paradoxically represented an alternative to the standard beauty ideal. Like the street style star and the personal style blogger, two other figures of twenty-first-century popular fashion, she personified the ideal of individual style, seemingly bucking set trends to create her own unique looks. Throughout the period of festival fashion's growth from 2005 to 2013, however, the ideal of individual style also transformed: from a resource mobilized to challenge dominant fashion ideals into mainstream fashion doxa. Those young women who were able to inhabit the ideal subject position of festival fashion did so by mobilizing what I call alternative fashion capital. They proved themselves to be ideal subjects of twenty-first-century popular fashion, wherein the borders between alternative style and mainstream fashion cultures had begun to blur. And, through their presence at summer music festivals across the globe, they inserted these historically specific codes of fashion into indie, transforming British indie music culture into an international fashion phenomenon.

A festival look, mediated and merchandized

In an "Ask Hadley" feature that appeared on *The Guardian*'s website on June 20, 2010, the newspaper's fashion editor, Hadley Freeman, was posed the following question: "I am going to Glastonbury next weekend and I see from various magazines that I am meant to be sporting a 'festival look'. What is a 'festival look'?" In her signature witty style, Freeman responded, "There is no 'look'. There is only 'warmth' and 'ease of disrobing for Portaloo emergencies.'"[2] Freeman reiterated her views on festival fashion five years later, writing for the same newspaper, "In an ideal world, by which I mean my world, festival fashion consists of a plastic rubbish bag fashioned into a poncho; wellies covered in *E coli*; [and] absolutely no clothes." It is only then, Freeman continued, that "a festival attendee knows they have had a good weekend."[3] Despite Freeman's and others' protestations, the past decade has witnessed the emergence of a well-defined, commercial festival look—one that is regularly referred to within both media and marketing discourses as "boho chic."

Elizabeth Wilson has explored in depth the bohemian myth and the various historical figures—both famous and unknown—who personified it.[4] According to Wilson, the myth originated in the early nineteenth century, as a means of reframing the figure of the artist. Specifically, during this period, "the artist was identified as an antagonist of the dominant groups in society": i.e. the bourgeoisie. As a result, key characteristics of the bohemian figure were, among others, "transgression, excess, sexual outrage, eccentric behavior, [and] outrageous appearance."[5] In other words, through their obscure intellectual and artistic pursuits, their transgressive sexual identities, and their eccentric styles of dress, bohemians refused—or failed—to participate in polite society. Although the bohemian is largely an historical figure, Wilson also explores more contemporary figures—Marianne Faithfull and Kurt Cobain, for example—who through their rock 'n' roll lifestyles personified bohemian resistance to bourgeois norms. It was within rock's Bohemia, Simon Frith and Howard Horne explain, that the specific relationship of the rock star and his model girlfriend first emerged, and "the press was soon fascinated by the scruffy star/bourgeois girlfriend story—McCartney and Jane Asher, Jagger and Marianne Faithfull, Clapton and Alice Ormsby Gore."[6] To that list, one could add Pete Doherty and Kate Moss.

Moss was not merely a "bourgeois girlfriend," but carried the essence of Bohemia in her look and persona. Since her emergence onto the international fashion scene in the early 1990s, she has been known as both model and

"Free Spirit"—two of the roles available specifically to women within Bohemia.[7] In July 1990, she posed for her first major editorial for *The Face* called "The Third Summer of Love." Styled by Melanie Ward and photographed by Corinne Day, Moss appears on the beach, playful and childlike. Three years later, Day photographed Moss for the lingerie editorial "Under Exposure" that appeared in the March 1993 edition of *Vogue*. This second shoot proved to be incredibly controversial as the use of Moss's still childlike body to model underwear was seen by many as pornographic.[8] Amid the controversy, Moss' career was launched, and throughout the following years, she would be referred to as the anti-supermodel or the super-waif. Her playful, childlike presence on the runways and in the pages of *Vogue* and other high fashion magazines served as an aesthetic challenge to the hard bodies of the supermodels of the 1980s and early 1990s. Indeed, Moss' beauty rested in its seeming "effortlessness" and "realness." She gained widespread popularity not for being physically perfect (like the supermodels of the 1980s), but rather for being an average girl from Croydon, South London who did not have to try hard to be graceful and beautiful. In an article about Moss in the August 1994 issue of British *Vogue*, the magazine's then-fashion director Lucinda Chambers argued, "That aura of normality … is the reason the kids follow her like a pop star—she's not the ultimate body like Helena Christensen or sharp and extraordinary like Linda Evangelista, but she is accessible."[9] In her essay on "Nobodies in Fashion Photography," Kate Rhodes explains, "Moss embodied the fairytale switch from 'found' woman-child into professional model before the eyes of magazine readers seduced by the possibility of continuous self-transformation."[10] By the early 2000s, this former "woman-child" had become the face of British fashion, not least through her multi-year contract with British heritage brand Burberry. In many of those campaign images, her hair is tousled and she laughs free-spiritedly, just as she did in her semi-nude romp on the beach with Day back in 1990. Through her relationship with Doherty, Moss was transformed into another Bohemian feminine ideal: Artist's Muse, "adored for her beauty, charm and fascination; her role was to provide a genius with both stability and inspiration, thus enabling him to produce masterpieces."[11] During their courtship, Moss served as inspiration for several songs that Doherty wrote for his band Babyshambles, while also providing back-up vocals and receiving co-writing credits. At the same time, however, her creative genius largely outshone his. That is, in contrast to the majority of bohemian women who came before her, whose own artistic talents were suppressed in order to support those of their romantic partners,[12] Moss flourished during this period, specifically in relation to the art of dress. Known throughout her career for her unique ability to mix designer and second-hand garments,[13] Moss' rock 'n' roll look at Glastonbury 2005 contributed to her self-actualization as a style star, not least because of the seeming limitless coverage it received in the popular fashion media (and tabloid gossip pages) (Figure 5).

Figure 5 Kate Moss and Pete Doherty, Glastonbury, June 25, 2005. © MJ Kim/Getty Images.

Moss had attended Glastonbury in the several years preceding 2005, developing with other British celebrities—notably, actress Sienna Miller and TV presenter Cat Deeley—a fashionable festival-oriented look that consisted of flowing dresses, low-slung belts, and suede booties. In 2005, however, Moss changed the script of what festival-wear could—and should—look like, appearing in what are known now as some of the most iconic looks of her twenty-five-year celebrity career. Photographs taken at the 2005 festival show Moss in two looks. In the first, she wears micro-shorts and a black waistcoat. In the second, she wears a black, leather belt slung low over a vintage, gold microdress that barely covers her backside. Her vintage gold mini-dress with fraying hems and her straggly and unwashed hair both contributed to the construction of a classic bohemian image: the "poor look."[14] Her emaciated frame signified not a lack of food, but rather an indulgence in smoking, drinking, and taking drugs. (Later that year, she would be caught up in a cocaine scandal.) Her Glastonbury 2005 outfits thus served to solidify her identity as a "dissident person"[15]—a controversial figure who, despite her money and social connections, lived (and largely continues to live) a life outside of bourgeois norms. Moss' Glastonbury 2005 outfits also created the template for festival fashion. In the words of Michael Hogan of *The Guardian*, in 2005 Moss "single-handedly invented festival fashion."[16]

Glastonbury—officially, The Glastonbury Festival for Contemporary Performing Arts—is a five-day, destination festival that has been held almost every year since 1970 on festival-creator Michael Eavis's farm in Pilton, Somerset, England. Its founding was contemporaneous to the mega-festivals of Woodstock (1969) and Isle of Wight (1968–70), now part of popular culture history as sites through which the hippy counterculture took shape. Unlike these other two, however, Glastonbury started small and grew over the years. By the 1990s, the festival became a rite of passage for many young people in the UK. The US saw the founding of Lollapalooza; the UK witnessed the birth of a range of festivals, catered to diverse music tastes. As Danny Scott explained in the May 1993 issue of *The Face*, "Today's festival lines up Primal Scream with Tom Jones, The Orb with guitar mashers like Faith No More—attracting ravers and grungers, crusties and parents, hippies and indie kids."[17] His words were followed by a two-page map of the UK, complete with locations of festivals and which ones would attract each group of young people.[18] Glastonbury came to take pride of place within the British festival circuit in the early 1990s; in Scott's words, "it is generally agreed that at Glastonbury '92 the festival came of age: it now has something for everyone."[19] It also gained notoriety for its routinely bad weather—an identifying characteristic it continued to bear throughout the 2000s and 2010s. Accordingly, the popular presses are filled with personal accounts by musicians, fans, and journalists, detailing the discomfort—and, at times, the horror—of being on a country farm during a rainstorm. Such accounts simultaneously underscore their speakers' credibility. For example, in 2013, radio disc-jockey and television presenter Lauren Laverne recounted for *The Guardian* her first Glastonbury experience as part of the band Kenickie:

> The first time I went to Glastonbury I was 19 and it rained. The weather wasn't just biblical: it was Old Testament. Specifically, the book of Job. My friends and I were in a band at the time, and due to play, but the stage sank into the rapidly expanding quagmire beneath it, and the gig was cancelled. [...] We arrived in carelessly impractical, carefully selected charity-shop garb which fared so badly in the Somerset monsoon we were forced to discard it item by item as events unfolded. By the time we drove back to London, we were in knickers and bin bags—even our tour manager, a tattooed ex-punk in his 30s.[20]

Through experiences such as these, Laverne and others quickly learned that wellington boots—a.k.a. "wellies"—were a Glastonbury "must." The early 2000s saw some tepid discussion within the fashion press as to whether to wear plain or patterned versions of the rubber boots.[21] What Moss contributed to the Glastonbury festival's welly-clad look was, in the words of *The Guardian's* Hadley Freeman, "those delicately angled knees."[22] That is, by pairing her Hunter wellies with a vintage, gold mini-dress (and, on another day, hotpants and a waistcoat), Moss transformed the rain boots from a necessity into a must-have accessory, the combination of short garments and tall boots showing off her enviably svelte legs. In the "Spy" section of the September 2009 issue of British *Vogue*, these two looks were paid homage in a segment subtitled "Trends: Hotpants vs. Minidresses," in which street style photographs of young celebrities and musicians attending Glastonbury were organized into the two categories.[23]

If Moss is known as the originator of festival fashion, British television presenter Alexa Chung has been identified as its main innovator. In 2008, Chung added her own unique twist to the look, accessorizing her wellies with thigh-high stockings and pairing the boots with cut-off denim shorts, a breton top, a black leather jacket, and a Chanel quilted purse (Figure 6). Since then, she has regularly appeared in photographable ensembles, lounging in the VIP area at Glastonbury or DJing at one of Coachella's many invitation-only pool parties. One garment she and her former boyfriend Alex Turner of the band Arctic Monkeys are recognized for having

Figure 6 TV presenter Alexa Chung and her then-boyfriend Alex Turner of the Arctic Monkeys at Glastonbury 2008. © Danny Martindale/Getty Images.

popularized is the wax jacket, pictured on Turner above. Like wellington boots, the wax jacket is a staple of an English country lifestyle, its waxy coating protecting wearers from blustery winds and misting rains. Both Chung's preferred brand of wax jacket and Moss's preferred brand of wellington boots—Barbour and Hunter, respectively—are well-known British heritage brands. Wilson explains, "Bohemia in Britain had always been closer than elsewhere to upper-class raffishness and eccentricity."[24] Within the Moss- and Chung-inspired Glastonbury looks, it seems, this connection to the appearance and lifestyle of the landed English aristocracy takes material form. An American *Vogue* print editorial from September 2013 furthers this connection. The editorial—"Ragged Glory"—is photographed by Mario Testino and features British models/"bright young things" Edie Campbell and Otis Ferry as they "take a caravan of the season's coolest rock-'n'-roll looks out for a tour of the English Countryside."[25] The motivation behind the shoot, according to editor Anna Wintour, was to celebrate "the bohemian rock chick, that wild child of Glastonbury and Coachella,"[26] who emerged as a significant figure in "the season's central narrative."[27] The "English Countryside" documented within the editorial hardly resembles the muddy grounds of Glastonbury, however. Instead, the two models traipse through a meadow in one photograph; in another, they ride together on horseback; in a third, other models (Ferry's actual brothers) join them at a makeshift campground. In this final scene, the models pile onto a worn, leather sofa positioned in front of two retro camper vans. In typical *Vogue* fashion, the editorial builds an aesthetic fantasy of festival life unrecognizable to participants. The garments featured, moreover, are designer-made, many from the Saint Laurent by Hedi Slimane collections.

In 2010, Coachella overtook Glastonbury as the preeminent destination festival—a transition that heralded the consolidation of a highly commercialized "boho chic" festival look. Asked by *The Guardian* in 2011 to write a response to the question "Why the big fuss about Coachella?," anthropologist Wendy Fonarow explained that "With so many artists overlapping [at the various major music festivals], it's important the destination festival become its own brand."[28] Coachella's "brand" is constituted through sun, celebrities, and "boho chic"—a brand that is in very obvious ways more compelling than Glastonbury's brand of rain, mud, and wellies. In a video she made for *The Guardian* website in 2014, fashion editor Jess Cartner-Morley (somewhat reluctantly) reflected on the increased prominence of Coachella, explaining,

Festival fashion used to mean wellies and parkas, and now it means vintage kimonos, wedges and crop tops. The reason for this is quite simple. It's photos of Victoria's Secret models at Coachella get a lot more hits than photos of [British musician] Florence Welch in her overalls at Glastonbury. […] The Palm Springs desert vision of "festival chic" has completely trampled all over the Somerset field vision.[29]

In the early 2010s Victoria's Secret model Alessandra Ambrosio became a familiar face within festival fashion imagery. Often pictured with either her young daughter or her fellow models, she traipses across Coachella's dusty desert festival grounds, dressed in a version of contemporary "boho chic": floppy hats, crop-tops, fringed suede satchels, turquoise jewelry, cowboy boots, peasant tops, and aviator sunglasses, among other items (Figure 7). Looking to translate her festival-ready image into financial gain, Ambrosio developed her own line of jewelry—ále by Alessandra—for

Figure 7 Alessandra Ambrosio and fellow models and friends at Coachella 2016. © Bauer-Griffin/Getty Images.

Baublebar: metal armbands, necklaces with quartz stones, and one multi-chained necklace called "Festival tassle strands."

Alongside photographs of Ambrosio and other Hollywood celebrity attendees—Kate Bosworth, Diane Kruger, and Kendall and Kylie Jenner, to name a few—articles describing the "boho chic" festival look proliferated throughout the fashion media of the early 2010s. For example, in a 2014 feature for vogue.com, Laird Borrelli-Persson uses images from the *Vogue* archive to write lessons for festival dressing. She uses an image from the 2014 Bruce Weber "Ragged Glory" editorial (discussed above) to make the point that "Short isn't the only option: You can't go wrong with a long, flowy skirt," and she uses photographs of Princess Elizabeth of Toro and Marisa Mell from the June 1969 and March 1, 1968 issues, respectively, to make the point "Be ab fab." Both women are pictured in crop-tops.[30] Whereas *Vogue* has access to hundreds of archival photographs, through which to outline the "boho chic" look—floppy hats, fringe, flowing hair, flower prints, "ethnic" accessories, crochet and lace, and flowing skirts—other media outlets provide readers/viewers with direct suggestions as to which garments currently on sale could be used to produce the look. Indeed, in *The Guardian* video discussed above, after lamenting the rise of the Coachella-inspired look, Cartner-Morley went on to show viewers some flowing kimonos and other "completely impractical" jackets as well as a T-shirt that had been "Californized"—that is, "turned into a crop-top with no sleeves to expose your very tanned belly button"—from current designer collections and high street shops.[31] Cartner-Morley's mocking terminology perhaps betrays her low regard for the seemingly commercialized fate of festival fashion. Back in 2009 she wrote, "The idea is to look like you are dressed for a festival, not like everyone else at the festival," when advising readers of *The Guardian* to avoid both the Kate Moss for Topshop and Matthew Williamson for H&M collections. The two ranges, she explained, were "standard-issue for festival posers."[32]

Topshop was quick to realize that the word "festival" offered a framework for marketing and merchandizing its goods. In the summer of 2013, the British high street giant published a festival guide.[33] In the years preceding, it had published numerous free magazines, often with features on new models and other young fashion professionals as well as fashion editorials exclusively using Topshop garments. The festival guide included a selection of the summer collection highlights;[34] a guide to lesser-known festivals, including Oya Festival in Norway and Fuji Rock Festival in Japan;[35] and short profiles on four of the hottest emerging musicians that year.[36] The guide also featured stills from a film called *The Road to Coachella*, starring Los Angeles-based actress and it-girl Kate Bosworth, made by her husband filmmaker Michael Polish.[37] Featuring a range of Topshop garments, including a "festival gillet" priced at £295 and "festival feather wings" priced at £35, the film shows a tangle-haired Bosworth wandering in the California wilderness. Alongside denim shorts, flower crowns, tasselled dresses, and suede booties, for sale in Topshop was the bohemian ideal of the "boho chic" festival look, first embodied by Kate Moss and now personified by the models and it-girls of Coachella. In the following years, other high street stores would follow suit, directly mobilizing the idea of the summer music festival within the merchandizing of goods. At the end of June 2014, in the weeks leading up to Glastonbury, the stores lining London's Oxford Street featured their festival collections. Upon stepping into Topshop, for example, consumers were confronted with the store's multi-colored culottes, crocheted tops, floppy hats, ankle boots, kimono-style jackets, and various flower headbands and headpieces.[38] Upstairs on the men's floor, mannequins were dressed in shorts-and-vests combinations; anoraks and denim jackets hung on rails; and straw hats were strewn about tabletops. Across Regent Street, H&M's window and in-store displays were dedicated to its "H&M Loves Music" campaign, which featured a video documenting a day in the life of two H&M-clad festival attendees who were en route to Coachella—a storyline not dissimilar to Topshop's *Road to Coachella* film from a year earlier.[39] At either end of Oxford Street, the windows of Primark stores declared, "Life is a festival."[40] There, mannequins were dressed in denim micro-shorts, lacy playsuits, flowing dresses belted with braided leather, and sheer and crocheted vests layered over bikini tops. New Look, Urban Outfitters, River Island, Miss Selfridges, and even Uniqlo each had their own window and in-store displays dedicated to the festival season (Figure 8).[41]

In New York, too, stores saw the marketing potential in festival fashion. In April 2016, for example, in the weeks corresponding with Coachella, the shop windows of Union Square branch of Forever 21 announced the American fast fashion retail giant's "Festival Goals." It was a two-window display that featured crocheted dresses and bell-bottomed slacks, suede jackets, floppy hats, fringed purses, and heeled wedge sandals.[42] Even the revered Manhattan department store Bloomingdale's saw a merchandizing opportunity with festival fashion (Figure 9). In its Lexington Avenue-facing windows, famous for their yearly Christmas displays, the department store featured a six-window display under the title "Festival Bound." The tagline read, "It's where style and sound converge, and it's hard to tell which came

Figure 8 A "boho chic"-themed window display at Miss Selfridge, London, June 2014. Photo Rachel Lifter.

Figure 9 A festival-focused display in a Lexington Avenue-facing window of Bloomingdale's, NYC, April 2016. Photo Rachel Lifter.

first—the music or the fashion." Each window featured several garments essential to any "Festival Survival Kit," including maxi skirts, fringed phone bags, festival throws blankets, denim shorts, mirrored sunglasses, and "new bohemian dress."[43]

New festival-oriented products emerged on the high street and on festival grounds: flower headbands and flash tattoos (Figure 10). Flower headbands are typical of the bohemian look, perhaps *the* accessory most frequently identified as part of the hippie wardrobe of the 1960s. The headbands of the 2010s varied greatly from those worn at Woodstock 1969, however. Although some were still made from cut flowers, the great majority were synthetic, procurable at high street stores, such as H&M, or at stalls on festival grounds. Further, although some still featured a thin band of daisy-like blooms to be interwoven into the wearer's hair, others consisted of a band of large, plump blooms to be placed atop the wearer's head, as if a crown. A more recent phenomenon—flash tattoos—are gold and silver temporary body adornments that mimic the look of armbands, necklaces, face decorations, and, of course, tattoos. They give one the appearance of wearing metal jewelry—a key element of the "boho chic" festival fashion

Figure 10 A stall selling flower crowns and offering to apply "metallic temporary tattoos" at Governors Ball NYC, June 2015. Photo Rachel Lifter.

look, as noted above—without the burden of actually wearing multiple heavy pieces.

Over the course of a decade, then, festival fashion and the boho chic look became a major industry trend. And yet, as this section has shown, the market value of festival fashion goods is tied directly to the symbolic value of the festival fashion images that circulate globally. As Driely S.—a photographer who has shot Coachella—explained,

> I make money from Coachella photos year-round. That stuff sells like crazy. The first year I shot it, I couldn't even believe it. Especially European magazines; they're suckers for it. they love that shit. [...] I'll sell an average of $3,000 worth of photos *a month* of Coachella alone.[44]

The symbolically high value of festival fashion images is due largely to the idealized female figure who stars in them. Who are these women? And why do they hold elite status within contemporary popular fashion culture?

A new figure of fashion: The stylish woman

Like the "new man" of the 1980s, the idealized figure of festival fashion was a figure of representation.[45] Festival fashion representations largely fall into two categories: those that attempt to outline and define the festival look—many of which were referenced in the preceding section of this chapter—and those that document interesting and innovative festival ensembles. The latter form of representation follows the format of street style photography: that is, photographs documenting and celebrating the ensembles worn by people encountered on the street. It is within the street style version of festival fashion imagery that the festival fashionista appears, recognized for her individual style.

As Agnès Rocamora and Alistair O'Neill explain, contemporary street style fashion imagery has its origins in the 1980s within the British alternative style magazine *i-D* and, more specifically, the "straight-up" fashion image that was its "visual signature."[46] The straight-up was a photograph taken of a person, randomly stopped on the street and wearing his/her own clothes. Elliot Smedley describes the straight-up both "as portraiture and as social documentation," as the goal was not to photograph fashionable display, but rather to document "real" styles and "real" identities.[47] Val Williams identifies the ensembles featured in the straight-up photographs as mix-'n'-match assemblages of clothes, "ranging from expensive to high street to secondhand."[48] Rocamora and O'Neill suggest that these ensembles were understood as being "combined in apparent disregard of dominant fashion codes,"[49] and, as a result, the "ordinary individuals" featured in the photographs were understood to be "creators in their own right."[50] Referencing Sarah Thornton's work, Angela McRobbie argues that the only people represented in *i-D* were those with "subcultural capital": in other words, those people who were hip and in the know.[51] As such, Caroline Evans notes, this "taxonomy of fashionable beings" produced within the pages of *i-D* "began to constitute a discourse of fashionability"[52]—one that stood in direct contrast to the mainstream fashion doxa of the decade and its promotion of top-down, designer-led fashion trends. Underpinning this alternative "discourse of fashionability" was the notion of individual style.

Today, the fashion discourse of individual style is one of several mainstream fashion doxa—a historical shift effected by increasing popularity of street style fashion imagery and the emergence of personal style blogging.[53] In the 2000s, "straight-up"-inspired street style images proliferated throughout the fashion media. In what is arguably the first scholarly work pointing to this shift, Rocamora and O'Neill highlight the "institutionalization of vox pop fashion images" across the popular fashion media in the 2000s,[54] with titles ranging "from the British *Independent on Sunday* to the French *Jalouse* or the aptly titled Japanese *Street*" all featuring "straight-up"-inspired images.[55] Street style images appeared not only within the print media, but also online via the establishment and exponential growth of street style blogs: for example, The Sartorialist (est. 2005) and Facehunter (est. 2006).[56] The proliferation of this type of fashion imagery—attractive to media sources big and small because of its time- and cost-efficiency—has had the effect of inserting the discourse of individual style into mainstream popular fashion. Personal style blogging has also played a role in effecting this shift. As Rosie Findlay notes, personal style blogging "first crystallized as a distinct subgenre of blogging [in] 2004–6."[57] Quoting her own earlier work, she continues, "Of paramount importance on these early blogs, as well as those that followed them, were their 'blogger's personal style and their individual perspective on fashion as constituted in their own life.'"[58] As Rocamora discusses, personal style blogs allow users "to display their new acquisitions, their rediscovery of an old piece of clothing, or their new way of mixing things together on their body"[59]: in other words, their individual style. She continues, by dressing the body, showing off the ensembles via images posted to their blogs, and contextualizing the images through narratives concerning the motivations behind each look, "bloggers partake in processes of identity construction"—of self-construction.[60]

Significantly, this process of self-construction has become intertwined with bloggers' increasing visibility and expanding professional roles within the contemporary fashion industry. Findlay explains that, whereas the first-wave blogs "were permeated by a sense of outsiders looking in, and not necessarily with the desire to be included,"[61] the second wave of blogging, which spanned 2008–10, was marked by a "mentality of seeing a blog as an opportunity to generate income [...] or to establish a professional platform as an author on style (as well as a kind of celebrity status)."[62] As Monica Titton notes, it is precisely by mobilizing their individuality—i.e. what sets their looks apart from mainstream fashion trends—that bloggers establish themselves within the industry.[63] Over time, however, the distinction between bloggers' individual looks and established trends has seemed to fade away, not least because popular bloggers, like The Man Repeller and The Blonde Salad, are frequently gifted items from designer collections. The distinction between street style looks and mainstream trends has also blurred. As Sophie Woodward argues in her article, "The Myth of Street Style," "The mediated version of street style, present in fashion magazines, has mutated: the subversive has become the ordinary."[64]

It is in the context of this historical shift—the mainstreaming and commodification of the discourse on individual style—that contemporary festival fashion representations documenting and celebrating the sartorial innovativeness of their subjects can be analyzed. Take, for example, a segment on *mode.com* called "Best Dressed at Governor's Ball 2014." One festival attendee is identified as "the prime example of how to dress for a festival without repurposing what the masses believe to be festival style." She wears a button-down, sleeveless shirt with the bottom tied in such a way as to make the shirt a crop-top, high-waisted tailored shorts, round sunglasses, and chunky sandals. The article's editors continue, "Snaps for her high waist and red lip—understated glamour, darling." Another young woman featured in the same article wears a white lace skirt over a slip, a crocheted crop-top, and an Aztec-print over-the-shoulder bag. Her caption reads, "This crocheted babe skillfully combined textures to create the perfect boho outfit."[65] Readers are invited to celebrate these two young women for their sartorial innovativeness, their individual accents; however, the looks they produce do not depart from contemporary popular fashion trends. To the contrary, their looks are best described as twists on the well-defined "boho chic" festival look, outlined in the preceding section of this chapter. The key difference between these street style-inspired festival fashion images and those within which journalists outline the key elements of the festival look and provide suggestions for readers as to which garments to buy is that, within the former, festival attendees are endowed with the nebulous quality of individual style.

Several feminist scholars have explored how the endowing of young women with ideal qualities is, in fact, a form of regulation and control. Anita Harris's *Future Girl* is a landmark study on this theme.[66] Harris writes in response to late modernity—a period in which "The benchmark for achieving a successful identity is no longer adherence to a set of normative characteristics, but instead a capacity for self-invention."[67] She continues, the young woman is created as the ideal subject of this culture, endowed with and "celebrated for her 'desire, determination and confidence' to take charge of her life, seize changes, and achieve her goals."[68] Embedded within this celebration, however, is regulation. In Harris's words, "There is a process of creation and control at work in the act of regarding young women as the winners in a new world."[69] Angela McRobbie's *The Aftermath of Feminism* draws on and extends Harris' work in relation to, what she identifies as "a new sexual contract currently being made available to young women, primarily in the West."[70] She uses the Deleuzian term luminosity to conceptualize how this contract is offered to young women. It creates "a spotlight so that they can become visible in a certain kind of way"—"a moving spotlight," moreover, that "softens, dramatizes and disguises the regulative dynamics" at play within it.[71] In relation to fashion and beauty, "The young woman is congratulated, reprimanded and encouraged to embark on a new regime of self-perfectibility."[72] What differs about McRobbie's argument from those of Sandra Lee Bartky and Susan Bordo, who were writing about similar performances of gender in the early 1990s, is that, according to McRobbie, by the 2000s patriachy's coercive grip is understood to have disappeared.[73] Within contemporary culture, therefore, performing femininity is to be understood not as a requirement under the male gaze, but as a choice that young women make for themselves, about themselves. In other words, the pursuit of self-perfectibility is understood as an opportunity, not a burden. One of the ways in which this "opportunity" is realized, I would argue, is through the demonstration of individual style.

Following Harris and McRobbie, individual style is not to be understood as a quality that young women possess, but rather as an interpellative device—a historically specific ideal through which some young women are recognized as stylish subjects. About Asian superblogging, Minh-Ha T. Pham formulates a similar argument. Pham places under analysis blogger

Susanna Lau's—a.k.a. Susie Bubble—success in order to make visible "the cultural economic conditions that make possible historical articulations of success."[74] That is, Pham considers the British born, ethnically Chinese Lau not as "an exceptional figure of success," but rather as *an embodied sign,* representative of "the technical, cultural, and economic forces" that have articulated success around Lau's British-Chineseness.[75] Following Pham's analysis of Lau, we can consider the stars of contemporary festival fashion images not as "exceptional figures," but as the embodiment of a certain "historical articulation" of ideal femininity. This ideal can be described as an ability to participate in a trend *not* because one is simply "following the trend," but rather because one is mobilizing one's individual style. And yet, whereas blogger Lau's style is identifiably offbeat and quirky, the looks shown in street style-inspired festival fashion representations fail to diverge from the relatively strict codes of festival fashion, as outlined in the preceding section. Judith Butler's articulation of the soul proves useful in theorizing the relationship between following the festival fashion trend and individuating one's look. According to Butler, "the soul is [...] a figure of interior psychic space inscribed *on* the body as a social signification that perpetually renounces itself as such."[76] Similarly, individual style is a normative ideal that is inscribed on the body, simultaneously foregrounding the idea of something interior to its subjects and hiding from view the "fashion and beauty system" that is, in fact, its originating source.[77]

It is, perhaps, no wonder then that models and celebrities—the very embodiment of fashionable ideals—feature so prominently in festival fashion representations as examples of festival attendees demonstrating their individual style. For example, *vogue.com*'s "The best street style looks from Coachella 2015" featured models, celebrities, and "it girls" Gigi Hadid, Kendall and Kylie Jenner, Alexa Chung, Diane Kruger, and Kate Bosworth.[78] Writing in 2011 for the British weekly *Grazia*, Polly Vernon explained, "It's at festivals that a celebrity's true style credentials shine through. There, where they're away from hot water, blow-dries, last-minute designer call-ins and the tweakings of super-stylists."[79] Not all journalists are as blindly celebratory. In a 2013 article for *The Guardian*, for example, in a discussion of Alexa Chung's long-sleeved-button-down-shirt-and-denim-shorts-and-high-top-Converse look from Coachella that year, Anna-Marie Crowhurst noted that Chung's look (as well as those of all celebrities) had been carefully chosen with the help of their managers and stylists. Despite this, Crowhurst acknowledged, "Chung has patented the concepts of 'effortless,' 'making sure I don't look as though I carefully chose this outfit with my stylist' and 'disregarding the fact that a long-sleeved shirt might be a bit warm for this particular occasion.'"[80] In recent years, the "particular occasion" of the summer music festival has become an important event in the social—and thus professional—calendars of models and celebrities. As Elizabeth Wissinger argues, socializing is part of models' work, as models have to "present themselves as 'in the know' as part of a community, an important player in the field of modeling" in order to secure work.[81] Like the parties and nightclubs that Wissinger mentions, festivals like Coachella provide an opportunity for models to be seen and photographed in the hopes of attracting the attention of brands.

Within street style-inspired festival fashion representations, however, these photographs of models and celebrities are intermixed with photographs of "normal" festival attendees, the great majority of whom, like their model-counterparts, have the slender, white bodies favored by the fashion industry. The bodily carriage of these "normal" young women reveals that they, too, are familiar with the "techniques of the body" associated with fashionable display.[82] The young women pose, facing the camera, often resting their weight on one leg with the other leg turned to the side—a stance that has a slimming effect. If the chosen festival attendee does not know how to pose, moreover, the photographer might take the opportunity to guide her. At the 2015 Governors Ball, for example, a photographer, who had stationed himself in a thruway on the festival grounds, upon which the setting sun cast a warm light, approached me. I was wearing a pair of cropped, flared jeans, and the photographer asked me to twist my body to the side, so as to accentuate the flare in the late afternoon light. (Unfortunately, he did not also advise me to stop squinting my eyes and pursing my lips.) At the same event I also witnessed a photographer, commissioned by a major fashion magazine, direct a young woman to walk several steps, spreading out her ankle-length "boho chic" dress, while he took her picture. In one sense, then, these photographers serve as agents of the interpellative discourse of individual style. That is, if the "normal" young woman called by this discourse does not know how to respond, the photographer will help her into position.

Performing individual style: Mobilizing alternative fashion capital

How and by what means did young women respond to the interpellative call of individual style? By mixing and matching second-hand and high street garments into individualized looks. Whereas almost all of my female respondents drew on the discourse of mixing and matching within their interviews, only those who possessed what I call alternative fashion capital were able to inhabit the ideal of individual style successfully. They were able to use the festival, moreover, as a space to interact with other young women, who were also endowed with the nebulous quality of individual style. For other respondents, however, the ideal of individual style proved inaccessible, the festival serving as a regulatory space throughout which the gaze of fashion could exercise its power.

Mixing and matching

In the early twenty-first century, a discourse on mixing and matching came to dominate how young women spoke about their dress practices. Sophie Woodward makes this point in her article "The Myth of Street Style."[83] There, she analyzes contemporary street style representations in dialogue with interviews with young people she met on the street or in bars—a methodology that greatly resembled my own. For Woodward, contemporary street style images "show 'ordinary' people plucked off the street, an ordinariness underlined by their inevitable comment that the outfit was sourced from charity shops or ('vintage'), and a high street shop perceived to be 'cool,' such as Topshop."[84] She explains that her respondents internalized this "new 'myth of fashionability'" perpetuated within such imagery.[85] Her respondents articulate that they like second-hand sources for "unique" garments that others might not have;[86] at the same time, unlike subculturalists, they "do not emphasize wanting to completely repudiate the styles of the mainstream."[87] Like Woodward's respondents, almost all of my female respondents relied on the discourse of mixing and matching when discussing their ensembles, at the time of interview and in regard to their everyday dress practices, more generally.[88] For example, Joan—a respondent interviewed with her boyfriend, Jack, outside of the East End Thrift Store in Whitechapel, London—explained,

> With high street clothes, you go out and see about ten other people wearing that dress or top, so vintage items tend to be more unique. Um ... I'm not really sure ... I just like the style of vintage clothing. I prefer that. I like mixing it with high street items to make a bit of a unique look.

Joan's comments were repeated by other female—and some male—respondents. For example, Sam and Nancy—two respondents from Canada, who were interviewed at the Great Escape Festival in Brighton—explained,

Nancy: You can find tons of it [vintage clothing in Canada], so there's like, thrift-department-stores, and that's where I do a lot of shopping. Yeah, it's good to mix that in with basics.

Sam: You can totally like, I think, create like a good look by mixing older shit and mixing it with newer stuff. It's easy. You don't have to spend a lot of money, and you can usually find stuff you want to wear.

In so speaking, these respondents signal that it is up to them, as agents within the self-stylization process, to select an ensemble from the available options. Like in the analysis of my male respondents' discourses, presented in the preceding chapter, Ted Polhemus's work on postmodern style resonates to an extent, as these respondents claim to be mixing different looks in their own individual identity projects.[89] Within my female respondents' practices, however, the limitless stylistic options, of which Polhemus speaks, are narrowed to two sources: second-hand and high street clothing shops. The current practice of mixing and matching is not a postmodern stylistic free-for-all, but rather a historically specific mode of engaging in popular fashion culture. For Woodward, the repetitiveness of the discourse of mixing and matching, within both street style images and her respondents' interviews, signals that the extraordinary art of street style has mutated into the routine practice of mainstream fashion, "the subversive has become the ordinary."[90]

The discourse of mixing and matching also underpins twenty-first-century marketing discourses. Pronouncements to "mix it up" appeared throughout the popular fashion media in the late 2000s. For example, an editorial in the August 10, 2009 issue of *Grazia* was entitled "The Mega-Mix." The tagline to the five-page editorial read, "Mix up your knits, jeans and basic tees with glamorous 'look at me' accessories to give your dress-down style a new-season update."[91] Similarly, one of the means through which Topshop worked to advertise its garments in its 2009 Autumn/Winter Style Guide was to display the garments through visual "mix and match" equations, literally showing readers how to mix and match their garments. Black harem trousers, a crop-top, and a denim shirt was one of the combinations featured.[92] Woodward also notes that "the mix-and-match aesthetic […] is perpetuated through fashion magazines as stylists' 'style tips.'"[93] Thus, in addition to street style and festival fashion images as well as blogger posts, the ideal of individual style is constituted through marketing materials focused on "mixing it up." In short, the line dividing street style and marketing material has begun to blur. Now, readers are prompted to "buy the look" that a celebrity has worn on the street, and a magazine will give suggestions as to shops and brands.

Although most of my respondents mobilized the discourse of mixing and matching, few also revealed the keen competences they employed when engaging in such a dress practice. The concept of "competence" is well developed within discussions of lesbian spectators of fashion imagery.[94] Responding to psychoanalytic work on "the gaze," Caroline Evans and Lorraine Gamman argue that it is impossible to theorize a singular "lesbian gaze." Engaging with Reina Lewis' analysis of Della Grace's photographs, they argue that these images "address and form the spectator because of the spectator's relationship to knowledge about specific objects and products" and *not* because of the spectator's identity status as lesbian.[95] In other words, reading images has to do more with competences one might have developed as part of a lesbian subculture than it has to do with the essentialist category of "lesbian." Lewis goes on to draw on this idea of "subcultural competences" in her later analysis of the ways in which some lesbian spectators can find "lesbian subcultural referents and cross-gendered lesbian erotics" in the fashion narratives presented in mainstream magazine titles, such as *Vogue Italia*.[96] Similarly, my respondents employed certain competences, gained from participation in the popular fashion and music scenes, when engaging with the regime of popular fashion representations of mixing and matching and individual style. These viewing competences were then recoded into forms of cultural capital as these young women engaged in the dress practice of mixing and matching. For example, Abby was interviewed at Broadway Market in Hackney, London with her boyfriend, Eric, whose response was discussed in the preceding chapter. She described her ensemble at the time of the interview:

> The top is a vintage one that was two pounds from Oxfam in Brighton. The shorts are high-waisted, acid-wash denim, and they're from Topshop. And the jelly shoes are a few years old; they were from Office a few years ago. And the headscarf's vintage, and the glasses I've got from Vegas, and they're fold up ones.

Within this short description, Abby demonstrated that she knew how to speak about and describe her clothing through popular fashion terminology. She was not wearing shorts, but rather "high-waisted, acid-wash denim" shorts. Moreover, in her description of her shoes, she was quick to note that they were several years old, bringing attention to the fact that she was aware that the trend for jelly shoes happened several years before our interview in 2009. At other points in the interview, Abby demonstrated knowledge about shopping second-hand. Originally from Leicester, she compared Leicester to London, suggesting that, although there are more options for vintage shopping in London, the prices are better in Leicester.

Silvia and Kara also demonstrated a breadth of knowledge about trends, shopping sites, and the media. The two women were approached for interview outside of Beyond Retro on Cheshire Street. It was a Saturday, and they were hanging out and shopping in the Brick Lane area of London. Although originally from Middlesborough, the women had been living in London for five years at the time of interview and demonstrated an interest in the city's second-hand shopping spaces. For example, during the interview, they compared the second-hand stores of the Brick Lane area with the stalls in Camden. Like Abby, they complained about the price of second-hand garments in London, where, it seemed to them, "a lot of the good stuff goes straight away, and you're left with over-priced rubbish" (Kara). During the course of the interview, moreover, they mentioned old films as inspiration for their dress. In her analysis of second-hand selling and shopping, McRobbie identifies old films as key markers of second-hand subcultural capital. She writes, "The sources which are raided for 'new' second-hand ideas are frequently old films, old art photographs, 'great' novels, documentary footage and textual material."[97] Silvia and Kara's interests and dress inspirations extended beyond anachronistic cultural texts, however. They were effusive in their praise of Chanel and mentioned Balmain as another fashion house, whose designs inspired them. They were similarly excited about Topshop. As Silvia said, "It just moves, Topshop. You go in … I think everything you look at in magazines … it's not an exact copy, but it's … Every style is represented in Topshop. Everything from the catwalk they bring out." The two respondents' equal praise for high-end fashion houses and the high street giant brings attention to a postmodern blurring of the boundaries between high and low culture.[98] Moreover, their equal praise for second-hand clothing sources alongside those sources that are actively interwoven into the established fashion system reveals another type of blurring: that between an alternative fashion culture and the established fashion industry.

This blurring of alternative style and mainstream fashion cultures emerged in the broader discussion of what inspires Silvia and Kara, as well.

On the one hand, Kara listed a variety of high fashion and niche fashion magazines that she reads:

> I love *Purple* magazine, *Interview* magazine—that's probably my favourite. *Vogue, Harpers, Nylon*—it's a bit young sometimes. *Blackbook's* really good ... just kind of anything I see that I think looks interesting. *10 Magazine* is good, *Wonderland* ... but they're all too overpriced ...

In so doing, she recognizes the "authority" of these magazines and their producers. *Vogue* is routinely identified as an "authority" on fashion.[99] In fact, it identifies itself as "the fashion bible." However, as Ane Lynge-Jorlén argues, niche fashion magazines "that merge high fashion with art and style cultures, often targeting both men and women," similarly vie for prominent positioning within the field of fashion media.[100] Kara's naming of these magazines reveals that her internalization of—her agreement to—the "authority" of these publications as well as to her elite fashion knowledge. Whereas many people have heard of *Vogue*, it is for the most part only members of the field of fashion that know *10 Magazine* and other niche fashion magazine titles. Yet, at another point in the interview, Kara and Silvia discussed the significance of "street fashion." Rocamora and O'Neill argue that "the street" is constituted through "the differential relation that unites this term to the catwalk and its associated realm of high fashion."[101] That is, Silvia and Kara claim to be inspired both by high fashion (brands and magazines) and its relative opposite ("the street"). Underpinning their discourse is an understanding that second-hand and high street shops, as well as high fashion and street style, are oppositionally placed fashion cultures. It is up to each young woman, moreover, to integrate the two sides within her own individual acts of self-creation.

The form of capital these women mobilize in their acts of self-creation might best be called alternative fashion capital, combining elements of both the "subcultural capital" of youth cultures and the high "fashion capital" mobilized by industry players.[102] It is this form of capital, moreover, that is prioritized within a fashion culture obsessed with mixing and matching second-hand and high street garments, a fashion culture that idealizes individual style. Thus, those young women who possess alternative fashion capital are able to use the ordinary practice of mixing and matching to inhabit the twenty-first-century ideal of individual style.

Festival spaces

The festival space transforms the individualized practice of mixing and matching into an intersubjective practice of taking inspiration from others' individual style. Several of my female respondents reproduced the notion of "the street" within their interviews. For them, it was a space where they could engage in certain practices of looking at others. In so speaking, they claimed to take on a role that resembles that of the *flâneur*, gazing at others within their milieu. For some, this process of looking at others was integral to their own creative processes of ensemble creation. For example, Rebecca from London stated,

> Like I know this girl who wears her hair up all the time with these really cool scarves. And I was like, "that looks really cool, but I want to do it my own way". So I started doing a little beehive, so yeah. So you kind of … I got a leather jacket, and someone else was like, "Oh, I really like that", so went and got one in a different style, so everyone kind of feeds off each other in a way. Like you wouldn't look at what someone's wearing and say, "I'm going to go to Topshop and buy exactly what she's wearing". You think like, "Oh, she's got an eighties jacket. That's pretty cool. But she's got it in red, and I'm going to try and find one more … that has a higher waist" or something like that because she's a different shape to me, or whatever.

Similarly, Nancy discussed her experiences working at American Apparel in Canada. She stated,

> I mean, when you go out, sometimes I see a girl wearing something that I think is really cool, and I'm like, "Oh, I could try that". And yeah, I used to work in a retail store, and I guess the other employees … like we had to wear American Apparel all the time, but like people would get creative with it, so it is nice to see what other people are doing.

Whereas "the street" is a discursive trope, the American Apparel shop, in which Nancy worked, and the festival site offer physical spaces where one can engage in the intersubjective practice of looking at and taking inspiration from others.

The spatial organization of festivals allows for engagement in seemingly egalitarian practices of looking. In an analysis of London Fashion Week,

Joanne Entwistle and Agnès Rocamora examine how participants engage in a process of "seeing and being seen."[103] Drawing on Michel Foucault's discussion of the way in which space facilitates certain modes of looking, they argue that, within the arena of the catwalk theater, "The gaze circulates *around* the space [...] so that all players are both subject and object of the gaze in the game of visibility."[104] As the runway juts through the center of the audience, dividing it into two sides, those people seated on each side "become part of the spectacle as one's eyes are directed across the stage to bodies seated on the other side."[105] This game of "seeing and being seen" works to reproduce the power relations of the field of fashion. As those people with the most fashion capital sit in the front row and those with little fashion capital are relegated to the standing area, "differences are visibly mapped out onto the space itself."[106] Like the catwalk theater, festivals produce certain practices of gazing by and among attendees. Festivals consist of large masses of land, divided up into smaller areas, each focused around a stage for performance. This layout facilitates a relationship between performers and audience, wherein those people in the audience watch the performers who, because of the stage lighting, have difficulty seeing audience members. There are also wide areas of space on festival sites, where those festival-goers who are not watching specific performers can hang out, relax, and have food. These spaces allow for people to sit and observe others. These spaces, moreover, are arguably egalitarian, wherein all those people moving through the main festival site have the ability to look at others within their milieu.

Michel Maffesoli's concept of the "neo-tribe" can be called on to analyze the social formation that emerges during festivals.[107] According to Maffesoli, there are no rigid boundaries defining neo-tribes. Instead, "neo-tribalism is characterized by fluidity, occasional gatherings and dispersal."[108] Neo-tribes "are fragile but for that very instant the object of significant emotional investment."[109] What is significant to neo-tribes is not whether they will persist, but rather "what is important is the energy expended on constituting the group *as such*."[110] In one sense, festival-goers form a neo-tribe, bound, at least in part, by their practices of looking at one another. They create a form of sociality, in which the process of creating the self can be performed intersubjectively, through looking at and taking influence from other people endowed with the nebulous quality of individual style. Christina and Jill, interviewed at Field Day Festival in London, evidence this point. Speaking specifically about the festival, they stated,

Jill: We've just sat all day going, "Oh, that's nice" or "I don't like what they're wearing".

RL: Well, [the festival] is a good place to watch.

Jill: It's inspiring to watch what other people are doing, what other people are wearing, where other people go, what kind of music people listen to. I really like things like that.

RL: Anything interesting you've seen today?

Christina: A lot of crop-tops. But like, I really like the crop-top, but I like it with a high-waisted thing, so there's only a bit of skin, and some people are showing too much.

Jill: Checked shirts … a lot of checked shirts, which is good … maybe a little bit overdone now.

At the time of interview, Jill was wearing a Barbour coat over a denim waistcoat, a floral-print T-shirt, a pair of leggings, and some plimsoll shoes. Christina was wearing brogues and leggings from Topshop, an American Apparel hoodie, and a vintage scarf that was her mom's. Drawing attention to certain garments and trends—i.e. crop-tops and checked shirts—the women bring attention to the specificities of the well-defined festival look, outlined in the first section of this chapter. Implicit in their identification of these garments is the fact that not everyone at a festival meets the stylistic criteria necessary in order to participate in the practices of "looking and being looked at" that these young women enjoy. Rather, the only people who are allowed to join in the neo-tribe are those that first meet the sartorial entrance criteria: wearing a semblance of the appropriate festival fashion look, whether the Barbour coat of Jill, Christina's bohemian vintage scarf, or the crop-tops of other attendees. Following Lacan, Evans and Gamman indicate that there is a difference between "looking" and "gazing," suggesting that the former is "associated with the eye" and the latter "with the phallus."[111] This distinction matters when considering the way in which the gaze is used as an instrument of power. Here, these women's gaze functions to separate those people who look the part and are endowed with individual style from those who do not and are not.

How Nicole and Iris, two women approached for interview at the 1234 Shoreditch festival, discussed their ensembles for the day is of particular relevance to a discussion of power, the gaze, and fashion. Neither woman was from London; Nicole was from Manchester and Iris from Bristol. The two friends met up at the festival to see their favorite part-indie, part-glam musician perform. In response to a question about what influences their looks, the women stated,

> *Iris*: Well like now. Because we're at a festival, obviously you don't want to look too dressy because you're outside. So you want to wear something casual, but you don't want to be completely boring.
>
> *Nicole*: Yeah, I mean, everyone here looks really good. Everyone's made a really big effort. I feel a bit underdressed, but at the same time, I wouldn't have brought anything dressier to wear … trying to find a compromise between price and style.

In contrast to the majority of my respondents, who drew on the well-rehearsed discourse of mixing and matching to discuss their ensembles, Nicole and Iris use a different set of languages to describe their festival looks, speaking instead about a "dress code" and indicating their fear of looking out of place by being underdressed. The festival "dress code" was identified in different ways by some of the other female respondents, as well. For example, Tanya and Danielle—two respondents from Bristol who were interviewed at Reading Festival—noted that the looks they were wearing were their "informal" looks. They would have to put on more "formal" attire to go to work. Efrat Tseëlon argues that, in contrast to men, women are not constructed as having an inner essence.[112] Rather, they present multiple selves through their dress. Understood through Erving Goffman's dramaturgy, she argues that this act is an investment—however minor—in a certain version of the self.[113] Following Tseëlon, it can be argued that, in moving between different looks, the above-quoted female respondents perform femininity. Following Goffman, moreover, the festival is one situation that demands a context-specific feminine performance of "mixing and matching" and looking around/being looked at. For these women, festival femininity is just one of the several femininities they perform. Returning to Nicole and Iris' above-quoted discussion, that others are "making an effort" to meet the festival dress code serves as a point of anxiety for Nicole. Foucault's work on the panoptical gaze can help make sense of Nicole's anxiety.[114] For these women, the threat of the observer's gaze forces them to police themselves by dressing the part of the "festival-goer." In the space of the festival, however, the gaze does not emanate from a central watchtower, but is located in the looks of the other festival-goers. That is, it is a "female gaze" exercised by other young women who are engaging in similar dress practices in response to this cultural moment.[115]

Further, what Bartky, drawing on Foucault's panopticon, identified in 1990 as the gaze of "an anonymous patriarchal Other" seems to affect Rebecca and Silvia's dress practices and senses of self, too.[116] Because of their curvy body shapes, these interviewees claimed that they never wear skinny jeans, even though it is the only style of jeans that they appreciated aesthetically. At different points in this chapter, Rebecca and Silvia have been identified as young women who demonstrated alternative fashion capital and an eagerness to engage with other young women endowed with individual style. And yet, their confidence is compromised by a gaze that works to police women into conditioning their bodies to meet contemporary ideals of beauty. For these female respondents and others, constructing the self demands both bowing to the regulatory norms that determine what an "acceptable" female body looks like *and* responding to the interpellative call of individual style.

Festival masculinities

And what about the slender, white boys of indie? How were they visualized and materialized through the representational and market practices of festival fashion? In the summer of 2014, menswear collections of London's high street stores, similar to their womenswear counterparts, were merchandized through the trope of the festival.[117] Topman, for example, had the word "festival" painted onto a handful of walls and structural supporting columns that framed a section of the menswear shop floor populated with anoraks, denim and cotton khaki shorts, patterned short-sleeved button-down shirts, and a range of printed T-shirts and vests. Alone, the word "festival" highlights the occasion to wear such garments without directly acknowledging "festival fashion" as a trend. Similar displays appeared up and down Oxford Street. When not directly labeled under the term "festival," these collections were identifiable by other means. One Oxford Street window display, for example, featured a variety of printed-shirt-and-denim-shorts combinations in front of a ten-foot mask that resembled the top of the totem poles produced by Native American tribes in Alaska and the Pacific Northwest. Analyzed in greater detail in the following chapter, the visual world of festival fashion uncritically cites Native American cultures: for example, in festival-goers' wearing of ceremonial headdresses. Visual references to Native American tribes also inform the variety of prints that proliferate throughout festival-ready menswear collections, in both pattern and colorway. In-the-know shoppers can thus recognize the garments on display as "festival-ready" without overt prompting through labels like "festival" and "festival fashion."

Although neatly laid out for him, the young man who embraced this festival-ready wardrobe was vulnerable to criticisms of "trying too hard." Especially for young, male festival attendees in Britain, indie's anti-fashion ideologies, analyzed in the preceding chapter, also framed young men's engagement with the festival trend. An article by Alex Needham for *The Guardian* exemplified the censure one might receive. Written from a British perspective, Needham is relentless in his criticism of the men who frequent Coachella. Particularly irksome to him is the fashionable tendency to go shirtless on the festival's desert grounds. "Tattooed, ripped and plucked, there's a chest displayed for every taste—unless you're a fan of the pasty British pigeon chest and fuzzy beer belly, both of which are conspicuous by their absence."[118] In an analysis of the attitudes and embodied practices of male models, Entwistle notes that her UK-based respondents scoffed at the idea of working on and toning their bodies. In contrast, her US-based respondents identified both working out and tanning as important modes of body work.[119] She explains this difference in relation to "cultural variation." "In the UK there is a reticence to appear to take too much interest in your appearance and to appear like 'you love yourself.'"[120] Such reticence underpins Needham's criticisms of Coachella's male attendees, whom he labels "bros." According to him, "bros" are identifiable by their "sweaty chests, flip-flops and very short shorts" and have flocked to Coachella with the rise of EDM music there.[121] Such negative characterizations of subcultural newcomers are hardly new. In her analysis of 1990s club culture, for example, Sarah Thornton explains how labels, such as "Sharon and Tracy" and "Acid Teds," were used to refer to the unwelcome participants of dance culture—those people whose presence at raves and underground clubs signified that such events were becoming too visible, too mainstream.[122] She explains that, whether or not such mainstreams actually existed, the use of these categorizations "reveals [much] about the cultural values and social world of hardcore clubbers."[123] The same goes for contemporary summer music festivals and the journalists, fashion editors, photographers, and attendees who produce the value systems that sustain them. That "the bros" seem to be more interested in the feminized acts of bodily display—showing off their "sweaty chests" and "short shorts"—and less interested in the masculinized art of music appreciation makes them especially susceptible to disdain. Perhaps even more than the phenomenon of festival fashion itself, the presence of "the bros" at festivals like Coachella and

Governors Ball signifies the mainstreaming of indie music culture and thus a threat to those people who hold its values dear.

For some, especially those proponents of indie music culture in Britain, this threat is tied directly to the Americanization of the summer music festival, which I have charted in relation to how Coachella has replaced Glastonbury in the festival fashionable imagination. Needham concludes, "While practicality still rules the day at Glastonbury, at Coachella you're expected to suffer to look good."[124] Here, "practicality" alludes to the continuing need to wear the "unfashionable" footwear of wellies to make it through Glastonbury's mud and muck. In so speaking, however, Needham neatly avoids the fact that wellies had become over the preceding decade one of the central features of a British-in-origin, fashionable festival look. His words thus speak not to a fundamental difference between the two festivals, but rather to a set of British indie values that seemed to be under threat. Indeed, the fashioning and the Americanization of the summer music festival challenged the frames through which indie music culture cohered. That is, the bodies of the Coachella bros, alongside those of their fashionably dressed female counterparts, represent a series of destabilizations of British indie music culture in regard to Englishness, "authentic" masculinity, and music. The following chapter continues to explore these destabilizations, specifically in relation to the centrality of whiteness to twenty-first-century indie.

CHAPTER 4
PRINTS, PAINTS, AND CROP-TOPS: THE EMERGENCE OF AFRO-DIASPORIC FESTIVAL FASHION

Through analysis of festival fashion, the preceding chapter explored a transformation in indie in the twenty-first century: its fashioning, its feminizing, and its internationalization. And yet, like the slender indie guitar player, the ideal woman of festival fashion was racially coded as white, idealized through her visibility at Glastonbury in the English countryside and Coachella in California's Indio Valley. The mid-2010s saw a racialized recoding of festival fashion, however, due to prolific media coverage of Brooklyn's Afropunk Fest—a two-day summer music festival that features black musicians and attracts a majority black and mixed-race audience. The looks worn by Afropunk Fest's female, male, and non-binary attendees reanimate a long tradition of diasporic black style as a form of political-sartorial resistance to white hegemony. They are syncretic looks, combining elements of the set festival look—crop-tops and flower headbands—with Afro-diasporic aesthetics: natural hair, dashikis, and Yoruba facepaint, for example. This chapter is about these sartorial displays of Afro-diasporic blackness and also about their representation in the mainstream media. It shows how American media titles—*Vogue*, the *New York Times*, and *Elle*, for example—embraced the newly mainstreamed ideal of individual style and, through this, forged a representational space for Afropunk Fest's sartorial play to be seen widely. Through such representation, moreover, Afro-diasporic blackness was inserted into the visual imaginary of twenty-first-century indie and, more broadly, that of twenty-first-century popular fashion.

Origins: *Afropunk: The Movie*

The origins of Afropunk Fest lie in James Spooner's 2003 documentary film *Afropunk: The Movie*, originally called "The Rock and Roll Nigger Experience."[1] Through interviews and footage of live shows, the film explores how a handful of young African Americans participated in and identified with the overwhelmingly white punk scene of the late twentieth and early twenty-first century. Spooner's goal with the documentary was to make these black punks visible. As he explained to Rawiya Kameir of *The Fader*,

I wasn't seeing myself represented at all in the subcultures I was attracted to and I really wanted to ask some question about why that was. By the time the film came out in 2003, [there] wasn't really a lot of room for black kids who wanted to do anything outside of pop bottles.[2] Coupled with 2003-era digital media—YouTube and MySpace didn't exist yet—that meant there wasn't a lot of access to other things. I remember Googling "black punk" and there was one thing that came up, and it was an essay on prison rape. That was it.

Spooner concluded, "There were zero conversations happening around black punk rockers or black alternative anything."[3]

The broader socio-political question of cultural legibility underpins *Afropunk: The Movie*'s narrative. As Mark Anthony Neal explains in his book *Looking for Leroy: Illegible Black Masculinities*, there are specific scripts through which black masculinity is made recognizable: the trope of "the angry, disaffected urban black male,"[4] for example, and also the "decidedly unsophisticated images of pimps and petty criminals [...] hip-hop thugs and strip-club denizens."[5] Similarly, as Aisha Durham notes within an analysis of Beyoncé's "Check on It" music video, within what she calls a hip-hop dreamworld women are frequently assigned to play one of two set roles: "the respectable race-loyal queen and the promiscuous, classless ho."[6] To what extent, Neal asks, can these racialized—and racist—tropes be challenged, queered. "By 'queer' I am alluding not only to the obvious ambiguities associated with queering sexualities [...] but also to queerness as a radical rescripting of the accepted performances of a heteronormative black masculinity."[7] Referring to Leroy, the character from the 1980s' television show *Fame*, for whom he titles his book, Neal writes, "Leroy represents a black masculinity that was 'illegible' to many."[8]

Neal's formulation of "illegible" black identities provides a framework for understanding how the identities of the young, black men and women featured in *Afropunk: The Movie* are performed and materialized. Many of the male and female subjects of Spooner's film discuss their inability to connect with contemporary black culture and, more specifically, the subject positions provided within hip-hop. As one respondent within the film says, "A lot of black people, in my opinion, have a tunnel vision of what black should be, and black people can't stray outside of that. 'It's wrong. You can't do that'"[9] In contrast, *Afropunk: The Movie* shows how punk—an overwhelmingly white cultural form—offers these young people a set of performative repertoires and semiotic codes, through which to create their identities. Several respondents, for example, talk about the thrill of entering the mosh pit. There is both the potential of physical injury from being punched or kicked by another person in the pit and a sense of camaraderie that, somewhat paradoxically, emerges from such intimate and aggressive contact. These black punk identities made visible within Spooner's documentary are difficult to decipher. Although not named as such, this cultural illegibility is noted by some of the documentary's respondents. Some interviewees speak, for example, of scolding by their parents or teasing from members of their communities for dressing in punk-inspired ensembles. One interviewee speaks about managing such responses by toning down his look when running errands in his neighborhood. In short, he makes his body more culturally legible in order to avoid bullying and/or censure.

As the remainder of this chapter shows, the question of cultural legibility also frames analysis of the performance and representation of blackness at Afropunk Fest in the mid-2010s. On the one hand, the event offers, to borrow Neal's phrasing, a "radical rescripting of the accepted performances" of urban blackness. As Simbarashe Cha, a fashion photographer who covered the event from 2012 to 2015, explained to me,

> The first thing that I noticed was how much style there was, and the second thing I noticed was that for such a large event that was almost exclusively young black attendees, there were no tensions, no stereotypical assumptions about what might happen if you get large groups of young black people together. Everyone that was there was showing love, everyone seemed to be in support of each other, there in love for the music.[10]

In place of the urban stereotypes of the gang member and drug dealer, on the grounds of and in photographs of Afropunk Fest, a form of contemporary Afro-cosmopolitan blackness emerges. Clothing and adornment play a large role in this rescripting of metropolitan blackness—a blackness illegible within both the tropes of urban blackness *and* the discursive framework of festival fashion. That is, like the black punk of the early 2000s, the black style star of the mid-2010s Afropunk Fest was not the idealized subject of its chosen cultural formation: punk and festival fashion, respectively. By

107

drawing on the signs and symbols of a formation that was racially coded as white, however, both figures offer new ways of thinking about blackness: specifically, blackness as forged within what Stuart Hall calls "the mixed, contradictory, hybrid spaces of popular culture."[11] As the chapter shows, however, unlike the black punk, the Afropunk Fest style star quickly became an object of fashionable fascination, transformed from an illegible black subject into an ideal subject of festival fashion, twenty-first-century indie, and popular fashion, more broadly.

The exponential rise of Afropunk Fest

The first Afropunk Fest—held in 2005 at the Brooklyn Academy of Music (BAM)—was intended to provide a physical meeting space for the geographically dispersed young people, who until that point had been communicating on the Afropunk online message-board. For the first festival Spooner and his co-founder Matthew Morgan curated a series of films at BAM and organized a handful of shows at legendary venue CBGB's in Manhattan.[12] "Back then," Spooner explained to Rawiya Kameir of *The Fader*,

> I only had two rules. One, you had to be good. And B, you had to have a black singer. I got into a shit-ton of fights about it. There was a band and the keyboard player was black. Like, no, you can't play. The keyboardist is welcome to do a solo show. But no one is looking at the keyboard player, everyone is looking at the singer. So, those were my rules.[13]

The decision to move the festival to Commodore Barry Park, according to Spooner, was impromptu, as attendees decided to organize a picnic on the final day of the 2005 festival.[14] Since then, Afropunk Fest has remained in Commodore Barry Park, but has ballooned in size and cultural visibility. As Brian Josephs of *Vice* wrote, "from 2003 to 2015, Afropunk hasn't just grown—it's been reimagined."[15]

Kameir and Josephs' articles were two among a spate of journalistic pieces that appeared in 2015, attempting to make sense of how the festival had changed since 2005. Not only did 2015 mark the ten-year anniversary of the festival, it also marked the first year that attendees had to pay for entrance: $70 for a weekend ticket. Despite this change, attendance numbers continued to rise, by the mid-2010s into the high tens of thousands. Journalistic pieces like Kameir and Josephs' appeared in a range of publications: from the music magazines *Fader* and *Pitchfork*, to the youth-oriented *Vice*, and also the elite *The New Yorker*. As article titles "Is Afropunk Fest No Longer Punk?" and "Gentrifying Afropunk" reveal, underpinning reportage across publications were the central questions: what happens when a subcultural movement like Afropunk becomes a mainstream phenomenon? Does it lose its power and politics?[16] For example, Hannah Giorgis of *The New Yorker* observed, "While this move toward attracting wider audiences has worked, it's also shifted the focus away from the movement's origins—and pushed out punk fans in the process."[17] One of those alienated fans was James Spooner himself, who left the festival in 2008, and was replaced as an organizer by Jocelyn Cooper.

Concerns over the ideological costs of mainstreaming also guided festival co-organizers Morgan and Cooper, as they shepherded Afropunk Fest into this new, bigger phase. Centrally, they redefined the term "Afropunk" from signifying a small group of black punks to encompassing more broadly "the other Black experience," as the movement's tagline reads.[18] As Ian F. Blair of *Pitchfork* noted, "those at the helm of the festival decided to redefine it, converting Afropunk from a subculture with a distinct identity into a fluid idea that could be broadly applied across the spectrum of blackness."[19] As Josephs of *Vice* explained, "There were others living in boxes, too: alternative hip-hop, alternative R&B, LGBT members, the natural hair community, etc. A more wider [*sic*] definition of Afropunk—'freedom,' as Cooper puts it— worked as an umbrella for all those facets of the black experience."[20] Today, Afropunk Fest "rules" read, "No Sexism, No Racism, No Ableism, No Ageism, No Homophobia, No Fatphobia, No Transphobia, No Hatefulness."[21] Similarly, the Afropunk website and its social media platforms feature articles and posts having to deal with a range of current political issues that inform the black experience, more broadly, tagging these posts with #blacklivesmatter, #blackjoy, and #blackgirlmagic, among other hashtags. In short, Afropunk's political message has been diversified, advocating for a range of perspectives, all included under the umbrella of the "the other Black experience."

Alongside Afropunk's message, the festival itself has expanded. Specifically, it has expanded into a global movement. Afropunk Fests are celebrated in Paris, Atlanta, London, and Johannesburg, alongside Brooklyn, with future plans for Brazil. To put on the larger festival each year, Afropunk has developed partnerships with a range of sponsors, from the black hair care retailer Carol's Daughter, to the multinational companies Toyota and Red Bull, to New York cultural institutions The Metropolitan Museum of Art and the radio network WNYC.[22] As Dick Hebdige writes, the ideological level is just one site of a subculture's potential incorporation. The other is the commercial level.[23] On this theme, marketer Rob Fields has written multiple times for *Forbes*, outlining "the opportunity marketers were missing out on by not engaging the audience that supports Afropunk."[24] One of Fields' expert interviewees explained,

> Afropunk represents the idea of cross-culturalism. Years ago, it would've been about celebrating our culture and heritage within our cultural group. That's the beauty of cross-culturalism: You're not only able to celebrate your culture within your group, but across multiple cultures. Initially, it was hard for brands to get their arms around Afropunk because they were still thinking mono (white, the old "general" market) or multi (non-white cultures, but separate). These days, cross culturalism plays very well in the minds of millennials.[25]

Throughout, the movement's organizers have attempted to temper the festival's rapid expansion by foregrounding activism. In Cooper's words, "We only want to work with brands that are authentic to the event. That want to speak to the community 365 days a year."[26] For example, at the 2016 festival Toyota Latino sponsored a performance featuring the Colombian group ChocQuib Town, in which participants held up signs reading "Our differences give us strength" and similar slogans, while Brooklyn- and Newark-based documentary photographer Ruddy Roye took pictures of the performance. In 2017, Toyota once again sponsored the festival, this time educating attendees about its hybrid technologies. Further, in addition to stalls for vendors, Afropunk Fest has a specific area—Activism Row—where organizations, such as Bridging Access to Care and Black Lives Matter, can interact with interested attendees. In 2016, volunteers were helping attendees register to vote in the American general election, and a member of the Brooklyn fire department was on site, recruiting potential future fire fighters. Criticized for charging entrance to the festival in 2015, its organizers made sure that a number of volunteer opportunities were made available for attendees who could not, or did not want to, pay the entrance fee.

In ways both unforeseen and uncontrolled by Afropunk Fest's co-organizers, fashion has become in recent years a central focal point, around which the festival experience rotates and from which its image radiates. In 2012, several publications began documenting the looks of the festival's attendees. One piece, published on *Noisey*, presented the photographer Nicholas Gazin's first-hand account of what he saw at Afropunk.[27] There are images of black and white attendees (one white male attendee wearing a dashiki); a close-up shot of two young women wearing loose Afros; and a photograph of a young black woman in a Lolita-inspired ensemble, among other photographs. He writes in his account of the weekend, "When Tunde from TV on the Radio came on stage to give the final performance of the festival he greeted the 30,000 people with 'All the most beautiful people in Brooklyn are here. As well as the ugliest. And the middling ones.'" Two other publications that covered Afropunk Fest that year—*Essence* and *Vogue Italia*'s "The Black Blog"—placed a greater emphasis on the "beautiful" attendees, documenting their ensembles through photographs and, in the case of *Essence*, captions.[28] *Essence* is a fashion, beauty, and lifestyle magazine catering to African American women, and its documentation of Afropunk Fest 2012 celebrated the looks of some of the festival's black female attendees. Its festival coverage that year followed the street style formula characteristic to festival fashion representations. Attendees are pictured in full-body portrait shots; they are identified by their names, occupations, and a catchphrase; and the sources of their garments are listed. For example, one student was given the tagline "Hipster Swag," and her outfit consisted of "an H&M top, thrift shirt, vintage rings and Doc Marten boots." Many mainstream publications list sources, as part of advertising and revenue schemes with big brands. By highlighting the mix of vintage and first-hand garments, the magazine draws on the fashionable discourse of mixing and matching, which was discussed in the preceding chapter. In contrast, in its coverage of the 2012 festival, *Vogue Italia*'s "The Black Blog" featured a series of photographs of black attendees, both male and female, all of whom wore edgy looks.[29] The subjects of the *Vogue.it* images wear jumpsuits, oversized and torn shirts as well as wide-brimmed hats and geometric patterned sunglasses. It is in these *Vogue.it* images, moreover, that one sees the hints of what would become in the following years one of the Afropunk look's defining features: a mix of typical festival fashion garments—cropped tops and denim cut-offs—and garments that signaled an association with the African diaspora—headwraps, dashikis, and natural hairstyles. The festival co-organizers discussed this fashionable development in 2014 with *i-D*:

> *Interviewer*: It's an incredibly stylish festival I've never seen so many cool looking kids in one spot.
>
> *Matthew Morgan*: Yeah, they're so stylish. It's become such a part of the festival, which I was a little scared of. I didn't want it to become a fashion show. It could have been kind of corny, but we haven't initiated it—they're bringing who they are.

Jocelyn Cooper: There was a girl last year wearing a black veil. Someone interviewed her and said, "What's up with the veil?" and she was like, "I'm wearing the veil because I've come to everybody's funeral … because I'm killing it."[30]

An Afro-diasporic festival look, performed

The contemporary Afropunk Fest look is constructed through the stylization of hair, clothing, and other forms of bodily adornment, such as face paint. As fashion studies scholar Carol Tulloch explains, "style" is a necessary concept within the analysis of "black people and the African diaspora […] their construction of self, and/or the use or production of garments and accessories in that process."[31] As the preceding chapter showed, however, individual style is also a historically specific ideal through which young women—and, here, men, and non-binary people, as well—are interpellated into the contemporary fashion system. These two articulations of style—the historical practice and the historically specific ideal—intersect within the materialization, performance, and representation of the Afropunk Fest look.

The black punks featured in *Afropunk: The Movie* rarely speak about their clothing, opting for the most part to wear loose jeans and non-descript T-shirts at home and on stage. The exception to this rule is Tamar-kali Brown, a twenty-eight-year-old woman from Brooklyn and one of the film's main subjects. Brown explains that she was drawn to punk by its distinctive set of visual signs and symbols. She says,

> Growing up, I had access to these images of, you know, folks in the bush, tribal peoples, what have you. And I remember them being really striking and moving me. Just because I really saw just the stark beauty in it all. So when I first started seeing images in punk—this really bright coloured hair, safety pin piercings and things like that—it was pretty much on that same level, just a contemporary Euro-centric version of what people in the bush were doing. All these things that, you know, existed before. Now that because I know exactly what I'm being and like I have no fear around it, I'm very clear, my choice to look the way I do is based on relating to traditionally African aesthetic, but it was through punk initially that I had those senses reawakened.[32]

She continues later in the film, "in my mind, me and my crew were on some sort of hardcore black nationalist type shit. But to the average person, we were just doing some white shit."[33] Within these comments, Brown mobilizes two contradictory logics. By using the term "in the bush" to refer to African peoples, she draws on a "naturalistic" logic that frames Africa, Africans, and thus blackness as closer to nature. By consciously using the signs and symbols of a white subcultural formation to fashion her "hardcore black nationalist" look, she practices a "syncretic" logic that troubles the boundaries between dominant white culture and subordinated forms of blackness. Both logics are also at play within the contemporary Afropunk look.

The conceptual framework used above, which posits "naturalistic" and "syncretic" "logics of black stylization" in opposition to one another, was formulated by cultural theorist Kobena Mercer.[34] In his essay "Black Hair / Style Politics," Mercer introduces, compares, and contrasts these two logics, locating each within the different historical moments it was fashioned through hairstyling practices. He argues that both logics function as political-stylistic responses to the racism of dominant culture, and he frames his analysis largely through the subcultural work from the Centre for Contemporary Cultural Studies. Mercer is more critical of the naturalistic logic—a logic that is embodied within two hairstyles under his analysis: the Afro and dreadlocks. He explains about the Afro: it does not have "roots" within an Africa of lived experience; rather, the style draws on the idea of "Africa" to "[champion] an aesthetic of nature that opposed itself to any artifice as a sign of corrupting Eurocentric influence."[35] His criticism of this logic comes from the fact that it is precisely this Africa–nature connection that was used to justify institutional practices of racism from the eighteenth century: specifically, the enslavement of African peoples in the Americas. Nonetheless, he concedes, the naturalistic logic proved extremely potent during the Civil Rights movement of the mid-twentieth century, wherein the Afro was "stylistically *cultivated* and politically *constructed* in a particular historical moment as part of a strategic contestation of white dominance and the cultural power of whiteness."[36] For Mercer, syncretic practices of black stylization offer more nuanced "responses to the racism of the dominant culture" because they also "involve acts of appropriation from that same 'master' culture through which 'syncretic' forms of diasporean culture have evolved."[37] He speaks about the "creolizing" art of jazz music[38] and also the conk—a hairstyle worn by black men in the 1940s, which "involved a violent technology of straightening" and left its wearers' hair with a reddish hue. He explains, "the political economy of the conk rested on its ambiguity. [...] To assume that black men conked up *en masse* because they secretly wanted to become 'red-heads' would be way off the mark."[39] Rather, "by flouting convention with varying degrees of artifice such techniques of black stylization participated in a defiant 'dandyism,' fronting out oppression by the artful manipulation of appearances."[40] Within her book *Slaves to Fashion: Black Dandyism and the Styling of Black Diasporic Identity*, Monica Miller takes up the themes of dandyism and syncretic stylization.[41] For her, "black dandies are creatures of invention who continually and characteristically break down limiting identity markers and propose new, more fluid categories within which to constitute themselves."[42] Within a discussion of the black dandies of the Harlem Renaissance, she explains that this practice of reconstitution involved drawing on "both European and African and American origins."[43] Whereas the leaders of the Harlem Renaissance attempted to articulate an authentic black modernism, she counters, the "failure [of the dandy] to espouse or promulgate a blackness that could be packaged as 'the' or 'a' New Negro aesthetic is precisely that which identifies the movement as a success."[44] In other words, it is the dandy's syncretic identity, his racial (and gender and sexual) indeterminacy—*not* some claim to an "authentic" and ultimately static blackness—that makes him a figure who can challenge "the racism of dominant culture."[45] She uses the term cosmopolitanism to make sense of these contradictions underpinning the black dandy's identity, explaining, "Black and blackness are themselves signs of diaspora, of a cosmopolitanism that African subjects did not choose but from which they necessarily reimagined themselves."[46] Her point echoes one Stuart Hall made in his famous essay, "What is This 'Black' in Black Popular Culture?". He writes that black cultural forms—and, here, we can include clothing styles—"are the product of partial synchronization, of engagement across cultural boundaries, of the confluence of more than one cultural tradition, of the negotiations of dominant and subordinate positions, of the subterranean strategies of recoding and transcoding, of critical signification, of signifying. Always these forms are impure, to some degree hybridized from a vernacular base."[47]

The Afropunk Fest look draws on naturalistic logics; it is also an example of a syncretic, hybridized, cosmopolitan blackness. Central within the Afropunk look are three elements: natural hair, African printed garments, and Yoruba-inspired facepaints. Through this combination of Afro-inspired elements, the contemporary Afropunk Fest look mimics this mid-century progressive black style of the Civil Rights and Black Power movements, fomenting a form of stylistic rebellion through the rejection of dominant white culture's signs and symbols. And yet, the contemporary Afropunk Fest look also radically updates this pose for the new millennium: through the proliferation of a variety of natural texture hairstyles; through the integration of typical festival fashion garments, such as crop-tops and denim shorts; and through the use of facepaints to perform a festival site-specific form of Afro-diasporic identity. The end result is a hybrid look, forged at the intersections of black style and festival fashion. It thus offers a new—and historically specific—way of imagining blackness, but also posts up new exclusions around how blackness is idealized and performed.

Hair

Black hair is both politicized and political. As Mercer explains, black hair is "symbolic material"[48] that "has been historically *devalued* as the most visible stigmata of blackness"[49] within dominant "ideologies of 'the beautiful.'"[50] As symbolic material, he continues, black hair can be fashioned as "aesthetic 'solutions' to a range of 'problems' created by ideologies of race and racism."[51] Different hairstyles produce different solutions, however. Noliwe Rooks opens her book *Hair Raising: Beauty, Culture, and African American Women* with an illustrative vignette from her own life, through which she outlines two opposing strategies of aesthetic stylization.[52] That is, as a thirteen-year-old girl, when she decided she wanted to straighten her hair, she got "caught between competing definitions of Black Power, Black Community, and Black Pride."[53] Her mother—an activist—outright refused to allow her to "capitulat[e] to the values of the dominant culture,"[54] whereas her grandmother—"a card-carrying member of a pre-integration, southern, middle-class, African-American community"[55]— facilitated her first beauty shop visit. According to her grandmother, "straightening my hair would give me an advantage in the world."[56] Rooks explains, "Whereas neither road led to a desire for whiteness or white culture, both routes led to very specific assumptions about my place in relation to other African Americans and the larger white society."[57] The two, opposing political-aesthetic strategies that Rooks outlines can be historicized within the mid-twentieth century. It was then, during the Civil Rights era, that the Afro emerged as a potent symbol of black resistance to dominant, white culture. In her book *Liberated Threads: Black Women, Style, and the Global Politics of Soul*, Tanisha Ford explains, although men and women had been wearing the Afro throughout the 1960s, Angela Davis' arrest in 1970 served to solidify a set of meanings around and through the hairstyle.[58] Scholars and journalists of the time identified it "as a symbol of her resistance to the cultural and political status quo"[59] and/or as "visual shorthand for revolutionary glamour."[60] Ford continues, Davis' "revolutionary glamour" subsequently served as a model of

Figure 11 Afropunk 2015 attendee. © Diane Allford.

inspiration for many young women of the trans-Atlantic African diaspora, for whom hair and clothing styles served as the means through which to fashion black activism.[61]

Davis' famous Afro is cited performatively within the contemporary Afropunk Fest look, as male and female attendees brush their natural textured hair into halo shapes, and publications are quick to use these looks as "visual shorthand for" a new era of "revolutionary glamour," to borrow Ford's phrasing.[62] One 2015 attendee received much attention for her Afro-ed look, not least because she coupled her six-inch halo Afro with a bright red, halter-top body suit, and high-waisted, flared blue jeans (Figure 11). Her image served as the cover photo within a street style feature for *Vogue.com* called "The Bold and the Beautiful: The Best Street Style at Afropunk," wherein photographer Ben Rasmussen collaborated with Senior Fashion Writer Marjon Carlos to document the looks of twenty-three male and female festival attendees on Polaroid film.[63] Her image also appeared in a photograph Diane Allford took for an online feature in *Coloures*—a now (at the time of publication in 2019) defunct online beauty site for black women.[64] The feature was called "15 Stunning Photos of Black Women Slaying AFROPUNK"—a title that uses the queer-in-origin and used-by-millennials term "slay" to recall the "Black is Beautiful" mantra of the Civil Rights generation. The attendee's image also appeared on Afropunk's own Instagram feed. There, Ruddy Roye, the Jamaican-born, Brooklyn- and Newark-based photographer, who was commissioned by Afropunk to document activism at that year's festival, used the posting to draw together the themes of punk, black activism, and the mistreatment of black people at the hands of the police. His caption to the Instagram post includes the following: "Her inspiration for her look is, of course, Pam Grier, but her friends think she looks like Angela Davis. It is the feeling of activism that drives her and the reason she wanted to attend Afropunk 2015. 'What happened to Sandra Bland was nothing new. What she went through was what black people have been experiencing for years,' she said."[65]

Through visual emphasis, a playful choice of words, or direct discussion of police violence against black people, each of these features uses this particular attendee's Angela Davis-esque look to bring attention to the ongoing need for Civil Rights-era activism, in positive action *and* in aesthetic style, in the mid-2010s—a historical moment characterized in part by a vigorous and violent debate over the statement "black lives matter." Photographer Driely S. pushed this political message further. In 2016, she was both one of Afropunk's house photographers, producing content for their website and social media, and shooting photo and video for several other publications. Among the many photographs she and her team of assistants took over the course of the weekend, one stood out. The subject's hair was partially teased out into an Afro and partially formed into dreadlocks, and he stood for his portrait under a sprinkler in the playground area of Commodore Barry Park. He wore denim overalls over his bare chest and a bit of material tied around his hair as a headband. As he posed for his portrait, he held his fist straight out in front of himself. Sensing the political potential of the image, S. guided her subject to raise his fist high in the air in the Black Power salute.[66] Her work is discussed again at the end of the chapter.

And yet, the Afro is just one among a variety of natural textured hairstyles that appear on Afropunk Fest grounds and in the photographs documenting the event. As Tiffany M. Gill explains, there has been a proliferation of natural texture hairstyles in the twenty-first century. She writes, "The term *natural* [...] is currently used to denote a wide range of aesthetic choices for African-descended women's hair that includes everything from short Afros to long, wavy textures, braids (with or without the use of hair extensions), twists, dreadlocks, and every variation in between."[67] Afropunk Fest functions as display grounds, of sorts, for these many styles. Captured in my own photographs of the event, shared on thousands of attendees' social media accounts, and documented by professional photographers, who were commissioned by various media outlets to cover the event, are dreadlocks, shaven heads, partially shaven heads, Afros, Afro puffs, Bantu knots, thin braids, thick braids, thick and thin twists, loose curls, tight curls, and hair of varying hues: black and brown, but also bleached blond, red, orange, green, blue, purple, blue-purple, pink, and white, as well as combinations of multiple colors. Some attendees used extensions to add color and/or length to their hair; others relied upon their natural hair for texture and style.

Publications highlight and celebrate this cornucopia of natural textured hairstyles within their coverage of Afropunk Fest. In 2014, for example, *Vogue.com* commissioned the artist Awol Erizku to photograph hair portraits of some of the festival's performers and attendees—a group of men and women, whom *Vogue.com* writer Marjon Carlos called within the feature's copy a "prideful pack."[68] That same year, *Essence.com* did a feature on "Hair Street Style," prompting its readers to "Enjoy the front row of our favorite hairstyles from ladies who mixed, mingled and enjoyed music's most distinct performances at the 10th annual AfroPunk Festival."[69] And in 2016, *Teenvogue.com* used the opportunity of that year's Afropunk Fest Paris to offer some "natural hair inspiration" to its readers.[70] The twelve-image slideshow featured photographs of female performers and attendees with short captions that both championed the featured looks and offered advice as to how readers could recreate them at home. For example, the caption to an image of three attendees, whose natural hair fell into different curl patterns, read, "These women are a perfect example of why you should never be afraid to let your natural hair flag fly. It's super important to moisturize naturally curly strands, so be sure to treat them to weekly deep conditioning treatments like the Carol's Daughter Monoi Repairing Hair Mask."[71]

Interwoven within this media coverage are three themes: self- and race pride, black womanhood and, finally, the role of the black haircare industry within the articulation and formation of the first two. As scholars of African American history and beauty culture have shown, these three themes have been intertwined throughout the twentieth and early twenty-first centuries. Rooks, for example, tells the entrepreneurial biography of Madam C.J. Walker, the famed African-American millionairess, who made her fortune in black hair care at the beginning of the twentieth century. Walker was born into slavery, but managed to move from field hand, to laundress, to cook and "from there I *promoted myself* into the business of manufacturing hair and goods and preparations."[72] The emphasis on self-promotion is significant. As Rooks explains, "Walker placed herself firmly within the dominant culture's tenet of each person pulling themselves up by their bootstraps,"[73] offering herself as a model entrepreneur for other black women to follow toward economic independence, not least by becoming saleswomen for her products.[74] Central within Walker's advertising imagery were photographs of Walker, herself; she was not only a model entrepreneur, but the model demonstrating the effectiveness of her hair-lengthening cream. As Rooks examines, one photograph shows Walker as a young woman, looking away from the camera, shy and embarrassed; she has short hair. Two other photographs show Walker as a mature woman, confident in her status, stature, and pose; her hair is long. Rooks explains, "The change, however, will not be characterized by acceptance within the dominant culture but rather will consist of enhanced internal feelings of self-pride and resistance to that culture."[75] Gill extends the history of the black haircare industry in her book *Beauty Shop Politics: African American Women's Activism in the Beauty Industry*.[76] She addresses Madam Walker and her fellow "beauty pioneer" Annie Malone,[77] before exploring other twentieth-century examples demonstrative of her argument that "the black beauty industry must be understood as providing one of the most important opportunities for black women to assert leadership in their communities and in the larger political arena."[78] She speaks of amnesty trips to Europe that the United Beauty School Owners and Teacher's Association took in 1954 and 1960, which "help[ed] to elevate African American beauticians as the global standard bearers of black beauty and hair care,"[79] boosting their image as respectable black businesswomen within both the American beauty industry and the African diaspora, more broadly. She also identifies the role of salons as a site for the dissemination of political material throughout the Civil Rights movement, explaining, it was "space frequented by a varied group of African American women that was hidden from those with a competing agenda."[80] The beauty salon was also a space that fostered "the ability to gather in a place of pampering and self-care [which] led to community activism."[81] As Maxine Leeds Craig explains in her book *Ain't I a Beauty Queen? Black Women, Beauty, and the Politics of Race*, however, the transition from the Civil Rights Movement to the Black Power Movement was signaled in part through women's abandonment of salon-straightened hairstyles.[82] First cultivated "on black college campuses and in Civil Rights Movement organizations," the natural would become a way for people, even those people not directly engaged in Civil Rights politics, to "join the abstract community of proud black men and women."[83] The natural, which quickly turned into the Afro style, functioned at the level of confrontation as opposed to integration. "It was proof that the Eurocentric beauty standard had been overturned, and as a result, the brown skin and tightly curled hair that had been black women's 'problems' were suddenly their joys."[84]

This overturning offered a new framework for black women to cultivate self- and race pride without having to process their hair with heat. As one activist Craig quotes explained, "There was a part of it that felt so magical and so true and honest. The realization that we could be who we were and be beautiful. It provided me with a level of confidence that I'd never known in my life before. There was community in the beauty standard."[85] Craig notes that the Afro turned first into a mass-market object—the Afro wig—before fading out of fashion in the late 1970s, to be replaced by new techniques of hair straightening that involved chemicals. Those chemicals were the critical focus of comedian Chris Rock's 2009 documentary *Good Hair*, the tagline of which was "Sit back and relax," where "relax" means both to rest and to straighten one's hair chemically—a painful process.[86] At the beginning of the twenty-first century, Gill explains, natural hairstyles have come back into fashion.[87] What's more, she shows, the discussion around natural hair and that around the haircare products most successfully used to cultivate natural textured hairstyles have moved online. The local salon has been replaced by "Nappturality.com or the more than 133 million 'natural hair blogs' that emerge through … a Google search [...] As such, these websites provide a rich archive for exploring issues of identity, entrepreneurship, and community in black women's lives."[88] These new digitally mediated sites are complex and at times contradictory. On the one hand, they promote a sense of self-worth that is tied to digital connectivity. As Gill argues, "Tagging a selfie '#TeamNatural' does not simply assert one's individual beauty, but connects a personal quest for affirmation to a wider community."[89] On the other, she explains, that access to these sites and modes of acceptable participation can be "e-policed." She gives the example of some sites "ban[ning] certain words: relaxed, straighten, good hair, bad hair, texturizer."[90] In the twenty-first century, then, natural hair serves as an expression of self- and race pride *and* as "the new normal in Black haircare" with its own rules and regulations as to who can participate and how they can take part.[91]

Young women and men who chose not to—or whose hair cannot— conform to the contemporary natural ideal in any of its varied forms are of course welcome on the grounds of Afropunk Fest, as are white attendees, those of other ethnicities, and those who are not dressed up; however, none of these groups are likely to be chosen by style hunters and photographers to pose for images that will represent the event throughout a range of independent and mass media. As Cha explained, he has been told that his street style portraiture at and of Afropunk Fest "looks like Coachella" and that, instead, he could try to represent the festival by taking photos of "people who look 'weirder.'" It is routine practice within festival documentation for photographers to seek out extreme looks that are made to stand in for festival as a whole; as another photographer with whom I briefly spoke explained, "I'm on assignment and I'm looking to capture the general fashion of the festival, whatever that is. But I'm also looking for people that are a little bit different than your super cool but beautiful people."[92] Counterposed to Coachella, however, "weird" is racialized, a cultural mechanism through which black bodies are fetishized and Othered. An elaborate natural hairstyle might serve as "weird" enough to make it into coverage of the event; so too might an ensemble that features Afro-diasporic aesthetics. I will outline these aesthetics now before exploring in more detail mainstream media representations of Afropunk Fest, how they frame its image, sometimes fetishizing it and sometimes using it to challenge dominant, white-orientated codes of fashion and beauty.

Paints, prints, and crop-tops

At Afropunk Fest 2015, under a tree close to the smallest of Afropunk's three stages, a group of young women had set up a small face-painting station. Their sign read, "Tribal = Facepaint." It continued, "the white paint is symbolic for purity, wearing them pays homage to our ancestors and *creates* social awareness to our culture in the present time and living status. The patterns are solely beautification and are custom to your faces [*sic*] desire."[93] Many attendees stood in line to have the white paint applied to their faces; far more were seen walking around the festival later with a variety of painted designs, arching over their eyebrows and across their cheeks. Perhaps responding to the language of the face-painting station, one week after the 2015 festival, a contributor to the online magazine *Those People* reprimanded the festival's attendees in a piece entitled, "Black America, Please Stop Appropriating African Clothing and Tribal Marks … Yes, that Means Everyone at Afropunk Too."[94] She writes,

> Black Twitter is littered with countless examples of the uproar that ensues when White people appropriate *Black culture*. Words such as *fancy dress, mockery* and *profiteering* are thrown around quite freely, but no one seems to realize that this selfsame violation is committed against us Africans—all under the guise of tribal fashion and connection to *The Motherland*.[95]

It is equally insensitive, she continues, when someone is "wearing a Fulani septum ring, rocking a djellaba, [and is] painted with Yoruba-like tribal marks."[96] The practice of imagining Africa through dress practice is longstanding. As Ford explains, within the global black freedom struggle of the mid-twentieth century, "Black women […] explicitly aimed to reconnect themselves to both real and imagined precolonial cultures in order to redefine notions of beauty, black womanhood, and style on their own terms."[97] On the Afro-diasporic imagination, Stuart Hall says, "I have had to say to people before, 'Africa is alive and well in the diaspora.'" But, he continues,

> the Africa we left 400 years ago under the conditions of slavery, transportation and the Middle Passage has not been waiting for us—unchanged—to go back to, either in our heads or in our bodies. That Africa, far from being just the ancestral home, is the subject of the most brutal and devastating modern forms of exploitation. It is the subject and the object of the most vicious forms of contemporary neoliberalism, victim of the strategies of the new forms of geopolitical power, as well as ravaged by civil war, poverty, hunger, the rivalry of competing gangs and corrupt governing powers and elites.[98]

Identifying herself as an African, and perhaps mirroring Hall's point, the article's author responds to the festival's diasporic imagining of Africa:

> I get that Black America's history is one marred with so many injustices that I would never claim to understand. The emergence of a unified voice that is strong and proud is one that I respect and continue to

applaud, but please also understand the need for *us* to be heard, too. Please don't trample our rights fighting for yours.[99]

The author's critique is atypical: the only piece I found which directly criticizes Afropunk Fest and black American practices of adornment. Perhaps unintentionally, it calls for a comparative analysis of the global iterations of Afropunk Fest to examine how Afro-diasporic festival fashion is performed across the varying geographies of the diaspora. Hall again: "of course there is the most profound connection between the African diasporas of the Caribbean, the US, of Brazil and Latin America and the diasporas of London or Paris, but these different 'Africas', though deeply interconnected, historically, cannot be 'the same' any longer. [...] Each has negotiated its relation to the West, to the surrounding world, differently."[100] Her critique is also typical; she mobilizes the framework of "cultural appropriation," which circulates widely within popular fashion discourses of twenty-first-century North America.[101]

Festival fashion is frequently addressed in discussions of cultural appropriation. In the years preceding Afropunk Fest's rise to fashionable prominence, "ethnic" trends that strove for a bohemian quality through tropes of the "exotic" started to pervade festival fashion: feathered headdresses and gemstone-encrusted bindis. The two trends received much backlash for their uncritical appropriation of sacred objects from Native American/Indigenous groups and Hinduism, respectively.[102] More broadly, mainstream fashion trends in North America and Western Europe routinely appropriate objects from minority, Asian, and African cultures, drawing on and reproducing a range of exoticizing tropes, historically and today.[103] As Elizabeth Wilson explains, bohemians, in their critique of mainstream culture, have frequently "turned a romantic eye on distant cultures, and searched for a spontaneity and authenticity in simpler societies which, they felt, no longer existed in their own."[104] Whereas the nineteenth-century bohemians "who desired to escape Western civilization did not yet understand how exploitative this might be,"[105] twenty-first-century festival attendees, to put it bluntly, should know better. Accordingly, the Montreal-based Osheaga festival banned headdresses from festival grounds in 2015. Discussions of cultural appropriation thus introduce questions of politics and ethnic privilege into summer music festivals.

Or, rather, reintroduce. In the late 1960s and early 1970s, summer music festivals signified politically, serving as testaments to the civil unrest of the period. This point is evidenced in documentaries made at the time. Michael

Wadleigh's *Woodstock: Three Days of Peace and Music*, for example, conveys the mass gathering of young people as an idyllic retreat;[106] the documentary film starts with bucolic scenes of fields, men calmly working to erect the event's central stage. The film also points to generational conflict. For example, a pair of young people describe to the camera how their parents fail to understand their lifestyle. Her mother thinks she is going to hell and his father asked if he was in a communist training center.[107] As indicated by the reference to communism, the generational divide that shaped late 1960s popular culture in the US and UK was also a political divide. Young attendees of summer music festivals sought freedom and equality; the older generation saw their practices as political subversion. This contrast emerges in another documentary produced at the time: Murray Lerner's *Message to Love*, filmed at the 1970 Isle of Wight festival off the southern coast of Britain, which saw 600,000 attendees from Britain and internationally.[108] The film starts with an interview from a local old-timer: "There is no doubt in my mind and a number of other responsible people, that this isn't just hippy fun. Behind it is black power, and behind that is communism."[109] Black power played a central role at 1972's Wattstax festival, which was documented by Mel Stuart in the 1973 film *Wattstax*.[110] The benefit concert was held by Stax Records in the Los Angeles Colosseum in honor of the seventh anniversary of the 1965 riots in Watts, California, which pitted the African American community against the police. The documentary starts with Reverend Jesse Jackson leading the assembled concert-goers in the Black National Anthem, fists raised in the Black Power salute. In addition to concert footage, the documentary features intimate interviews, including with comedian Richard Pryor, about the conditions of black life in America as well as relationships between black men and women. Some of the commentary resonates with the themes that animate the current Black Lives Matter movement. Pryor asks, for example, how a police officer can "accidentally" shoot a black man in the chest six times. To the laughter of his assembled audience, he puts on a goofy voice caricaturing that of a white police officer and says, "Well, my gun fell and just went crazy!"[111]

Festivals have evolved over the years, changing with festival-goers' mutating tastes. Writing in 1993 for *The Face*, contributor Danny Scott provides an account of transitions in the British festival scene: from "lots of groovy bands, lots of groovy kids, a sense of belonging and a feeling that communal existence was still a spiritual thing" to "loud guitars, male bonding and rock chicks in unsightly leather bodices" in the late 1970s and early 1980s.[112] He calls this period "the heyday of the 'rock festival'" and notes that "they were dreadfully unfriendly places too. Each person or group got their own bit of grass, laid down their grubby plastic sheet … and prepared to do bloody battle with anyone who invaded their personal space."[113] Another shift happened in the late 1980s and early 1990s: an expansion in festival offerings, responding to the surge in popularity of rave and dance acts as well as the American-in-origin hip-hop phenomenon.[114] Scott cites the booker of the Reading Festival: "People were there to be entertained, and we needed to present different types of acts."[115] Seattle-in-origin Nirvana played Reading in both 1991 and 1992, as they rose to global pop domination. So too in 1992 did New York-based hip-hop group Public Enemy. Scott also gives the example of Glastonbury, which was founded in 1971 and remained a laid-back idyll during the "heyday of the rock festival." According to Scott, when given the opportunity to include a dance stage in 1990, the festival's founder Michael Eavis declined: "perhaps unsurprisingly, the thought of thousands of blissed-out boys and babes and the adverse media they would attract worried Eavis."[116] Nonetheless, he continues, "dance music did find a way into Glastonbury, band by band, sound system by sound system, and it didn't take the country's club-goers too long to embrace the festival scene."[117]

In the early twenty-first century, the summer music festival continues to be a site wherein rock, dance music, and hip-hop intersect. This eclectic mash-up of sounds has faced resistance from some people who hold rock and indie values dear. For example, the preceding chapter ended with a discussion of Alex Needham's criticism of Coachella "bros," who he claims appeared at the festival with the rise of electronic dance music there.[118] Again, the bros, so far as Needham is concerned, are more concerned with displaying their bodies than appreciating music, his words steeped in the values of rock authenticity, which were discussed in Chapter 2. Before Coachella, American hip-hop artist Jay Z's headlining slot at Glastonbury 2008 was lamented by some. Oasis's Noel Gallagher, for example, is quoted as saying, "I'm not having hip-hop at Glastonbury. It's wrong."[119] In the following years, American R'n'B/pop superstars Beyoncé and Kanye West would also headline the British festival. Thus, whereas some might see festivals as predominantly rock-oriented spaces, they are in fact sites that morph with popular tastes. On this point, about the 2013 Pitchfork festival, organized by the indie-oriented, music taste-making website of the same name, *New York Times* music critic Jon Caramanica said,

> This year was the first year that felt bigger to me. This felt like a genuine American festival, now admittedly small scale. […] There is literally no reason Kanye West couldn't headline this festival. […] I would not

have thought that three [or four years ago]. This is the first year that I went in and I said "this feels not just like an approximation of Pitchfork taste, but an approximation of overall where movements in music are headed."[120]

These transformations are commercial; festivals seek out the acts that will sell the most tickets. And yet the commercial is also political. By diversifying their music offerings, summer music festivals in Britain, North America, and elsewhere are questioning and challenging—intentionally and unintentionally—what festival culture can look and sound like.

In the 2010s, summer music festivals are—to the surprise of many—emerging as spaces to imagine blackness, often outside of the determining frame of hip-hop. Afropunk Fest, with its origins in a movement focused on the black punk experience, is at the forefront of this metamorphosis. Witnessed on festival grounds are practices of imagining Africa, in sound and vision, that simultaneously invoke Africa—both "real and imagined"[121]—and articulate a cosmopolitanism that is unique to the diasporic experience. Regarding sartorial imaginings: one of the young women I interviewed at Afropunk Fest 2015 stated, "I'm wearing the dashiki as solidarity with black people around the world and because it matches my hair, so that's why I have it on." Her dashiki—bright blue with accents of green, yellow, orange, and black—did indeed provide a pleasant color-contrast to the bright purple extensions braided into her waist-length hair. One media site focused on black beauty culture included a photograph of this young woman within its online coverage of the event. In the photograph, she beams at the camera, clearly enjoying her time on festival grounds. As Mercer explains, the dashiki was commonly worn within the Civil Rights era, specifically as part of a dress code associated with Black Muslim organizations.[122] That is, "elements of 'traditional' African dress—tunics and dashikis, head-wraps and skullcaps, elaborate beads and embroidery—all suggested that black people were contracting out of Westernness and identifying with all things African as a positive alternative."[123] Although many Afropunk Fest attendees undoubtedly wear Afrocentric garments in the everyday lives, others use the opportunity of the festival to celebrate their Afrocentricity through dress. What's more, Afropunk Fest attendees are not only "contracting out of Westernness," they are also confronting contemporary forms of bigotry, not least through slogan T-shirts and hats. Many attendees wear garments with political messages. For example, for her performance at Afropunk Fest 2015, Lionbabe wore a vest that read "Very Black." Another attendee of the 2015 festival wore a hat with the letters MLNN—signifying melanin, the pigment of black skin and hair. And, a woman pictured in *Buzzfeed*'s coverage of the festival in 2014—a photo essay called "31 Ridiculously Gorgeous People at Afropunk"—was pictured wearing high-waisted white, wide-leg jeans and a black T-shirt with the name "Mike Brown" printed in white.[124] Michael Brown had been killed by the white police officer Darren Wilson just weeks before that year's festival. She had altered the T-shirt, cutting off the collar and several inches at the bottom, so as to transform it into a V-neck crop. The look is both political and fashion-forward, not least because she accessorized with some sweet animal ears worn over her naturally styled hair.

As this cropped T-shirt and the preceding examples indicate, the Afropunk look is also a syncretic product, forged through Afro-diasporic and political signifiers and objects and garments from mainstream popular fashion. In other words, the Afropunk look is both political black style and festival fashion. The outfits on display combine dashikis, head-wraps, and political slogan T-shirts with crop-tops, headbands, headdresses, and other "festival fashion" garments, typically sourced in high street stores. For example, one woman, with whom I spoke at Afropunk Fest 2015, explained her outfit as follows: "I was feeling like a 'native-American-type-of-Afro-bohemian-vibe-thing,' so I did a headdress similar to a Burning Man-Mohawk headdress. The pants are from yesterday; they're like Afro, Afro-American-designed pants, and then my top is from American Apparel, and it's just a bralet." Another one of my interviewees wore a piece of "Nigerian cloth, handmade" that she sourced in Brooklyn. It appeared that she had wrapped the material—white with a black geometric pattern—around her strapless bra, so as to fashion it into a crop-top. She also wore orange palazzo pants that she identified as from Thailand and a cowrie shell necklace that she purchased at H&M. "I was so surprised that they had something so ethnic and cultural," she explained. "I was like, 'Let me go ahead and anoint it and make it something special.'" Her friend, whom I also interviewed, explained that her aunt brought her from Turkey the black crop-top with white bell sleeves that she was wearing. She wore high-waisted dark blue jeans, cuffed, with black Doc Martens boots. She was most interested in describing her bracelets: one was a gift; she could not remember the source of another; "one is from H&M; a Chinese lady gave me this one; and I bought this one at an Afro-indie store in the city." Her many-colored head-wrap was sourced from an African Store on Church Ave in Brooklyn. She explained further that the friend she was with did her face make-up: white paint, decorated as to make circles around each eye, extending above the eyebrow. Another pair I met described their outfits as such:

Respondent 1: I'm wearing a black romper with a belly dancing belt: nice and basic and comfy ... with my purple hair, yeah! I literally just dyed it a week ago. It was an experiment, but it turned out pretty cool.

Respondent 2: I'm wearing a piece from Free People, and it's Bali-inspired, so an Indian vibe with lots of embroidery. I work for the company, and that was like a key point in our summer industry and our main point in look. So it was a big trend on India this summer, so I was just finishing out the trend.

These respondents' discussion of mixing and matching "ethnic" and mainstream garments was typical. So too was the paradoxical practice of identifying the garments sourced in high street stores as the part of the look that had "ethnic" appeal. Black and mixed-race women were not the only attendees dressing up in such mix 'n' match ensembles. A young man from London, interviewed within the *New York Times* coverage of the 2015 festival, explained that he was wearing "a traditional Yoruba gown," over cuffed trousers and Converse high-tops.[125]

Are these ensembles examples of black style a form of political practice or are they versions of the now standardized festival fashion look, layered with Afro-diasporic inflections? They are both, and it is precisely the look's ability to be both familiar and politically different that turned Afropunk Fest into a fashion media event.[126]

Documenting Afropunk Fest: Fashion media representations of blackness

Between 2012 and 2015, there was an exponential increase in photographers documenting Afropunk Fest. My own experiences at the festival mirror these shifts. In the first year that I attended—2013—the only time I saw multiple cameras was when I and my fellow attendees desperately scrambled to get smartphone photos of movie star Will Smith, who was at the festival to support his wife Jada Pinkett Smith's nu metal band Wicked Wisdom. In 2015, however, when I decided to do research at the festival, I realized that the many photographers around me, many of whom toted professional-grade DSLR cameras, better played the role of "festival ethnographer" than I did. As Brent Luvaas explores, street style photographers share a "common project with visual anthropologists and scholars of fashion"[127] in that they are similarly "singling out those distinctive individuals in these places that we saw as capable of speaking to larger cultural processes at work."[128] Street style photographers are able to do this work much more quickly and efficiently than academics. Unburdened by information sheets and participant consent forms, photographers must simply indicate to potential subjects with as little as a nod of the head that they want to take their picture, often followed by an exchange of Instagram handles and/or a discussion as to which publication would be running the photograph. Over the course of 2015 and 2016, I met a range of photographers, both amateur and professional, who were attempting to document the festival's look and its energy. I met students, independent photographers and filmmakers, art bloggers, political bloggers, fashion forecasters, and casting agents. Many of the independent photographers spent time talking with their subjects, building connections, and laying the groundwork for future collaboration. One photographer explained, "I'm here just networking. [...] I love taking photos of people. And there's a lot of different people out here. There's a chance to connect, meet new folks. Contact, you never know." Another person spoke to me about his blog and fashion line, identifying the former as "a pro-black blog" with a focus on "style, black history and clothes." A third person I spoke with was an art blogger. He was there taking pictures both of stylish attendees and of "photographers photographing the people." He explained, "I've seen people that I follow on Instagram and got a chance to photograph them, which was really a coup for me. Afropunk Fest thus serves as an important meeting place for people, often with their own brands, who want to meet others interested in interrogating blackness. The festival has also become a central location for publications to get street style footage. At Afropunk Fests 2015 and 2016 there were freelance photographers, who worked for a range of publications: *BET, Ebony, Essence, Fashion Bomb Daily, Yahoo, Fader, Buzzfeed, Teen Vogue, Vogue Italia, Elle, W*, a Japanese magazine called *Warp*, and Getty Images. Within days of the festival—or often that very day—they would submit their photographs, which would then be uploaded instantly onto the publications' websites. In the preceding chapter I argued that the gaze circulating around the festival was an intersubjective one, wherein those people with alternative fashion capital could take inspiration from one another within their own practices of self-fashioning. By the mid-2010s, at Afropunk Fest, however, the gaze that circulated was one produced through the demands of social and digital media (Figure 12).

Figure 12 At right, at least five photographers—both professional and amateur—capture the looks of four attendees at Afropunk Fest 2015. Photo Rachel Lifter.

A changing mediascape

In the mid-1990s, Sarah Thornton argued for a sustained consideration of how media representation informs subcultural formation. Responding to Stanley Cohen's earlier work, wherein he explores how the mass media belatedly and misleadingly described the altercations between the Mods and the Rockers in Brighton in the mid-1960s, Thornton argues, "'Subcultures' do not germinate from a seed and grow by force of their own energy into mysterious 'movements' only to be belatedly digested by the media. Rather, media and other culture industries are there and effective right from the start. They are central to the process of subcultural formation."[129] To prove her point, she identifies and explores how different media voices contributed to the production of the mid-1990s British club cultures. The "moral panic" produced by the mass media, for example, works "as a form of hype."[130] Arguing against Cohen, she continues, "derogatory media coverage is not the verdict but the essence of [subcultural] resistance."[131] In contrast, niche media—she identifies this media category as consisting of the music and style press—"categorize social groups, arrange sounds, itemize attire and label everything. They baptize scenes and generate the self-consciousness required to maintain cultural distinctions."[132] Her final category—micromedia—consists of ephemera, such as flyers, that serve to bring a group together, to organize those who are "'in the know' or in the 'right place at the right time.'"[133]

Thornton's categories can be updated and redeveloped to account for the media representation of Afropunk Fest in the mid-2010s. Here, social media—Instagram, Facebook, and Snapchat—have replaced flyers as the means through which young people are brought together in the right place at the right time. The Afropunk website serves as its own form of niche media. Through stories posted to the website directly and then linked to via the Afropunk Instagram and Twitter accounts, the organization outlines its own definition of what the Afropunk movement is and is about. Regular Instagram posts include an "Afro of the Day" feature and images of black women and men, tagged with the hashtags #BlackGirlMagic and #BlackBoyMagic. The website features articles that are identified by category: race, sex and gender, art, fashion, music, film/TV and activism, among other themes.[134] In short, "the self-consciousness required to maintain cultural distinctions"[135] is produced in-house, by Afropunk's own media-making machine. Finally, standing in for the mass media is the contemporary mainstream fashion press, which includes fashion titles such as *Vogue*, *Vogue Italia*, and *W* as well as more generalized titles that have devoted fashion and style sections, including the *New York Times*, *i-D*, *Vice*, *Fader*, and *Buzzfeed*.[136] Whereas the mass media produced a "moral panic" around the community of baggy-trouser-wearing ravers under Thornton's analysis, today's fashion presses regard Afropunk Fest in a far more positive light. Within the mainstream fashion press, Afropunk Fest represents a once-yearly display of black cosmopolitan fashionability. It is what photographer Cha has called "black fashion week."

Why does the mainstream fashion press cover Afropunk Fest? And why is its mode of representation wholly positive? The answer to these questions lies in the historical developments charted in the preceding chapter. That is, the mainstreaming of the fashion discourse of individual style has provided a context through which the mainstream fashion press can recognize Afropunk Fest and celebrate the looks on display as both "unique" festival ensembles and politically conscious articulations of contemporary blackness. As an object of fashion representation, blackness has a tense history. Within a broader discussion of fashion modeling, sociologist Elizabeth Wissinger explains that blackness is represented through the "twin pillars of exoticism and exclusion."[137] Black models are frequently excluded from runway presentations and fashion editorials. When they are featured, moreover, they often have to either downplay their "Otherness"—a strategy only available to light-skinned models of color—or "[ramp] up one's 'ethnicity.'"[138] Ashley Mears—another sociologist studying models—calls these two looks "ethnicity lite" and "exotic ethnicity."[139] The former "blends mainstream white beauty ideals with just a touch of otherness,"[140] and the latter offers "a radical departure from the white frame […] best represented by Alec Wek, a famous once-bald Sudanese model with very dark skin."[141] As Wissinger notes, it is not only through skin color that exoticism is performed, but also through styling and setting. She gives the famous example of a *Harper's Bazaar* spread from 1999, in which the black British supermodel Naomi Campbell, clad in a leopard-print dress, seems to be racing a cheetah along the plains of Serengeti National Park.[142] In contrast to the racialized body ideals demanded within high fashion editorial imagery, the ideal of individual style is theoretically more open to non-white bodies, not least because of the dubious associations between "individual style" and "the street," "the street" and blackness. By taking up the truths of the ideal of individual style, the fashion press is thus able to recognize black people as fashionable without engaging in broader questions about the lack of black models on runways and in advertisements nor about the polarizing terms of editorial representation.

A second set of questions emerges: When did the mainstream fashion press embrace the discourse of individual style? And why? This story of shifting values has British and American variants. As Ane Lynge-Jorlén charts, in the 1980s, the British media landscape witnessed a polarization with the founding of three London-based youth cultural publications: *i-D*, *The Face*, and *Blitz*. Together, they were identified as a new genre of media—the style press.[143] The style magazines were aimed at young people and made by young people, whatever their gender. Paul Jobling writes that these magazines attempted "to tap both the imagination and the wherewithal of young adults who had grown up in the shadow of punk."[144] They allowed a space for young people to create their own images, which, as Lynge-Jorlén argues, led to a "ubiquitous sense of self-promotion [as the style magazines] showed the styles of friends of the producers or the producers themselves, as well as how they partied."[145] This magazine culture and its alternative "discourse of fashionability"[146] was understood to stand in counter-position to the mainstream fashion media titles for women. As Agnès Rocamora suggests, the name of the genre—the *style* press—was coined "perhaps to reassure readers by keeping at bay the negative connotation attached to the femininity that the word 'fashion' still evokes."[147] Lynge-Jorlén continues, however, that in the 1990s the strict divisions between the fashion and the style press began to blur. Referencing Penny Martin, she notes that the emergence of the second wave of the style press in this decade—*SleazeNation, Dazed & Confused*, and *Raygun*—heralded a shift in the style publications in that the genre "became altogether glossier."[148] The high fashion media changed during the 1990s, as well. Jobling identifies the editorship of Alexandra Shulman marking a shift in British *Vogue*'s editorial voice.[149] Under her leadership it began to employ several of the photographers who had made their names at the style publications and also "to incorporate the type of street or grunge style iconography more usually associated with magazines like *The Face* and *i-D*."[150] Jobling points out that this incorporation of "grunge style" photography was not without opposition, as British *Vogue* readers responded negatively to the 1993 spread "Under Exposure," photographed by Corinne Day and featuring Kate Moss. He identifies the response to the editorial as one of the ways in which "the ensuing tension in incorporating what is acceptable in subcultural practice or alternative culture into the mainstream or dominant culture" manifests.[151] Nonetheless, Anna König similarly notes this shift in British *Vogue*'s representational forms.[152] She explains that "no title resonates with authority and history the way that *Vogue* does";[153] however, in analyzing the magazine's language over the period between 1980 and 2001, she observes "a shift from 'high culture' to 'popular culture' as the frame of reference."[154] She explains, "*Vogue* has tried to move on from its traditional and somewhat elitist roots and yet one cannot help wondering if this has, at times, been at the expense of an assured and recognizable identity."[155] To borrow from Pierre Bourdieu's framework for analyzing fields of cultural production, the recent history of the British fashion press demonstrates how the established media players—here: British *Vogue*—took up the "truths" of the newcomer's doxa on individual style.[156]

In contrast, there was no sustained threat to the authority of the established American fashion media during the 1980s and 1990s. Perhaps a contender was the teen magazine *Sassy*. Launched in 1988 and led by the twenty-four-year-old editor Jane Pratt, the magazine's mostly female staff produced written and visual stories about fashion, beauty, and boys through a distinctly feminist voice. Writers Kara Jesella and Marisa Meltzer pay tribute to the magazine in their book *How Sassy Changed My Life*, arguing that the magazine offered a radical new way of thinking about young femininity.[157] The ideal *Sassy* girl was the nerdy girl, the DIY girl, the unpopular-stroke-independent girl, who did not "get the guy," but also did not stake her worth on getting him. Jesella and Meltzer explain, the *Sassy* staff had a complex and somewhat contradictory approach to fashion and beauty culture. They were into indie music and riot grrrl and zine culture—all understood as frameworks for challenging mainstream ideals of beauty—but they also tried cellulite-reducing products because, in the words of *Sassy* writer Christina Kelly, "I have a pathological fear of cellulite."[158] *Sassy* thus offered a fun and irreverent approach to fashion and beauty—an approach to which many teen girls and adult woman were attracted. But *Sassy* was pitched to challenge the staple teen magazines *Seventeen* and *YM*, not the established fashion magazines *Vogue* and *Elle*. And when it was sold and revamped in 1996, its teen-oriented feminist discourses disappeared. According to media studies scholar Brooke Erin Duffy, it was the emergence of digital media at the turn of the twenty-first century, which eventually affected how mainstream women's magazine titles represented fashion.[159] She explains, established media titles realized that, firstly, they needed to develop digital content and, secondly, the digital platform demanded that they change their voice, as the online audience was perceived to be younger.[160] She gives the specific example of *Glamour* magazine, which pitched a 2012 digital campaign directly to millennials with the slogan "Never Drink and Text."[161] The relentless pace of the digital media also prompted American fashion titles to embrace street style and festival fashion as quick and relatively inexpensive fashion content for their digital platforms. It was not until the 2010s, then, that the American media began to espouse the discourse of individual style, underpinning such fashion coverage, and thus a framework for representing blackness outside of the polarizing tropes of traditional editorial imagery. At the same time, writers and editors like Marjon Carlos, whose work is discussed above, were pushing to expand these media titles' fashion coverage to include the bodies and work of people of color."[162]

It is in light of these cultural shifts in traditional fashion media representation that one can reflect upon the proliferation of Afropunk Fest fashion images that appear across the digital pages of the American (and international) fashion media at the end of August in 2015, 2016, and 2017. Writing in the late 1970s, Dick Hebdige argues that the mainstream media can represent subculture in two ways. The first is by portraying subcultural participants as "folk devils," effectively exoticizing them.[163] The second is by minimizing the subcultural threat, saying "they're just like us." He talks about a 1977 article from *Woman's Own* called "Punks and Mothers," which put forward the message that the institution of the family was also important to punks.[164] Some contemporary representations of Afropunk Fest fall into the latter category: specifically, by refusing to explore style in the context of diasporic blackness, they frame black hair choices as merely that: aesthetic choices, individually made without political effect. And yet, such neutering can prove more complex than on first glance. Take, for example, *vogue.com*'s approach to black hair. In the days leading up to Afropunk Fest 2015, the website ran several articles celebrating the "Leading Ladies" of that year's line-up.[165] Central to the representation of the singers were descriptions of their hair. Jillian Hervey of the band Lionbabe was heralded for her "lion's mane (if you will) of tousled golden curls." Kelela was celebrated for her unique look of "dreads" and partially "shaven dome." And British-born SZA was commended for her "enviable and feathery bushel of cascading curls (which the singer recently dyed a Chaka Khan copper)."[166] These performers' hairstyles had been for the past several years—and continued to be—a point of interest for fans and beauty editors alike. Their looks at Afropunk Fest 2015 did not fail to disappoint. Assumedly with the help of her longtime hairstylist Chuck Amos, Hervey used vertical cornrows to shepherd her curly, blond tresses into a voluminous mohawk. Kelela surprised audiences by revealing that she had cut her formerly waist-length locs to her shoulders. And SZA revealed in the flesh her new copper hue, which was inspired, she had explained to Mackenzie Wagoner of *vogue.com* earlier in the year, by "'ginger babies'—including Lily Cole, Grace Coddington, Karen Elson, and Pippi Longstocking."[167] Missing from this coverage is a direct acknowledgment of blackness. And yet, through references to the white fashionable (and one fictional) figures Coddington, Elson, and Longstocking, the article—and SZA's hair practices, of which the article speaks—recalls the dandyism that Monica Miller outlines. Again, she writes, "black dandies are creatures of invention who continually and characteristically break down limiting identity markers and propose new, more fluid categories within which to constitute themselves."[168] The article extends Miller's formulation, moreover, offering up examples of *female* black dandies, who simultaneously break down limiting racial markers, such as hair, proposing new forms of fashionable black femininity: here, that combine the textures of black hair with the looks of redheads. One is reminded of Mercer's analysis of the conk—a style worn by black American men in the 1940s, which left their hair with a reddish hue. Again, Mercer writes, "To assume that black men conked up *en masse* because they secretly wanted to become 'redheads' would be way off the mark. [...] Far from an attempted simulation of whiteness, I think the dye was used as a stylized means of defying the 'natural' color codes of conventionality in order to highlight artifice, and hence exaggerate a sense of difference."[169] Here, difference might not simply signify racial difference, but also Afro-cosmopolitan creativity.

Beyond street style?

What do viewers see in media coverage of Afropunk Fest? A new form of the fetishization of black bodies or an articulation of a defiant Afro-cosmopolitanism? I will take this last section to explore examples that support the latter, as they pave the way for a new politics of identification within twenty-first-century indie and twenty-first-century popular culture, more broadly.

The first example is a 2015 photo/video editorial for *Vogue Italia*'s "The Black Blog." It was called "This is Afropunk," and to an extent it mimics the tropes of black exoticism typical to fashion editorial representation.[170] The editorial features four black models, each with natural hair, teased out for length and volume. The shoot took place on festival grounds, photographer Joanna Totolici positioning the models in front of the crowds of people who were milling about and/or enjoying a performance. Here, the fields of Commodore Barry Park are substituted for the plains of the Serengeti as a "natural" black environment; however, the shoot in no way works to build a connection between black bodies and nature, as the previously discussed Naomi Campbell shoot does—a connection, moreover, that has served as a justification for racism since the eighteenth century. Rather, the setting locates the models directly within a contemporary—and complex—iteration of blackness, as outlined in the preceding sub-sections. The styling add to this re-telling of blackness. The models wear a range of designer garments from designers Issey Miyake, Ashish, Sophie Andes Gascon, and Charles Harbison, among others. Many of the designer garments featured have bold prints, often with matching jackets and trousers. It is a look that Solange Knowles premiered three years earlier in the Melina Matsoukas-directed video for "Losing You."[171] Set in Cape Town's township of Langa, the video features Solange, a cast of her friends, and members of the Le Sape Society from the Democratic Republic of Congo, all performing a sort of black dandyism with and through contemporary high fashion garments. In the video, Knowles wears garments from Suno, Kenzo, Diane von Fursterburg, Opening Ceremony, and J. Crew. She wears matching sets: jackets and trousers, cardigans and shorts. The garments were selected by *Elle* South Africa fashion director Asanda Sizaniwas and styled by Ty Hunter. In both the "This is Afropunk" editorial and the "Losing You" video, a contemporary, bold, and *black* aesthetic is produced. The mixing and matching of garments engages in the historical practice of black style, and the bold geometric patterns mimic traditional African prints. What results—in Solange's video and "The Black Blog" editorial—is a highly fashioned image of contemporary Afro-cosmopolitan black identity.

The second example is the work of the Brooklyn-based, Brazilian photographer Driely S. S. had been photographing Afropunk Fest since 2013 and in 2016 was asked to be one of the Afropunk house photographers.[172] She was also courted that year by a range of mass media publications. Her photographic process involves first finding locations, considering how the light will fall at different times during the day. She then searches the festival for potential subjects, coaxing them back to her chosen locations. The end result is a fully fashioned editorial image. She recalled within the interview that at the 2015 festival she tried for hours to get an attendee—any attendee— to stand under a fountain that was spraying mist. Although invisible to the naked eye, the camera's lens would capture a rainbow rising above the subject's head. In 2016, in addition to the photographs she would submit to Afropunk, she decided to do street style for *Oyster* magazine in Australia and tintype photographs of musicians and fans that were published online at *W*. When we met in the weeks preceding the festival, she was in the process of holding individual meetings with all of the publications to consider where the best fit for her work would be. Her choices were political.

> Maybe three years ago, I pitched to a bunch of publications and they were like, "Sorry, that's not really the audience for our publication. We cover Coachella, but Afropunk is too niche." I was like, you're pretty much saying that like they're black people and you don't want to cover it because your audience isn't going to like this.

She continued, "Now, funny enough, everyone wants it." The difference in three years, she argues, is that now the Black Lives Matter movement is "trendy." "I was like, 'excuse me?' People are dying; it's not a bag, it's not going to go out of season. It's not 'trendy.' It's not how you approach it. It's really tricky."

S. had spoken about these issues with the festival's founders, who, she explained, promised her a small space backstage from which to stage her tintype portraits—a project that she had conceived of earlier that year as a tribute to the recently deceased Malian photographer Malick Sidibe, which involved a century-old form of photography that demands subjects sit still for five minutes as their images are transferred chemically to a metal plate. Regarding how to monitor other publications' representations of the festival, she suggested to the festival founders: let the publications in, let them cover the event, so that black people are represented within the mainstream media, and if something happens, "we can put them on blast after." For her own tintype portraits, she positioned both musicians and attendees in front of a striped backdrop, resembling one used by Sidibe in many of his black-and-white portraits of Malians. With this connection as context, the images function as fine art fashion photographs (Figure 13). For her street style portraits that year, she managed to get other attendees to stand in the mist-spraying fountain, this time suggesting to one subject that he raise his fist in the air in a black power salute—an exchange discussed already in this chapter. As she explained to me, the best approach is "to infiltrate the system from the inside out." She would submit that photograph and the other portraits she and her team took that day to the publications, for whom she was working. She would also over the next weeks receive requests for

Figure 13 Tintype by Driely S., Afropunk 2016. © Driely S.

syndication rights for other unused images. With a sigh, S. noted that she still gets many more requests for syndication rights of photographs she has taken at Coachella.

Perhaps even the look of Coachella is changing, however. In 2018, Beyoncé played the festival, staging an elaborate homage to the sounds and aesthetics of historically black colleges and universities. The performance was indeed spectacular, sonically and visually, widely celebrated as a history-making occasion. As one *Los Angeles Times* headline read, "Beyoncé Came to Coachella, and Disrupted its Entire Culture."[173] Other media articles, published in the days following her April 14 performance, articulated a similar attitude, celebrating how the star inserted black visual imagery and black politics into the overwhelmingly white cultural event. Even before Beyoncé's performance, however, change was afoot. Published in the hours leading up to her headlining set, another *Los Angeles Times* article proclaimed "Less Boho Chic, More Streetwear Style on the Coachella Fashion Scene for 2018."[174] Some of the looks featured in the fashion segment did indeed resemble the streetwear trend that has become a major part of 2010s fashion: fanny packs worn slung over shoulders and sweatpants cut slim to the leg. And yet, other featured garments could still be classified in the "boho chic" tradition: crop-tops, fringe, metallic body tattoos. A definitive difference between this article's festival fashion portraits and those of years past was that all but two of the featured attendees were people of color. "Streetwear" is routinely used to signify blackness—a linguistic technique that irks and infuriates black designers, who see themselves routinely placed in the "streetwear box" despite designing clothing for high fashion markets.[175] That linguistic framing is mobilized in the *Los Angeles Times* article; "streetwear" signifies black attendance at the festival and practices of black festival style. In spite of this questionable use of "streetwear" as a framing device, the article shows that, even before Beyoncé set foot on the Coachella stage, already changing was how that particular festival and festival culture, more broadly, were being represented by the media. In light of the rise of Afropunk Fest and the broader shifts in representation that have been explored in this chapter, both the Coachella image and that of indie are thrown up for discussion, to be imagined anew. So too the ideal figure of indie has been imagined anew; as this and the preceding chapter have shown, the commercial phenomenon of festival fashion and the broader discourse of "individual style" that underpins it have forged a space within indie through which women can see and perform themselves and—interconnectedly—blackness is imagined in new and exciting ways.

CHAPTER 5
BEYOND RETRO AND THE POP RAGTRADE

This chapter is about Beyond Retro—a London-based second-hand retailer that selects its product from the millions of tonnes of waste produced within the first-hand production cycle and aligns that product aesthetically with contemporaneous first-hand trends. It is emblematic of a new node in the second-hand retail sector, which seeks to offer second-hand products *en masse* and on trend: what I call, the pop ragtrade. How does analysis of Beyond Retro and the pop ragtrade contribute to the story of indie? Beyond Retro sells clothes and other fashionable objects used to construct the evolving indie look, in its stores in Britain and Sweden and internationally via its website. Also, like the music magazine editors and street style photographers, whose work I analyzed in Chapters 2 and 4, respectively, the owners and employees of Beyond Retro are "cultural intermediaries,"[1] whose creative professional labor—here, having to do with sourcing and organizing second-hand garments for sale—contributes to the evolution of indie and its look. Finally, like indie, Beyond Retro's path from East London warehouse to international fashion retailer was fueled by the growing currency of "individual style" within the popular fashion market. The case study thus offers another lens through which to consider the rise of this fashion doxa and its impact on the representation and performance of identities, within both indie and twenty-first-century popular fashion culture, more broadly.

A touchstone for this chapter is Angela McRobbie's 1989 essay "Second-hand Dresses and the Role of the Ragmarket."[2] McRobbie situates her analysis of second-hand retailers and shoppers within the tradition of postwar youth cultural research and the dialectics of subcultural style and mainstream fashion, upon which this research relied. She challenges the orthodoxies of this body of work, however. By highlighting the "entrepreneurial infrastructure" of the ragmarkets, she blurs the dividing line between authentic subcultural style and mainstream fashion, showing that the former too has a commercial element.[3] The instability of this border between subcultural second-hand practice and the mainstream fashion industry informs many of her subsequent points. For example, she speaks about "the opportunities which second-hand style has offered young people, at a time of recession, for participating in the fashion 'scene.'"[4] Also, she argues that it is not "any longer possible to pose the world of street style or second-hand style against that of either high fashion or high street fashion," giving the example of "young professionals, male and female," whose wardrobes "were almost, to the last sock or stocking, discovered, restored and worn by the young men and women who worked in, or hung around, Camden Market and a whole series of provincial ragmarkets, in the late 1970s and early 1980s."[5] It was in the ragmarkets, moreover, that young women could find affordable alternatives to the popular looks worn on stage, screen, and runway; "These included 1960s' cotton print 'shifts' like those worn by the girls in The Human League in the early 1980s (and in the summer of 1988 'high fashion' as defined by MaxMara and others)."[6] McRobbie's analysis continues to matter thirty years later because the symbiosis between second-hand style and mainstream fashion that she identified on the streets of London in the 1980s is now in the early twenty-first century happening on a global scale. Female entrepreneurs still work in the ragmarkets, but the second-hand business also has expanded exponentially. As Karen Tranberg Hansen explains, "Although the secondhand clothing trade has a long history, its economic power and global scope were never as vast as they have been since the early 1990s," the reasons she cites being the opening up of economies in the global south and increasing demand for second-hand product in Eastern Europe.[7] Today's global traders understand the recycling business, have an eye for detail and, to use McRobbie's words, have learned the value of "the skills of mending and restoring items and [...] where the best sources for their stock were to be found."[8] These skills are no longer only employed by "scouring the country for out-of-town markets, making trips to Amsterdam to pick up the long leather coats favoured by rich hippy types," however.[9] Rather, today, as Beyond Retro evidences, they are employed by scouring the millions of tonnes of waste produced in the first-hand retail cycle and reproducing that product as a second-hand mode of engaging in contemporary popular fashion.

Second-hand retailers: Staging creative consumption

Beyond Retro's flagship location on Cheshire Street in East London opened on September 11, 2001. As the store's owner Steven Bethell recounted, upon his return to New York from a trip to Africa, he stopped for a layover in

London, but got held up due to the September 11 attacks on the World Trade Center in New York.[10] The night of September 11, he was standing in the Cheshire Street location—a former dairy that, at that point, functioned as a warehouse for his stock of used clothing. At the time, Bethell was in the grading business, sorting used clothing into categories for new uses—a process discussed in detail below—and the company would sell some of the reusable pieces at various shops, stalls, and markets around the city, for example in Camden Stables. Bethell explained, "I remember the night, and I was thinking, 'Well, I'm stuck here anyway, so why don't I just open the doors?' And I just put an eight-foot board right in front of the store and said, 'We're selling clothes.'"

In the early 2000s, Cheshire Street was an unlikely location for a clothing shop of any sort. The street intersects with Brick Lane—the centerpiece of the East End's South Asian neighborhood; however, whereas Brick Lane saw much traffic due to its bustling restaurant scene, Cheshire Street was empty, without shops and restaurants. Throughout the following decade, Brick Lane would rapidly develop into a popular weekend destination for young people looking to eat out, shop second-hand, and dance the night away at newly established clubs and music venues. Acknowledging these developments, Jenna Rossi-Camus—a former employee—explained that because Beyond Retro's flagship store is so far down Cheshire Street, it represents the "frontier of Vintageland," her words distancing the store from the more regularly traversed, and arguably gentrified, Brick Lane shopping area.[11] She employs what Louise Crewe et al. have called location talk as a strategy for imagining the alternative, by identifying second-hand retail as located within alternative cities or parts of cities.[12] Here, Beyond Retro is not merely part of the hip Brick Lane area; it extends beyond it. Indeed, in turning off Brick Lane onto Cheshire Street, one must walk for ten minutes before arriving at the shop: first past several other second-hand stores and then past several local pubs, council estates, and even some disused buildings. As Amber Butchart, another former employee, recounted, "when I first started I would find needles outside in the morning." Rob Flowers, a third former employee interviewed, explained further, "Especially early on it was quite a hairy walk because there was nothing there. [...] You'd see people like halfway there being like, 'I'm going the wrong way,' but they'd finally get there."[13] Indeed, on my own first visit to Beyond Retro in 2009, I became nervous that I had gone too far and had somehow missed it, as I felt far from a recognizable shopping district. It was only the parade of yellow Beyond Retro shopping bags, adorned with the company's anchor logo, headed in the opposite direction that served to reassure me of my route. The building itself also induces confusion. That is, Beyond Retro's flagship store is an imposing red brick building with former windows filled in with gray, cement bricks. Graffiti marks the external walls of the building, and trash seems to accumulate alongside its base. The only signifiers that this building is not, in fact, abandoned are the Beyond Retro signs hanging from the front door and side wall, and the occasional group of young shoppers standing outside, smoking and chatting.

The store's interior resembles a warehouse or even open-air ragmarket that is overfilling with stock. The ceilings are high; the external brick walls remain visible through a thin coat of white paint; and much of the piping and electricity circuitry is visible. Upon first entering the Cheshire Street location, one is overwhelmed by the masses of clothing within the store, as there are thousands of pieces on display on the shop floor in the flagship location. Garments are displayed by type—for example, men's tartan shirts, playsuits, dresses, and shoes—and are marked with home-made signs made from printer paper pasted onto colored cardboard. Because no two second-hand garments are exactly the same, however, no rack of clothing is uniformly structured. Instead, the rack of men's tartan shirts, for example, includes shirts of varying colors and prints as well as shirts that have been worn to varying degrees. Differently sized shirts are all placed together, as opposed to

Figure 14 The scene inside Beyond Retro on Cheshire Street, 2017. © Don Stahl.

being organized through ascending size, as is the case in many first-hand retail sites. Similarly, the scarf-section consists of a giant box in which hundreds of scarves rest on top of and entwined with one another. This form of presenting clothing promotes a hunt. One must actively search through the rack of tartan shirts to find one of a preferable color, size, print, and degree of wornness; one must dive into the box of scarves to find one with a pattern one likes.

It is important to understand the retail design of Beyond Retro not as the accidental result of having too much stock, but rather as a specific merchandizing strategy, one that is typical of second-hand retailers (Figure 14). Sean Nixon suggests that retail design can be "understood [...] as working through the organization and incitement of identity."[14] In Beyond Retro the organization of garments works to produce a "creative" consumer: one who is able to move through the seeming disarray of garments on the shop floor to find "unique" pieces. Again, this strategy is typical of second-hand retailers and outlets. In a discussion of the Montreal second-hand shop Buddy Lee's, Alexandra Palmer argues that "This strategic merchandising of second hand clothes in both ordered, and seemingly, disordered manner recreates the experience of searching for treasures in a city market."[15] And, in her observational notes on a visit to Manchester UK's Afflecks Place—an indoor market, housing numerous second-hand and independent retailers— Crewe explains, "This is a place where you could quite literally lose yourself. [...] This all seems to be part and parcel of the Afflecks Place 'alternative' shopping experience where the rules of the game seem to be to break the rules of conventional consumption in terms of spatial layout, range of goods, price, rummagibility."[16]

"Rummagibility" holds much currency for second-hand shoppers. For example, Nicky Gregson and Crewe found that people preferred second-hand spaces that allowed them to hunt for garments themselves.[17] It is through this consumption-as-hunt that second-hand shoppers performatively produce themselves as creative subjects. Such performative acts are geographically and historically located. Hansen, for example, explores second-hand clothing consumption in Zambia, what is called *salaula*.[18] She examines how young men and women search through the second-hand markets, constructing looks from imported garments that both speak to "trends from across the world" and "local norms about bodies and dress."[19] Salaula is thus practiced in response to and in dialogue with global geopolitics and the flow of clothing from Western Europe and North America to secondary markets in South America, Eastern Europe, Asia, and, of course,

Africa—a process discussed in the following section. "Salaula," Hansen writes, "brings consumers into a bigger world: the world of awareness, of now."[20] In contrast, in Britain and North America in the first decades of the twenty-first century, consuming second-hand clothes has been theorized not as a means of engaging in global fashion trends, but rather as a mode of escaping them. Heike Jenss, for example, highlights the unique practice of 1960s styling in 1990s Germany, wherein participants use garments that were originally mass-produced and marketed in the 1960s "in a re-creation of the authenticity of the period."[21] Marilyn DeLong *et al.* argue that "In the twenty-first century knowing how to create a unique look in an otherwise bland mass-produced market may be a way to regain one's individuality through revaluing and reuse, and redefine fashion in the process."[22] As the preceding chapters have shown, however, "individual style" has changed status, moving from subcultural ideal to mainstream fashion doxa, perpetuated throughout the media and across the fashion market. Thus, performative attempts to claim individuality through second-hand garments must be requalified, understood now as a means of performing contemporary fashion, not escaping it. Palmer acknowledges this historical shift and second-hand clothing's role within it.[23] She suggests that second-hand has "shifted from subculture to mass culture" and highlights how second-hand garments are routinely used within the fashion media "as a sign of individuality and connoisseurship."[24] In using the term "connoisseurship," Palmer speaks to the knowledges employed in second-hand shopping. By identifying them as highly touted throughout the media, moreover, her work speaks to the mainstreaming of both second-hand consumption *and* its attendant knowledges.

In the 1980s and 1990s, second-hand knowledges were niche knowledges. As McRobbie explains, "The apparent democracy of the [second-hand] market, from which nobody is excluded on the grounds of cost, is tempered by the very precise tastes and desires of the second-hand searchers."[25] Thornton's concept of "subcultural capital," developed in the years following McRobbie's article, proves useful when thinking through the "precise tastes and desires of the second-hand searchers"; here, the markers of "subcultural capital" are an ability to pick and choose which items should be used a second time around—a basis of knowledge and skills that, although highly regarded within the spaces of the ragmarkets, was not widely celebrated throughout the fashion industry when McRobbie was writing in the late 1980s. Second-hand garments had begun to appear in the fashion media by that point, as McRobbie acknowledges. One place they were visible was in styled fashion editorials. For example, the stylist Melanie Ward and the photographer Corinne Day, who worked together on Kate Moss's debut editorial "Third Summer of Love" for *The Face* (July 1990), both recalled scouring second-hand ragmarkets to find garments to be used in the images they created.[26] They did not have access to designer garments, so they had to make do; the ragmarkets offered a treasure trove. Even when Ward did gain the clout to borrow designer garments when her career took off in the 1990s, she still mixed them with "found" things as a means of defining her styling aesthetic and practice.[27] Despite this media visibility—rather, through the mediated visibility of second-hand garments as unique, one-off pieces— these objects and the retailers, who sold them, continued to hold alternative status at the turn of the millennium. Writing over a decade after McRobbie, Crewe *et al.* identify the ongoing niche status of second-hand knowledges, highlighting "the importance of distinction through second-hand consumption, where innate knowledge and cultural capital enable entry into a secret style world where there's a wealth of knowledge." They qualify this second-hand know-how as "knowledge that can't be learnt or taught."[28]

And yet, in the twenty-first century, these knowledges are becoming less exclusive precisely because they are being taught. The media has played a key role here. In addition to styled editorials, one also sees second-hand clothes in fashion media segments, offering lessons about which garments to buy and where to buy them. For example, in a "More dash than cash" segment in the September 2009 issue of British *Vogue*, suggestions were made on wool blazers.[29] The suggested options were from Joseph (£495), Tommy Hilfiger (£280), and Beyond Retro (£15). According to Anna König, "*Vogue* frequently strikes the tone of the informed voice of authority imparting wisdom": here, where to find fashionable blazers.[30] Through *Vogue*'s "authoritative voice," Beyond Retro's garments are legitimated as affordable options for readers to buy.[31] This "authoritative voice" is visible within *Vogue*'s styled editorials, as well. For example, one caption to a leather-focused editorial featuring British it-girl Pixie Geldof suggested, "try Hi Star and Rellik for authentic Eighties jackets."[32] Again, Crewe *et al.* argue at the beginning of the 2000s that second-hand knowledges are not learned easily and retailers hold these knowledges dear: "a kind of secret language of distinction which confirms a complicity between the tastemakers and excludes the layperson who is always somehow bound to miss the point."[33] By the end of the decade, however, those knowledges have integrated into the mainstream, as *Vogue* lets readers in on key shopping sites for second-hand garments, albeit quite high-end ones.

Today, much like McRobbie argued in the late 1980s, second-hand dress emerges not as anti-fashion, but rather as a way of engaging with popular fashion and its imagination. Although some second-hand retailers still hold on to alternative value systems, others see opportunity in second-hand's fashionability. For example, one of the retro retailers, whom Crewe *et al.* interviewed in the late 1990s, explained that he bounced his stock off of what was selling in Topshop.[34] Crewe *et al.* talk about how such selling practices blur the discursive distinction between alternative and mainstream retail.[35] What has happened is that "these oppositional understandings [have been] brought increasingly into question" and what has "replaced them [are] notions of blurring, mixing, heterogeneity, even hybridity."[36] They conclude that this new historical framework offers both challenge and choice for retro retailers:

> For those retailers for whom understandings of retro retailing continue to rest on purity and authenticity, the choice would appear to be either to get out altogether or to retreat further into the more elitist, specialist niches of vintage clothing. For others, though, it is the complexities of trading "mixing-it" which, we suggest, will become critical. Indeed, as some of the main players on the high street—Top Shop being the obvious example—move into juxtapose second hand with new on their sales floor, the challenge for retro retailers is to handle this juxtaposition differently; to mobilize difference in ways which go beyond high-street retail practices. Suggesting how they might do this in practice is beyond the scope of this article, but the theoretical requirements are clear: to find new ways of re-imagining and mobilizing the place of "the alternative" within, rather than counterposed to, the mainstream.[37]

I have quoted Crewe *et al.* at length because they offer a prompt to which in the ensuing years Beyond Retro has responded directly. Beyond Retro imagines the "alternative" on a mass scale, thus making the acts of creative consumption accessible to a greater number of shoppers. In so doing, moreover, the company also impacts the commercial fashion industry, in both its values and its wastefulness.

The pop ragtrade, on trend and *en masse*

To understand fully how Beyond Retro works, one must familiarize oneself with Bank & Vogue—the second-hand commodity grading and brokering firm that Bethell and his wife started two decades ago. As Bethell explained within interview,

> We basically buy from charities like the Goodwill and Salvation Army and private collectors throughout Canada and the United States. And literally we buy tractor-trailer-loads of baled clothing. So, in a tractor-trailer-load you can fit 45,000 lbs (roughly 60,000 garments), and we sell those all over the world. We sell them in Central America, in South America, in Africa.

There are many uses for recycled textiles, the first of which is providing clothing for second-hand markets in Latin America, Africa, Eastern Europe, and Asia. Not all clothing sees a second life in this way, however. As Bethell noted within interview, there is no second-hand market for the Burberry- and London Fog-style "Mac" raincoats that have been a staple of British wardrobes since the nineteenth century. Accordingly, garments that cannot be reworn get put to other uses. As Bethell explains, there is the "shodding" business, wherein "wool coats [are] ground up for the batting for the insulation of your car or the wadding underneath your carpet"; the "wiper" business, "which is cutting up clothes, obviously, for rags"; and the "spinning" business, "where they de-arm things like wool sweaters and acrylic sweaters and re-yarn it." In contrast, "One of the sexier parts of the business," Bethell continued, "is the vintage business." "We have a team of people throughout the world, who stand on the conveyer belts and look for trend-facing or historically important pieces," Bethell explained. "That product goes to Beyond Retro, one of the ten Beyond Retro stores." On Beyond Retro's website is an infographic, answering the question: "The cycle of vintage: Just how do we get all those clothes, anyway?"[38] In abbreviated form, it details the processes of collection by charitable donation; sorting of clothing into that which can be reworn and that which will be repurposed into rags and insulation materials; selection of "on trend" pieces from the mountain of reusable garments; and shipment of these pieces to Beyond Retro shops in the UK and Sweden, where they will be priced and sold. These sourcing, sorting, and selling processes are performed through coordinated activity between, on the one side, the young and creative staff at Beyond Retro's central office in London and, on the other, the range of garment workers employed by Bank & Vogue across the globe. Far from trading in odd pieces acquired through flea markets and estate sales, Beyond Retro is trading in the great mass of global waste produced within a period of fast fashion.

What are offered in its ten brick and mortar stores and its online shop are second-hand garments in bulk and—crucially—on trend.[39]

Brokering firms, like Beyond Retro's parent company Bank & Vogue, play a major role within a global system of textile waste removal, recycling, and reselling. As noted in Bethell's discussion above, Bank & Vogue buys used goods in bulk from large charities and private sellers and sells this used product to various markets in South America, Asia, and Africa. As Hansen notes, little is known about the financial underpinnings of the global ragtrade, not least because the "face" of the ragtrade is that of charitable organizations.[40] She continues, "Most people who donate garments to charitable organizations are not aware of how their donations are disposed of. Put simply, consumers donate so much clothing that the charities cannot handle it."[41] As a result, charities sell donated goods to brokering and grading firms, using the money earned to engage in charitable projects.[42] Media portrayals of this process have been less than celebratory of the roles played by commercial firms, and questions arise as to who actually makes the most profit from the sale of donated clothes.[43] Nonetheless, Hansen argues, "The commercial connection in the flow of donated clothing need not be problematic."[44] As Jana Hawley writes, "This 'hidden' industry consists of more than 500 businesses that are able to divert more than 1.25 million tons of postconsumer textile waste annually," and 93 percent of this textile waste is recycled without any additional impact on the environment.[45] Hawley continues, "Although the primary goal for [textile grading firms] is to earn profits, the business owners are also very committed to environmental philosophies and take pride in their contribution to waste reduction"[46]—a theme central to Bethell's discourse, discussed in greater detail below. Much of the work of textile recycling occurs within sorting and grading plants, like the one operated by Bank & Vogue in Canada. In her ethnographic research on a British grading firm, Julie Botticello explores the agency of individual workers on the sorting line.[47] She discusses one Eastern European worker, who mobilizes her understanding of the Eastern European end-market within her selection of garments. That is, she would choose only the highest grade of second-hand garments to send to this market. Botticello explains further, when challenged by managers about her selectivity, she and other female line-workers "will take it upon themselves to slash some of the borderline ones with scissors to make their decisions irreversible."[48] Of course, selection processes are also dictated from above, by a system of classification developed by the facility.[49] It is in regard to this system of classification that Beyond Retro/Bank & Vogue proves most interesting.

That is, within Bank & Vogue sorting facilities, pickers follow trend reports produced by Beyond Retro's London-based product department.

Amber Butchart developed the role of trend-analyst for Beyond Retro. When she started at the Cheshire Street store, Beyond Retro had a tiny staff—there were only about five people at the Christmas party—and "everyone did a little bit of everything." Not only was the staff small, but the sorting processes were inefficient. Butchart explained, "At that time, product would arrive unsorted. We were just getting enormous bales, and you would just have to sort through it all there." She continued later in the interview, "You'd probably throw away like 70% of it. It would be like a bale of jeans or something, and it would just be *any* kind of jeans. So, you'd sort through it all, trying to pick out styles people might want to wear." As a result, she began producing "trend reports for the pickers to pick specific items—pieces we thought would do really well. And that process grew and developed over the course of the time I was there." By the time Butchart left Beyond Retro, the product department developed trend reports four times per year. By 2014, as Bethell explained to me, the trend reports were updated daily:

> We now, each one of the people standing in the factory picking clothes has a tablet which is attached to a server in the cloud of which every week our trend-based team in London says, "Hey, this is really relevant today, this week in East London," and we're sending out e-mails routinely about what's really relevant and what we really want to try to achieve within the four walls of the stores. So, it's not just picking nice clothes or historically relevant clothes, but about picking relevant clothes to the conversation of the day in London.

Rossi-Camus explained in greater detail "the conversation of the day in London." Speaking to me in 2009, Rossi-Camus described the trend reports as including "street-style pictures, pictures of famous people, people in bands, people who work here as well as labels or designer pieces—things that are sort of the icon, what we're trying to get many, many more copies of." She continued,

> At the same time that our pickers are picking right now, sort of, eighties Dynasty-era party dresses, while the fashion designers like Asos just came and they put a whole lot of jumpsuits and things with big shoulder pads and things with sparkly appliqués on denim. So, the same kind of product that we're looking for here is being produced. There's definitely a fashion *Zeitgeist* in all of it.

Festival fashion offers another opportunity for Beyond Retro to embrace the "fashion *Zeitgeist*." In the summer of 2014, for example, gathered together into a corner of Beyond Retro's Cheshire Street shop floor were denim cut-off shorts and waistcoats, tie-dyed shirts, colored anoraks, cropped shirts, crocheted sweaters, ponchos, and patterned wellington boots. Similarly, at Rokit—another major second-hand retailer on Brick Lane—dungaree shorts, jean cut-offs, colorful anoraks and windbreakers, denim jackets and overalls, as well as devil horns and Mickey Mouse ears were pulled into a back corner of the store.[50] Hand-painted signs tacked above such assemblages read "festival," thus identifying the merchandizing strategies of the second-hand stores. On August 4, 2017, Beyond Retro's weblog featured a posting entitled "Festival Wear." Using styled photographs with a model and product shots, the posting highlighted several items available at Beyond Retro, which would make the wearer "stand out from the crowd, come rain or shine!" Items included short dungarees (or shorteralls), jumpsuits, crop-tops, high-waisted shorts, and a fringed jacket.[51]

Producing second-hand product that resonates with contemporary high street trends can prove difficult, however. Butchart remembered roadblocks she and the staff encountered when trying to pull together their first festival pick in 2006:

> It was actually really, really difficult getting wellies at first because I remember asking for them for quite a long time. And it was funny, but it was like, we're kind of used to being able to get really bright, really fun wellies on the high street now, but at the time you couldn't. So, actually getting a pick of wellies that worked for us was really hard for a really long time, and suddenly they just exploded on the high street and you can then obviously see them coming through, like second-hand, in the grade.

One strategy that many second-hand retailers—including Beyond Retro—employ to make second-hand product relevant to contemporary fashion is alteration and upcycling. Beyond Retro's upcycling process started with another one of my interviewees—Dean Sidaway. Initially, Sidaway would come into Beyond Retro's Cheshire Street store one day a week to do the in-store displays. Shortly, his role grew into archiving rare garments and textiles and altering those that would not resell. He recalled, "We used to get these—I think they were kind of—1970s amazing prints and fabrics, but the ugliest dresses. And I used to cut the tops off and then put an elastic waistband on them, and then we'd sell them."[52] The practice of upcycling articulates a specific design aesthetic; it also has become one of several foci within the emergent body of research on sustainable fashion.[53] In her article "SLOW + FASHION—an Oxymoron—or a Promise for the Future …?," for example, Hazel Clark highlights the work of three small-scale fashion designers and companies who recycle used textiles and worn clothes to produce new designs.[54] London-based Worn Again, for example, produces sport shoes from recycled textiles "as diverse as men's suits, shirts, car seats, and prison blankets."[55] Also based in London, Junky Styling works directly with customers, reworking their old clothes into new designs.[56] Finally, there is TRAID—a British recycling firm that not only collects and resells used clothing *en masse*, but also redesigns garments under its TRAIDremade label.[57] The example of TRAID opens up a space through which to think about upcycling on a much larger scale. Indeed, what Sidaway started in the back room of the Cheshire Street store has become a major global operation for Beyond Retro.

As outlined on the company's website, Beyond Retro owns a factory in Northern India dedicated to the production of new clothes from recycled material. As Bethell explained to me within interview, the idea started with those Burberry and London Fog coats for which he could not find a market:

> Four years ago, everybody wanted to make a cotton shopper with your name on the side of it. And it kind of killed me a little bit to go and buy a brand-new cotton bag and silkscreen our name on it. It isn't really what we're about. […] So those sort of like Burberry and London Fog coats, we'd take those and cut out a pattern of a shopping bag and printed our logo on them. And I just thought this was a fun thing to do.

He continued, "we started very quickly developing this idea of taking old clothes—maybe the size is wrong, maybe there's something broken about it—and actually taking them and remanufacturing them into relevant clothes." Speaking in late 2014, he reported that the factory has a staff of almost 100 people, who make over 10,000 garments per month using fifty different SKUs.[58] In 2015, the company added to its website a story, introducing potential shoppers to the Beyond Retro Label Family. There, one can see photographs taken in the factory, many of which are portraits of factory workers holding a sign that reads "I made your clothes." As the website explains, "Led by Raw Material Manager Padmini and Master Tailor Laxman, our 85 full-time employees are paid fair market wages and benefits.

We've met our makers—and we'd like you to meet them too. These are the faces that make our Label range happen."[59] Like with sorting and picking, the manufacture of new garments is the result of coordinated action on the part of the London-based design team and the garment makers on the factory floor. Bethell explained,

> The trend department is in London, and they say, "Look, we know that camo—the original camo—is going be on trend this fall. We need to think about that." We have a designer in London [...] and we have a head of manufacturing who helps guide the facility. We do the toiles and the spec-tac in London, inspired by our archives department or inspired by a shape that we like or pattern that we think is on trend. We do the spec-tac, we do the toile and send that to the facility in India. Then we tell the facility, "Look, start picking green camo. Start picking 70s black leather. Start picking African print." And literally we have these piles of reserve fabric, and they go to those reserve fabrics, they pull from the fabrics. They pull the toile and the spec-tac, and on the base of that they start manufacturing. They'll sample an item for us.

Although zippers and trims are often sourced new, the patterns are cut from old garments. Images on the Beyond Retro website highlight this recycling, as site visitors can see both the new patterns, marked in chalk, and the unpicked seams of former garments.

Crucially, Beyond Retro upcycles garments and objects *en masse*, producing hundreds of copies of a rucksack, for example (Figure 15). It is the size and scale of Beyond Retro's upcycling operation that distinguishes it from the small designers, identified by Clark. "There's the trick," Bethell explained: "It's one thing to design something pretty. But it's another thing to design something pretty from a waste product. And then it's another thing to design something pretty from a waste product but make 500 of them." As evident both on the website and within Bethell's discourse, this large-scale upcycling project is positioned as a counter to the wasteful practices of the mainstream fashion industry as well as the industry's history and ongoing problems with human rights abuses. Whereas many first-hand retailers claim ignorance to human rights violations, hiding behind legal layers of sub-contracting, Beyond Retro proudly claims both ownership of and management of the factory in India.

This discussion of Beyond Retro draws attention to a form of second-hand retail that differs considerably from the ragmarkets that McRobbie

Figure 15 Beyond Retro Label backpacks with a small poster illustrating the recycling process, Beyond Retro, Cheshire Street, 2017. © Don Stahl.

explored in the late 1980s. Then, McRobbie suggests, London's second-hand sources were more closely aligned with the city's urban markets that sprang up in working-class or immigrant communities than with "mainstream" clothing stores. She writes that the ragmarkets "offer an oasis of cheapness, where every market day is a 'sale'. They point back in time to an economy unaffected by cheque cards, credit cards and even set prices."[60] In contrast, Beyond Retro is a highly organized retailer that operates across multiple sites globally (including an online platform), manages thousands of tons of textile waste annually, and produces a second-hand product that aligns with contemporary popular trends. For McRobbie, the ragmarkets were a site of fashion because, as she explained in her book *British Fashion Design*, the story of British fashion has been less about individual designers and more about "fashion as a participative practice, a form of popular culture."[61] It was only at the end of the 1980s and beginning of the 1990s, she explained, that the figure of "the fashion designer as *auteur*" emerged, spurred on and constituted within the growth of the art schools.[62] The twenty-first-century fashion story, however, is perhaps one best told through conglomerates and major high street retailers, as fast fashion—and potential responses to it—dominates much discussion about and within the current fashion industry.

And yet, Beyond Retro and several other second-hand retailers make themselves visible within this current conglomerate-dominated environment, specifically by loaning garments to freelance stylists and the press, free of cost. "Early on," Bethell explained, "we realized that we were a very, very small fish in an enormous sea of retail in the UK." Nonetheless, Bethell continued, Beyond Retro had/has something first-hand retailers did/do not: "mass exclusivity."

> There weren't 300 SKUs in the store. There were 18,000 items in the store. So [stylists] have like an enormous amount of product to choose from through which they can style the look that they're trying to make. So, it was inspired from that whole guerilla marketing mentality, which is: the way we're going to succeed is by offering our strength and diversity of product we have.

Bethell's "guerilla marketing mentality" both demonstrates a reflexive understanding of the diverse inventory Beyond Retro has to offer and also reveals his keen understanding of shifts and changes in the production of fashion media and the ideals promoted within it. Beyond Retro's garments thus appear across a range of magazine titles—"from *Vogue* to *NME*, even like *Heat* and *The Sun*"[63]—and within varying segments: from styled fashion editorials to advice to readers on where to shop. Similarly, London-based Rokit routinely lends its garments to stylists, and California-based Wasteland has a "stylist rental policy" section on its website.[64] Far from fleeing mass media attention, such stores actively seek it in an attempt to bring attention to their second-hand product. But as these press loan policies make clear, Beyond Retro and other pop ragtraders are not merely taking advantage of this new ideal of individual style, seeing it as a means of inserting their product into many shoppers' wardrobes. Rather, they are active contributors to the construction of this fashionable discourse, inserting their garments into the popular fashion imagination, creating the need for their product. Further, Bethell's language speaks to Beyond Retro's ability to meet this growing need. By using the term SKU—which stands for stock keeping unit—he reveals that what is in his stores are not the treasured items, but massive amounts of retail inventory. His store is not overshadowed by the dominating fast fashion industry, a small subcultural response to the mainstream fashion system; rather, he has enough stock to compete—at least to a certain degree—with the high street, to participate in and drive mainstream fashion tastes.

Why do Beyond Retro's retailing strategies matter? For one, the scale of the company's endeavor makes it possible to see how an "alternative" product can function within the mainstream fashion system. Just like the twenty-first-century indie identities, explored in the preceding chapters, Beyond Retro's product is both commercially produced and cloaked in ideologies of the alternative: here, the trope of the creative consumer. Crewe *et al.* lament the incorporation of creativity into the mainstream because "it loses its creative potential, its alternative distinctiveness, its symbolic power."[65] But perhaps a different conclusion can be made of this transition. Perhaps it is not that creativity has lost its symbolic power, but rather that the mainstream fashion shopper—one who might be creating a Dior-Homme-inspired skinny look or participating in the mass-market festival fashion trend—now has access to that symbolic power, albeit in its altered commercial form. That symbolic power might no longer signify resistance against mainstream fashion, but it might also now be effectively employed within discussions of sustainability. As Bethell remarked, "We see our biggest competitor is Urban [Outfitters] or Topshop or um, you know that's really the ... It's the new guys that are our competition, not ... that's who we're chasing. We really want dollars from those guys to come into our pockets." In the first pages of this book's introduction, I cited McRobbie's recent point that, today, a range of industry players—students, freelance designers and even multinational brands—mobilize their alternative status for commercial gains and market advantages.[66] Although this practice "suggests that creative professionals are largely de-politicized," she argues, "this does not mean [the creative industry's] field of influence is totally depleted of cultural value."[67] Following McRobbie, then, perhaps Beyond Retro's repositioning in the fashion market has a bigger impact than its own profits; perhaps the repositioning of alternative second-hand retail within the global capitalist fashionscape is a step toward reimagining mass production and consumption, thereby addressing the environmental politics of sustainability.

CONCLUSION

This book has offered a photo album of fashionable snapshots that capture indie throughout its forty-year history. Evolving from niche independent music scene to Britpop sensation, indie proved that it was a cultural form open to change. But indie would not merely change in the decades following; it would be transformed. As *Fashioning Indie* showed, recognition by the fashion industry—its material producers and its meaning-makers—transformed indie from British music culture to international fashion phenomenon, from a predominantly white and male-oriented formation to a commercial space in which women could see and perform themselves and blackness could be imagined in new and exciting ways.

Of course, what is offered here is *one* story of indie's evolution from the 1980s until the present. Another author covering this period might focus on independent music production and distribution, charting these practices to their new home in the digital soundscape. Today, artists can record and mix music on their personal computers and upload their work on platforms such as Soundcloud, without influence from major labels or reliance upon traditional distribution methods. That other story would be focused on what David Hesmondhalgh calls the "institutional" logics of independent music-making, which he contrasts against the "political-aesthetic" logics of indie.[1] Focusing on the evolving aesthetics of indie, *Fashioning Indie* intentionally told a story of popular culture at its most commercial and, in doing so, engaged directly with the question of shifts in the cultural politics youth cultural forms.

In the early twenty-first century, indie was one of the dominant sounds and looks of popular culture. Skinny jeans became a staple wardrobe item for a generation of young men and women, and festival fashion was born, quickly claiming a position alongside beachwear on the summer fashion schedule that is both produced and followed by merchandizing teams. Chapters 1 and 2 took skinny jeans as a loose launching point and focused on the figure of the slender, white guitar-playing man. I illustrated in Chapter 1 how the significance of his slender body transformed as the skinny indie look gained attention: from awkward childishness in the 1980s, to rock swagger in the

1990s, to fashion iconicity in the 2000s. As a twenty-first-century fashion icon, the indie rocker's slender legs modeled authentic masculinity on Hedi Slimane's Dior Homme runways and in the high street collections enthralled with this new ideal of masculinity. As I showed in Chapter 2, however, reconciling indie's newfound fashion status with the values of authenticity proved a tall order for young male participants in twenty-first-century indie music culture, both as musicians and fans. Chapters 3, 4, and—to an extent—5 addressed the phenomenon of festival fashion and, in so doing, built a portrait of indie that extends beyond Britishness, music, and masculinity to incorporate analysis of the rise and increasing orthodoxy of the historically specific ideal of individual style. In Chapter 3, I identified individual style as a pernicious ideal that demands women follow set trends but only under the guise that they are not. Festival fashion is one place wherein this balancing act is undertaken; young women are prompted to buy ensembles from mass-market high street collections, but once on festival grounds they are required to demonstrate their individual style, if they are to be chosen to be snapped by street style photographers working for the fashion media. In Chapter 4, I explored how the mainstream fashion media's embrace of the ideal of individual style has provided a means of making a contemporary and cosmopolitan form of blackness visible within the current popular fashion imaginary. That is, the Afro-cosmopolitan looks displayed on the grounds of Brooklyn's Afropunk Fest are historically specific articulations of black style; they are also recognized within the contemporary fashion media and by industry players as performances of individual style. And in Chapter 5, I examined how the rise of the ideal of individual style effectively repositioned second-hand garments as key tools within the contemporary fashionable wardrobe. Seizing on this moment, Beyond Retro inserts its garments into the popular fashion imaginary through its media loans. More importantly, it meets the growing demand for fashionable second-hand garments by culling the millions of tonnes of fashionable waste that are produced within the first-hand fashion cycle each year and offering it to consumers as a means of engaging in popular fashion *and* creative consumption.

All of these chapters addressed the question of the cultural politics of youth culture: specifically, the dialectical tension between subcultural and commercial fashion practices. I attempted to show how this tension underpinned each figure and form under analysis: the indie rocker as an authentic fashion icon; the ideal woman of festival fashion as both on trend and bucking trends; the style stars of Afropunk Fest as both recognizable through the ideals of the moment and articulating black style as a longstanding form of critical cultural practice; and second-hand retail as trading an alternative product within the mainstream fashion system. Chapters 3, 4, and 5 also bring attention to new forms of cultural politics that can be seen within a post-incorporated indie. On cultural politics, Stuart Hall explains, "Cultural hegemony is never about pure victory or pure domination . . . ; it is never a zero-sum cultural game; it is always about shifting the balance of power in the relations of culture; it is always about changing the dispositions and the configurations of cultural power, not getting out of it."[2] As indie transformed from music subculture to fashion phenomenon, the "configurations of cultural power" that framed it also transformed. No longer in a position from which to mobilize a subcultural stance, twenty-first-century indie is a cultural space in which questions of visibility and sustainability can be explored. On visibility, I highlighted the reshaping of indie through its fashioning and feminizing (Chapter 3) as well as the emergence of a cosmopolitan blackness that demands a renewed understanding of the image and imaginary of twenty-first-century indie (Chapter 4). On sustainability, I foregrounded the role of second-hand goods as solutions to problems of fashion waste. These questions—visibility and sustainability—dominate popular and academic discussions of fashion today. What becomes clear to me, as I conclude the writing of this book, is that the book itself is then as much a product of its time as the phenomena it investigates. As both fashion and cultural theory are always evolving, new trends shaping how we see ourselves and interpret the world around us, it is important to capture each historical moment—what Stuart Hall would call "the present conjuncture"[3]—exploring its richness before it disappears, only to be replaced by other, equally significant, moments.

NOTES

Introduction

1. Dick Hebdige, *Subculture: The Meaning of Style* (London: Methuen, 1979).
2. Ibid., 94.
3. John Clarke, cited in Hebdige, *Subculture*, 95.
4. Hebdige, Ibid., 2.
5. Michel Foucault, *Discipline and Punish* (London: Penguin, 1977); *Archaeology of Knowledge* (London and New York: Routledge Classics, 2002).
6. Michel Foucault, *The Use of Pleasure. The History of Sexuality Volume 2* (London: Penguin, 1985). See also M. Foucault, "Technologies of the Self," in L.H. Martin, H. Gutman, and P.H. Hutton (eds) *Technologies of the Self: A Seminar with Michel Foucault* (Amherst: University of Massachusetts Press, 1988); M. Foucault, *Ethics: Subjectivity and Truth* (London: Penguin, 2000).
7. By "models for practice," I am referring directly to Foucault's essay "Ethics of the Concern for the Self as a Practice of Freedom." There, he writes, "I would say that if I am now interested in how the subject constitutes itself in an active fashion through practices of the self, these practices are nevertheless not something invented by the individual himself. They are models that he finds in his culture and are proposed, suggested, imposed upon him by his culture, his society, and his social group" (291), in Foucault, *Ethics: Subjectivity and Truth* (London: Penguin, 2000).
8. Angela McRobbie, *Be Creative: Making a Living in the New Culture Industries* (Cambridge and Malden, MA: Polity, 2016), 7–8.
9. Ibid., 8; McRobbie develops her argument here by drawing from Luc Boltanski and Eve Chiapello's analysis of earlier anti-capitalist discourses: specifically, "the artistic critique (an off-shoot of the student movement of the late 1960s, whose more political counterpart they label the 'social critique')" (8); see L. Boltanski and E. Chiapello, *The New Spirit of Capitalism* (London: Verso, 2005).
10. Simon Reynolds, *Rip it Up and Start Again: Post-punk 1978–1984* (London: Faber and Faber, 2005).
11. David Cavanagh, *The Creation Records Story: My Magpie Eyes are Hungry for the Prize* (London: Virgin Publishing, 2001); Lizzy Goodman, *Meet Me in the Bathroom: Rebirth and Rock and Roll in New York City 2001–2011* (New York: Dey Street Books, 2017); John Harris, *The Last Party: Britpop, Blair and the Demise of English Rock* (London and New York: Fourth Estate, 2003); Alex James,

Bit of a Blur (London: Abacus, 2008); Sam Knee, *A Scene In Between: Tripping through the Fashions of UK Indie Music 1980–1988* (London: Cicada Books, 2013); Sam Knee, *Untypical Girls: Styles and sounds of the transatlantic indie revolution* (London: Cicada Books, 2017); Simon Reynolds, *Rip it Up and Start Again: Post-punk 1978–1894* (Basingstoke: Macmillan, 1989); Louise Wener, *Just for One Day: Adventures in Britpop* (London: Ebury, 2010).

12. I base much of my analysis on "Sonic"—an exhibition of Slimane's photographs, which ran from September 18, 2014 to January 11, 2015 at the Fondation Pierre Bergé-Yves Saint Laurent in Paris. "Sonic" showcased Slimane's photographs of two music scenes, delineated by place and time-period: London (2003–7) and California (2007–14). The spatiotemporal trajectory of the exhibition followed Slimane's own creative and professional trajectories.

13. Nick Rees-Roberts, "Boys Keep Swinging: The Fashion Iconography of Hedi Slimane," in *Fashion Theory* 17, no. 1 (2013): 9.

14. Simon Frith and Howard Horne, *Art Into Pop* (London and New York: Methuen, 1987).

15. Agnès Rocamora, "Fields of Fashion: Critical Insights into Bourdieu's Sociology of Culture," in *Journal of Consumer Culture* 2, no. 3 (2002).

16. Janice Miller, *Fashion and Music* (London: Berg, 2011), 54; see also Sheila Whiteley, *Women and Popular Music: Sexuality, Identity and Subjectivity* (London: Routledge, 2001).

17. Helen Davies, "All Rock and Roll is Homosocial: The Representation of Women in the British Rock Music Press," in *Popular Music* 20, no. 3 (2001). See also Keith Negus, *Producing Pop: Culture and Conflict in the Popular Music Industry* (London and New York: E. Arnold, 1992).

18. Simon Frith, "Fragments of a Sociology of Rock Criticism," in S. Jones (ed.) *Pop Music and the Press* (Philadelphia, PA: Temple University Press, 2002).

19. See, for example, Georg Simmel, "Fashion," in Daniel Purdy (ed.) *The Rise of Fashion* (Minneapolis: University of Minnesota Press, 2004); Thorstein Veblen, "Dress as an Expression of a Pecuniary Culture," in M. Barnard (ed.) *Fashion Theory: A Reader* (London and New York: Routledge, 1997); J.C. Flügel, "The Great Masculine Renunciation and its Causes," in Purdy (ed.) *The Rise of Fashion*.

20. On disciplining the female body, see Sandra Lee Bartky, *Femininity and Domination: Studies in the Phenomenology of Oppression* (London and New York: Routledge, 1990). At the time of writing this introduction in 2018, there is much discussion in the press debating size and racial diversity on the runways and in fashion campaigns.

21. Agnès Rocamora and Alistair O'Neill, "Fashioning the Street: Images of the Street in the Fashion Media," in Eugenie Shinkle (ed.) *Fashion as Photograph: Viewing and Reviewing Images of Fashion* (London and New York: I.B. Tauris, 2008), 186.

22. Agnès Rocamora, "How New Are New Media? The Case of Fashion Blogs," in *Fashion Media: Past and Present*, Djurdja Bartlett, Shaun Cole, and Agnès Rocamora (eds) (London: Bloomsbury, 2013), 161. She continues, the "other media" that have

represented street style before blogging are *i-D* magazine in the 1980s as well as a number of print titles in the 1990s: *FRUiTS*, *STREET*, and *TUNE*.

23. Stuart Hall, "What is this 'Black' in Black Popular Culture?," in *Social Justice* 20, no, 1 & 2 (1993): 104–14; Kobena Mercer, *Welcome to the Jungle: New Positions in Black Cultural Studies* (London and New York: Routledge, 1994); Monica Miller, *Slaves to Fashion: Black Dandyism and the Styling of Black Diasporic Identity* (Durham, NC: Duke University Press, 2009).

24. Nicky Gregson and Louise Crewe, *Second-hand Cultures* (Oxford and New York: Berg, 2003).

25. McRobbie, "Second-hand Dresses and the Role of the Ragmarket," in A. McRobbie (ed.) *Zoot Suits and Second-hand Dresses: An Anthology of Fashion and Music* (Basingstoke: Macmillan, 1989).

26. Dapper Dan, cited in "A$AP Ferg Interviews Dapper Dan, A Harlem Legend & Fashion Icon," *MTV News*, August 16, 2017 [youtube.com, accessed December 8, 2018]; 5m12s.

27. See, for example, Valeriya Safronova, "Inside Dapper Dan and Gucci's Harlem Atelier," *New York Times*, March 20, 2018 [nytimes.com, accessed December 8, 2018].

28. Jennie Livingston (dir.), *Paris is Burning* (Miramax, 1990).

29. On New York's gay history, see: George Chauncey, *Gay New York: Gender, Urban Culture, and the Making of the Gay Male World 1890–1940* (New York: Basic Books, 1994). On *RuPaul's Drag Race*, see Jim Daems (ed.), *The Makeup of RuPaul's Drag Race: Essays of the Queen of Reality Shows* (Jefferson, NC: McFarland & Company, 2014).

30. Wandera Hussein, "Supreme's James Jebbia wins Menswear Designer of the Year at the 2018 CFDA Awards," *Fader*, June 5, 2018 [thefader.com; accessed December 8, 2018].

31. John Clarke, Stuart Hall, Tony Jefferson and Brian Roberts, "Subcultures, Cultures and Class," in S. Hall and T. Jefferson (eds) *Resistance through Rituals: Youth Subcultures in Post-war Britain. 2nd Edition* (London and New York: Routledge, 2006), 9.

Chapter 1

1. Sam Knee, *A Scene In Between: Tripping through the Fashions of UK Indie Music 1980–1988* (London: Cicada Books, 2013), 3.

2. Simon Reynolds, *Rip it Up and Start Again: Post-punk 1978–1984* (London: Faber and Faber, 2005).

3. David Cavanagh, *The Creation Records Story: My Magpie Eyes are Hungry for the Prize* (London: Virgin Publishing, 2001), 52.

4. Ibid., 150.

Notes

5. Ibid., 151.

6. David Hesmondhalgh, "Indie: The Institutional Politics and Aesthetics of a Popular Music Genre," in *Cultural Studies* 13, no. 1 (1999): 35.

7. Reynolds, *Rip it Up*, 93.

8. Iain McNay, cited in Reynolds, Ibid., 93.

9. Wendy Fonarow, *Empire of Dirt: The Aesthetics and Rituals of British Indie Music* (Middletown, CT: Wesleyan University Press, 2006), 34.

10. Reynolds, *Rip it Up*, 106. Reynolds also provides an in-depth discussion of Rough Trade: how it operated in the image of a cooperative; how it fostered fifty–fifty deals with bands; and how it supported other labels through loans and its distribution network, the Cartel (102–7).

11. Hesmondhalgh, "Indie: The Institutional Politics," 35.

12. Geoff Travis, cited in Cavanagh, *The Creation Records Story*, 39.

13. Roger Holland, *Sounds*, July 5, 1986: 21; emphasis in original.

14. Hesmondhalgh, "Indie: The Institutional Politics," 35.

15. Daniel Miller, cited in Reynolds, *Rip it Up*, 109.

16. Ibid.

17. John Harris, *The Last Party: Britpop, Blair and the Demise of English Rock* (London: Fourth Estate, 2003), 4.

18. Hesmondhalgh, "Indie: The Institutional Politics," 34.

19. Matthew Bannister, *White Boys, White Noise: Masculinities and 1980s Indie Guitar Rock* (Hampshire and Burlington, VT: Ashgate, 2006), 57.

20. Reynolds, *Rip it Up*, 519.

21. Hesmondhalgh, "Indie: The Institutional Politics," 38. Citing Will Straw, Hesmondhalgh argues that a similar shift was taking place in the North American indie scenes. He writes, "Will Straw has noted 'the enshrining of specific forms of connoisseurship as central to an involvement in alternative rock culture' from the mid-1980s on in the USA and Canada. Straw suggests that the interest within post-punk culture in the history of 'rock-based forms of recorded music' points to a much stronger link between post-punk and older, rock institutions than is generally recognized. The basis of the continuity between rock and post-punk alternative culture was, for Straw, their shared origin in a 'largely white bohemia'. Straw suggests that alternative rock culture is sexually as well as ethnically insular: collecting and studying old rock bands is a rite of passage for young men entering the 'scene'" (46).

22. Cavanagh, *The Creation Records Story*, 227.

23. Ibid., 228.

24. Reynolds, *Rip it Up*, 519.

25. Keith Cameron, *Sounds*, December 24/31, 1988: 10.

26. Ron Rom, *Sounds*, December 20/27, 1986: 8.

27. Dave Lemon Drops, cited in Mr. Spencer, *Sounds*, August 30, 1986: 39.

28. Bannister, *White Boys*, 62.

29. Ibid., 61.

30. Lawrence Felt, cited in Anon, *Art & Music*, Spring 2009: 40.

31. Phil Wilson, cited in Anon, Ibid.

32. Reynolds, *Rip it Up*, 522.

33. Simon Reynolds, "Against Health and Efficiency: Independent Music in the 1980s," in Angela McRobbie (ed.) *Zoot Suits and Second-hand Dresses: An Anthology of Fashion and Music* (Basingstoke: Macmillan, 1989), 250. See also Reynolds, *Rip it Up*, 522.

34. Cavanagh, *The Creation Records Story*, 190.

35. Reynolds, "Against Health and Efficiency," 251.

36. Stephen Pastel, cited in Cavanagh, *The Creation Records Story*, 190.

37. Pete Momtchiloff, cited in Anon, *Art & Music*, Spring 2009: 41.

38. Paul Kelly, cited in Ibid.

39. Stephen Pastel, cited in Knee, *A Scene In Between*, 38.

40. Amelia Fletcher, cited in Knee, Ibid., 98.

41. Bannister, *White Boys*, xxiv.

42. Ibid., 62.

43. Michael Kerr, cited in Knee, *A Scene In Between*, 61.

44. Amelia Fletcher, cited in Knee, Ibid., 99.

45. Angela McRobbie, "Second-hand Dresses and the Role of the Ragmarket," in McRobbie (ed.) *Zoot Suits and Second-hand Dresses*.

46. Ibid., 42.

47. Knee, *A Scene In Between*, 28-9.

48. McRobbie, "Second-hand Dresses," 42.

49. Knee, *A Scene In Between*, 86-7.

50. Ibid., 100-6.

51. McRobbie, "Second-hand Dresses," 42.

52. Anon, *The Face*, March 1987: 12.

53. William Leith, *i-D*, October 1986: 76-7.

54. Reynolds, "Against Health and Efficiency," 254-5.

55. Frank Mort, *Cultures of Consumption: Masculinities and Social Space in Late Twentieth-Century Britain* (London and New York: Routledge, 1996), 64.

56. Ibid., 56.

57. Ibid., 64.

58. Ibid., 64, 70; emphasis added.

59. Sean Nixon, "Exhibiting Masculinity," in Stuart Hall (ed.) *Representation: Cultural Representations and Signifying Practices* (London; Thousand Oaks, CA; New Delhi: Sage: 1997), 307.

60. Anon, *NME*, August 1, 1998: 33.

61. Johnny Cigarettes, *NME*, May 22, 1993: 37.

62. Anon, *Sounds*, October 27, 1990: 16.

63. Anon, *Sounds*, December 15, 1990: 22.

64. Anon, *Melody Maker*, September 12, 1992: 7.

65. Anon, *NME*, November 20, 1993: 36.

66. Nick Hornby, *High Fidelity* (New York: Riverhead Books, 1996), 63.

67. Helen Davies, "All Rock and Roll is Homosocial: The Representation of Women in the British Rock Music Press," in *Popular Music* 20, no. 3 (2001): 301–2.

68. Ibid., 301.

69. Angela McRobbie, *Postmodernism and Popular Culture* (London and New York: Routledge, 1994), 131.

70. See Angela McRobbie and Jenny Garber, "Girls and Subcultures," in Stuart Hall and Tony Jefferson (eds) *Resistance through Rituals: Youth Subcultures in Post-war Britain* (London: Routledge, 1993 [1976]).

71. See also Sam Knee, *Untypical Girls: Styles and sounds of the transatlantic indie revolution*, (London: Cicada Boks, 2017).

72. Bannister, *White Boys*, 104.

73. Brett Anderson, cited in Anon, *NME*, November 6, 1993: 27.

74. Noel McLaughlin, "Rock, Fashion and Performativity," in Stella Bruzzi and Pamela Church Gibson (eds) *Fashion Cultures: Theories, Explorations and Analysis* (London: Routledge, 2000).

75. Ibid., 277.

76. Ibid., 278.

77. Ibid., 279.

78. Ibid., 275.

79. John Harris, *The Last Party: Britpop, Blair and the Demise of English Rock* (London and New York: Fourth Estate, 2003), 318.

80. See David Cavanagh on the story of Creation Records.

81. Hesmondhalgh, "Indie: The Institutional Politics," 36.

82. Ibid., 34.

83. Ibid., 46.

84. Ibid., 56.

85. Ibid., 46.

86. Cavanagh, *The Creation Records Story*, 560.

87. Ibid., 530. See also Hesmondhalgh, "Indie: The Institutional Politics," 45–6.

88. Hesmondhalgh, "Indie: The Institutional Politics," 56.

89. John Harris, *NME*, January 7, 1995: 8.

90. Harris, *The Last Party*, xvi.

91. Alex James, *Bit of a Blur* (London: Abacus, 2008), 150.

92. See Harris, *The Last Party* for a full account of the story of Britpop.

93. James, *Bit of a Blur*, 83.

94. Harris, *The Last Party*, xviii.

95. Danny Scott, "Festivals!", *The Face*, May 1995: 171.

96. Ibid.

97. Rosalind Gill, "Power and the Production of Subjects: A Genealogy of the New Man and the New Lad," in Bethan Benthwell (ed.) *Masculinity and Men's Lifestyle Magazines* (Oxford and Malden, MA: Wiley Blackwell, 2003), 37.

98. See Sean Nixon, *Hard Looks: Masculinities, Spectatorship & Contemporary Consumption* (New York: St. Martin's Press, 1996).

99. Ben Crewe, *Representing Men: Cultural Production and Producers in Men's Magazine Market* (Oxford and New York: Berg, 2003), 125.

100. Ibid., 134.

101. Ibid., 142.

102. James, *Bit of a Blur*, 129.

103. Justine Frischmann, cited in Harris, *The Last Party*, 162.

104. Danny Scott, "Festivals!", *The Face*, May 1993: 171; emphasis in original.

105. Anon, *Melody Maker*, December 21/28, 1996: 49.

106. Sonya Aurora-Madan, cited in Avril Mair, *i-D*, June 1994: 6.

107. Rupa Huq, *Beyond Subculture: Pop, Youth and Identity in a Postcolonial World* (London and New York: Routledge, 2006), 35.

108. Davies, "All Rock and Roll is Homosocial," 302; emphasis in original.

109. Ibid., 303.

110. Louise Wener, *Just for One Day: Adventures in Britpop* (London: Ebury, 2010), 196; emphasis in original.

111. Ibid., 199.

112. See Mary Celeste Kearney, "The Missing Links: Riot Grrrl—Feminism—Lesbian Culture," in Sheila Whiteley (ed.) *Sexing the Groove: Popular Music and Gender* (London and New York: Routledge, 1997).

113. Wener, *Just for One Day*, 287.

114. Ibid.; See also Hesmondhalgh, "Indie: The Institutional Politics," 51–2, and Huq, *Beyond Subculture*, 144–5 for alternative readings of feminism within Britpop. Huq, for example, argues that "Female Britpop role models like riot grrrls reverse

the 'female' dummy stereotype as portrayed in Robert Palmer's 'Addicted to Love' video of the 1980s, where the self-aggrandising male is centre of attention backed by largely lifeless perfunctory females" (145).

115. Anon, Reviews, *The Face*, April 1994: 131.

116 Martin Wallace and Jarvis Cocker (dirs.), Babies, performed by Pulp, (Gift, 1992).

117. Scott, "Festivals!", *The Face*, May 1993: 57.

118. James, *Bit of a Blur*, 106.

119. Scott, "Festivals!", *The Face*, May 1995: 57.

120. Amy Raphael, "Sex on a stick?," *The Face*, March 1994: 68.

121. Ibid., 70.

122. Susan Corrigan, "Boys R Us," *i-D*, June 1995: 21.

123. Anon, *The Face*, March 1993: 93.

124. Tony Marcus, *i-D*, December 1993: 18.

125. Cliff Jones, "Looking for a New England," *The Face*, May 1994: 42.

126. Ibid.

127. Luella Bartley, *Dazed & Confused*, Issue 14, 1995: 9.

128. Tony Marcus, *i-D*, October 1994: 26.

129. Crewe, *Representing Men*, 134.

130. Jones, "Looking for a New England," 44.

131. Deena Weinstein, cited in Huq, *Beyond Subculture*, 139.

132. Bridget Foley, *Marc Jacobs* (New York: Assouline Publishing, 2004), 16.

133. Ted Polhemus, "From Sidewalk to Catwalk," in *Textile View Magazine* 27 (1994): 28–31.

134. Anon, *Vogue*, April 1993: 231; emphasis in original.

135. Edward Enninful, *i-D*, October 1994: 51.

136. John Robinson, *NME*, February 18, 1995: 20.

137. Mark Hooper, *i-D*, September 2001: 308.

138. Rob Sheffield, cited in Lizzy Goodman, *Meet Me in the Bathroom: Rebirth and Rock and Roll in New York City 2001–2011* (New York: Dey Street Books, 2017), 340.

139. Conor McNicholas, cited in Goodman, *Meet Me in the Bathroom*, 219.

140. Johnny Davis, *The Face*, July 2001: 103.

141. Ibid.

142. Marc Spitz, cited in Goodman, *Meet Me in the Bathroom*, 219.

143. Austin Scaggs, cited in Goodman, Ibid., 129.

144. Thomas Onarato, cited in Goodman, Ibid., 45.

145. Joe Levy, cited in Goodman, Ibid., 234.

146. Karen O., cited in Goodman, Ibid., 491.

147. Levy, cited in Goodman, Ibid., 234.

148. Christian Joy, interview with author, July 5, 2016. All further quotations from Joy are sourced from this interview.

149. Hedi Slimane, *Anthology of a Decade* (Zürich: JRP Ringier, 2012).

150. Kimberly Mack, "'There's No Home for You Here': Jack White and the Unsolvable Problem of Blues Authenticity," in *Popular Music and Society* 38, no. 2 (2015): 176.

151. Jason Baron, cited in Goodman, *Meet Me in the Bathroom*, 243.

152. Chris Lombardi, cited in Goodman, Ibid.

153. Nick Valensi, cited in Goodman, Ibid., 117.

154. April Long, cited in Goodman, Ibid., 219.

155. Anon, *NME*, December 22/29, 2001: 67.

156. Ibid.

157. Anon, *NME*, June 30, 2001: 4.

158. Luella Bartley, cited in Anon, Ibid.

159. Anon, "Stroke of Good Luck," *NME*, May 18, 2002: 14.

160. Ibid.

161. Anon, *NME*, November 29, 2003: 37.

162. Nathan Followill, cited in Goodman, *Meet Me in the Bathroom*, 408.

163. Ibid.

164. Anon, *NME*, January 31, 2004: 29.

Chapter 2

1. Craig McLean, "To Dior for," *The Guardian*, September 25, 2005 [theguardian.co.uk, accessed January 15, 2015].

2. Cathy Horyn, "That Man From Saint Laurent," *New York Times*, August 10, 1999 [nytimes.com, accessed February 28, 2017].

3. Jay McCauley Bowstead, "Hedi Slimane and the Reinvention of Menswear," in *Critical Studies in Men's Fashion* 2, no. 1 (2015): 39.

4. Charlie Porter, "Body Politic," *The Guardian*, June 30, 2001 [theguardian.com, accessed May 27, 2016].

5. Hedi Slimane, cited in Craig McLean, "To Dior for."

6. Sean Nixon, "Resignifying Masculinity: From 'New Man' to 'New Lad,'" in David Morley and Kevin Robins (eds) *British Cultural Studies: Geography, Nationality,*

Notes

and Identity (Oxford: Oxford University Press, 2001), 374. See also Frank Mort, *Cultures of Consumption: Masculinities and Social Space in Late Twentieth-Century Britain* (London and New York: Routledge, 1996); Sean Nixon, *Hard Looks: Masculinities, Spectatorship & Contemporary Consumption* (New York: Palgrave MacMillan, 1996).

7. Ibid.

8. Ibid., 379.

9. Janet Street Porter, "Editor-at-large: At Last—a Fashion Designer Who Tells Men it's OK to Look Like a Wimp," *The Independent*, February 1, 2004 [independent. co.uk; accessed April 20, 2015].

10. Simon Frith and Howard Horne, *Art into Pop* (London and New York: Methuen, 1987), 73.

11. Ibid., 89.

12. Ibid., 88.

13. Ibid., 89.

14. Ibid., 149.

15. Ibid., 90.

16. Ibid., 92.

17. Simon Frith and Angela McRobbie, "Rock and Sexuality," in Simon Frith and Andrew Goodwin (eds) *On Record: Rock, Pop & The Written Word* (London and New York: Routledge, 1990), 373.

18. Miles Socha, "Hedi's New Book: For Pete's Sake," *WWD*, June 7, 2005 [wwd.com, accessed February 28, 2017].

19. Hedi Slimane, cited in Hadley Freeman, "Dior Homme," *10 Men* A/W (2005): 130.

20. Hadley Freeman, "The Right Notes," *The Guardian*, February 4, 2005 [theguardian. com, accessed May 27, 2016].

21. Hedi Slimane, cited in Socha, "Hedi's New Book."

22. Pete Doherty, cited in Hadley Freeman, "Are You a Pete or are You a Bill?," *The Guardian*, July 11, 2005 [theguardian.com, accessed May 27, 2016].

23. Hedi Slimane, cited in Craig McLean, "To Dior for."

24. McLean, Ibid. He identifies this quotation in an image of "a page from Doherty's diary." I could not see that page, but the phrase is cited again in the image I mention, which was taken April 2005 and reappears in Slimane's later exhibition "Sonic."

25. Most of my analysis in this section is based on observation of "Sonic."

26. Nick Rees-Roberts, "Boys Keep Swinging: The Fashion Iconography of Hedi Slimane," in *Fashion Theory* 17, no. 1 (2013): 12.

27. See also Rees-Roberts, "Boys Keep Swinging."

28. Wendy Fonarow, *Empire of Dirt: The Aesthetics and Rituals of British Indie Music* (Middletown, CT: Wesleyan University Press, 2006), 191.

29. Lawrence Grossberg, "The Media Economy of Rock Culture: Cinema, Postmodernity and Authenticity," in Simon Frith *et al.* (eds) *Sound and Vision: The Music Video Reader* (London and New York: Routledge, 1993), 204.

30. Noel McLaughlin, "Rock, Fashion and Performativity," in Stella Bruzzi and Pamela Church Gibson (eds) *Fashion Cultures: Theories, Explorations and Analysis* (London and New York: Routledge, 2000), 268.

31. Grossberg speaks about a second form of authenticity "often linked with dance and black music, [which] locates authenticity in the construction of a rhythmic and sexual body. Often identifying sexual mobility and romance, it constructs a fantasy of the tortured individual struggling to transcend the conditions of their inadequacy" ("The Media Economy of Rock Culture," 202). McLaughlin critiques the "orthodox narrative of rock history," noting that "a key aspect of this has been the long-standing 'necessary connection' forged between black people, black culture (clothes and performance styles) and music-making: between blackness, the body, rhythm and sexuality" ("Rock, Fashion and Performativity," 269).

32. Richard Dyer, *The Matter of Images: Essays on Representation* (London and New York: Routledge, 1993), 143.

33. Frith and Horne, *Art into Pop*, 92. On gender in rock, see also Frith and McRobbie, "Rock and Sexuality." Also, as a response to his earlier essay with McRobbie: Simon Frith, "Afterthoughts," in *On Record: Rock, Pop & The Written Word*.

34. Dyer, *The Matter of Images*, 128.

35. Ibid., 130.

36. Cathy Horyn, "Where the Boys are is Where the Girls Should be," *New York Times*, February 1, 2005 [nytimes.com, accessed February 28, 2017].

37. Yuniya Kawamura, cited in Joanne Entwistle and Agnès Rocamora, "The Field of Fashion Materialized: A Study of London Fashion Week," in *Sociology* 40, no. 4 (2006): 742.

38. I would like to thank Don Stahl for helping me find the language to describe the soundtracks' sounds.

39. McLean, "To Dior for."

40. Frith and Horne, *Art into Pop*, 73.

41. Tim Blanks, "Runway: Fall 2005 Menswear: Dior Homme," *Vogue*, January 30, 2005 [vogue.com; accessed July 24, 2017].

42. Anon, "Autumn/Winter 2005 Menswear: Dior Homme," *Vogue*, January 31, 2005 [vogue.com; accessed July 24, 2017].

43. Tim Blanks, "Runway: Spring 2006 Menswear: Dior Homme," *Vogue*, July 7, 2005 [vogue.com; accessed July 24, 2017].

44. Hamish MacBain, *NME*, November 18, 2006: 34; emphasis in original.

Notes

45. Sarah Thornton, *Club Cultures: Music, Media and Subcultural Capital* (Middletown, CT: Wesleyan University Press, 1996).

46. Frith and Horne, *Art into Pop*, 124.

47. Ibid., 132.

48. Ibid., 145; emphasis in original.

49. Ibid., 151.

50. Ibid., 177; emphasis in original.

51. Johnny Borrell, cited in JS Rafaeli, "The Definitive History of Landfill Indie in Seven Songs, Narrated by Johnny Borrell," *Noisey*, April 5, 2016 [noisey.vice.com; accessed September 15, 2017].

52. Nikolai Fraiture, cited in Chuck Klosterman, "Gang of Five," *Spin*, December 2003: 73.

53. All interviews with young male participants in indie were conducted over the spring and summer of 2009. All names of respondents have been changed.

54. Noel McLaughlin, "Rock, Fashion and Performativity," 268.

55. Ibid., 269.

56. Ibid.

57. Helen Davies, "All Rock and Roll is Homosocial: The Representation of Women in the British Rock Music Press," in *Popular Music* 20, no. 3 (2001): 306.

58. Ibid.

59. Michael Agosta and Marcy Medina, "Alternative Styling," *WWD*, September 8, 2005 [wwd.com; accessed February 28, 2017].

60. Janice Miller, *Fashion and Music* (London: Berg, 2011), 25.

61. Ibid.

62. Marc Spitz, "The Rebirth of Cool," *Spin*, January 2003: 59.

63. Brandon Flowers, cited in Marc Spitz, "Gluttony, Envy, Wrath, Vanity, Avarice, Lust, and Sloth? We're Game," *Spin*, February 2005: 52.

64. Angela McRobbie, *British Fashion Design: Rag Trade or Image Industry* (London and New York: Routledge, 1998), 151.

65. Gester Gudmundsson, Ulf Lindberg, Morten Michelsen, and Hans Weisethaunet, "Brit Crit: Turning Points in British Rock Criticism, 1960–1990," in Steve Jones (ed.) *Pop Music and the Press* (Philadelphia: Temple University Press, 2002), 41.

66. Ibid., 51.

67. Steve Jones and Kevin Featherly, "Re-viewing Rock Writing: Narratives of Popular Music Criticism," in *Pop Music and the Press*, op cit., 19.

68. Ibid., 32.

69. Ibid., 33.

70. Ibid.

71. Gudmundsson *et al.*, "Brit Crit," 54.
72. Ibid., 55. *Sniffin' Glue* was a punk zine, first released in 1976.
73. Ibid., 56.
74. Ibid., 57.
75. McRobbie, *British Fashion Design*, 151.
76. Krissi Murison, *Nylon Guys*, September 2009, 97.
77. Adham Faramawy, interview with author, June 16, 2009..
78. Davies, "All Rock and Roll is Homosocial," 306.
79. Doug Brod, interview with author, June 23, 2017. All further quotations from Brod are sourced from this interview.
80. Michelle Egiziano, interview with author, August 23, 2017. All further quotations from Egiziano are sourced from this interview.
81. Simon Frith, "Fragments of a Sociology of Rock Criticism," in *Pop Music and the Press*, op cit., 243.
82. Ibid.
83. Anon, *NME*, November 29, 2003, 37.
84 Uncredited director, *On Call*, performed by Kings of Leon, (RCA, 2007).
85. Grossberg, "The Media Economy of Rock Culture," 204.
86. Spitz, "The Rebirth of Cool," 54.
87. Thornton, *Club Cultures*.
88. Ibid., 11.
89. Ibid., 11–12.
90. Agnès Rocamora, "Fields of Fashion: Critical Insights into Bourdieu's Sociology of Culture," *Journal of Consumer Culture* 2, no. 3 (2002).
91. Angela McRobbie, "Second-hand Dresses and the Role of the Ragmarket," in Angela McRobbie (ed.) *Zoot Suits and Second-hand Dresses: An Anthology of Fashion and Music* (Basingstoke: Macmillan, 1989), 29.
92. Thornton, *Club Cultures*, 12.
93. Ted Polhemus, "From Sidewalk to Catwalk," in *Textile View Magazine* 27 (1994): 31; see also Ted Polhemus, *Streetstyle: From Sidewalk to Catwalk* (London and New York: Thames and Hudson, 1994); *Stylesurfing: What to Wear in the 3rd Millennium* (London and New York: Thames and Hudson, 1996); "In the Supermarket of Style," in Steve Redhead *et al.* (eds) *The Clubcultures Reader: Readings in Popular Cultural Studies* (Oxford and Malden, MA: Blackwell Publishing, 1997), 130–3.
94. Polhemus, "In the Supermarket of Style," 131.
95. Agnès Rocamora and Alistair O'Neill, "Fashioning the Street: Images of the Street in the Fashion Media," in Eugenie Shinkle (ed.) *Fashion as Photograph: Viewing and Reviewing Images of Fashion* (London and New York: I.B. Tauris, 2008), 193.

Notes

96. Pierre Bourdieu, *Distinction: A Social Critique of the Judgement of Taste*, R. Nice (trans) (London and New York: Routledge, 1984).

97. On the Mods and the Rockers, see Stanley Cohen, *Folk Devils and Moral Panics: The Creation of the Mods and Rockers. 3rd Edition* (London and New York: Routledge, 2002 [1972]).

98. Dyer, *The Matter of Images*, 143.

99. Agnès Rocamora, "Fields of Fashion." See also Joanne Entwistle and Agnès Rocamora, "The Field of Fashion Materialized: A Study of London Fashion Week," *Sociology* 40, no. 4 (2006).

100. Tim Blanks, "Runway: Spring 2013 Ready-to-wear: Saint Laurent," *Vogue*, September 30, 2012 [vogue.com; accessed July 30, 2017].

101. Sarah Mower, "Runway: Spring 2016 Ready-to-wear: Saint Laurent," *Vogue*, October 5, 2015 [vogue.com; accessed July 30, 2017].

Chapter 3

1. Jess Cartner-Morley, "What to Wear at the Music Festivals," *The Guardian*, April 20, 2010 [theguardian.com, accessed April 20, 2015].

2. Hadley Freeman, "Ask Hadley," *The Guardian*, June 20, 2010 [theguardian.com, accessed April 20, 2015].

3. Hadley Freeman, "Since When Were Music Festivals Al Fresco Fashion Shows?," *The Guardian*, April 27, 2015 [theguardian.com, accessed May 20, 2015].

4. Elizabeth Wilson, *Bohemians: The Glamorous Outcasts* (New Brunswick, NJ: Rutgers University Press, 2000).

5. Ibid., 3.

6. Simon Frith and Howard Horne, *Art into Pop* (London: Methuen, 1987), 92.

7. Wilson, *Bohemians*, 86.

8. See Paul Jobling, *Fashion Spreads: Word and Image in Fashion Photography Since 1980* (Oxford and New York: Berg, 1999).

9. Lucinda Chambers, British *Vogue*, August 1994: 92.

10. Kate Rhodes, "The Elegance of the Everyday: Nobodies in Contemporary Fashion Photography," in Eugenie Shinkle (ed.) *Fashion as Photograph: Viewing and Reviewing Images of Fashion* (London and New York: I.B. Tauris, 2008), 205.

11. Wilson, *Bohemians*, 118.

12. See Wilson's chapter on "Feminine Roles" in *Bohemians*.

13. Angela Buttolph, *Kate Moss Style: Inside the World's Most Famous Wardrobe* (London: Random House, 2009).

14. Wilson, *Bohemians*, 165.

15. Ibid., 164.

16. Michael Hogan. "The 10 Best Kate Moss Moments," *The Guardian*, January 11, 2014 [theguardian.com, accessed April 20, 2015].

17. Danny Scott, "Festivals!," *The Face*, May 1993: 57.

18. Ibid., 60-1.

19. Ibid., 57.

20. Lauren Laverne, "Lauren Laverne on Fashion: What to Wear to a Festival," *The Guardian*, June 23, 2013 [theguardian.com, accessed April 20, 2015].

21. Hadley Freeman, "The World's Muddiest Catwalk," *The Guardian*, June 24, 2005 [theguardian.com, accessed April 20, 2015].

22. Ibid.

23. Anon, "Spy," British *Vogue*, September 2009: 140.

24. Wilson, *Bohemians*, 110.

25. Mario Testino (photographer), "Ragged Glory," *Vogue*, September 2013: 858.

26. Anna Wintour, "Letter from the Editor," *Vogue*, September 2013: 300.

27. Ibid., 288.

28. Wendy Fonarow, "Ask the Indie Professor: Why the Big Fuss over Coachella Festival?," *The Guardian*, April 13, 2011 [theguardian.com; accessed April 20, 2015].

29. Jess Cartner-Morley, Caterina Monzani and Ekaterina Ochagavia, "Glastonbury 2014: How to Dress for Festivals—Video," *The Guardian*, June 25, 2014 [theguardian.com, accessed April 20, 2015].

30. Laird Borrelli-Perrson, "Festival Dressing Done Right: 16 Inspirational Looks from the *Vogue* Archive," *Vogue*, April 16, 2014 [vogue.com, accessed May 20, 2015].

31. Jess Cartner-Morley *et al.*, "Glastonbury 2014."

32. Jess Cartner-Morley, "Field Dressing for Festivals," *The Guardian*, May 7, 2009 [theguardian.com, accessed April 20, 2015].

33. There is very little bibliographical information available about this guide, which was to be picked up by Topshop customers as they entered and exited the store in summer 2013. The magazine is made from non-glossy paper and includes no dates and only minimal contributor information about the photographers, stylists, and editors who worked on the various features.

34. Tung Walsh (photographer) and Anna Trevelyan (stylist), "Our Summer Edit," in Ibid., 4-9.

35. Anon, "A Festival World Tour," in Ibid., 10-11.

36. Hanna Hanra, "Our Sounds of the Summer," in Ibid., 12-13.

37. Michael Polish (director), "Here Comes the Sun: 'The Road to Coachella,'" in Ibid., 14-19.

38. Observation on June 25, 2014.

39. Ibid.

40. Observation on June 28, 2014.

41. Observations on June 25 and 28, 2014.

42. Observation on April 7, 2016.

43. Observation on April 19, 2016.

44. Driely S., interview with the author, August 2, 2016.

45. On the "new man," see Frank Mort, *Cultures of Consumption: Masculinities and Social Space in Late Twentieth-Century Britain* (London and New York: Routledge, 1996); Sean Nixon, *Hard Looks: Masculinities, Spectatorship & Contemporary Consumption* (New York: Palgrave MacMillan, 1996).

46. Agnès Rocamora and Alistair O'Neill, "Fashioning the Street: Images of the Street in the Fashion Media," in *Fashion as Photograph*, 186.

47. Elliot Smedley, "Escaping to Reality: Fashion Photography in the 1990s," in Stella Bruzzi and Pamela Church Gibson (eds) *Fashion Cultures: Theories, Explorations and Analysis* (London and New York: Routledge, 2000), 147.

48. Val Williams, *Look at Me: Fashion and Photography in Britain 1960 to the Present* (London: The British Council Visual Arts Publications, 1998), 112.

49. Rocamora and O'Neill, "Fashioning the Street," 186.

50. Ibid., 190.

51. Angela McRobbie, *British Fashion Design: From Rag Trade to Image Industry* (London and New York: Routledge, 1998), 154.

52. Caroline Evans, "Dreams That Only Money Can Buy ... Or, The Shy Tribe In Flight from Discourse," in *Fashion Theory* 1, no. 2 (1997): 176.

53. "Fashion discourse" and "fashion media discourse" are terms Rocamora develops, drawing on and combining Pierre Bourdieu's concepts "symbolic production" and "fields of cultural production" and Michel Foucault's concept of "discourse." See Chapter 3 in *Fashioning the City: Paris, Fashion and the Media* (London and New York: I.B. Tauris, 2009).

54. Rocamora and O'Neill, "Fashioning the Street," 185.

55. Ibid., 188.

56. For an in-depth analysis of The Sartorialist, see Esther Rosser, "Photographing Fashion: A Critical Look at the Sartorialist," in *Image & Narrative* 11, no. 4 (2010). She argues that "*this* blog is not the site of an expression of a truly 'alternative' fashion press," as the person whose ensemble is featured "is reduced, in the hands of Schuman, to a mere model; an expression of *his* [Schuman's] notion of fashion" (168; emphasis in original). See also Fiona Golfar, "Mr. Big Shot," British *Vogue*, September 2009, 303. On Facehunter, see Jess Berry, "Flâneurs of Fashion 2.0," in *SCAN: Journal of Media Arts Culture* (2010).

57. Rosie Findlay, "The Short, Passionate, and Close-knit History of Personal Style Blogs," in *Fashion Theory* 19, no. 2 (2015): 166.

58. Ibid., 167.

59. Agnès Rocamora, "Personal Fashion Blogs: Screens and Mirrors in Digital Self-portraits," in *Fashion Theory* 15, no. 4 (2011): 410.

60. Ibid., 411; Notable exceptions include Catherine Connell and Minh-Ha T. Pham, who similarly point to how blogging can foster shared identities and demonstrate collective dissent. Connell explores the *Fa(t)shion February* project that, through the online posting of images of fa(t)shionable women during the semi-annual fashion months, "celebrates and proliferates images of *unruly bodies*." Pham looks at how fashion blogging techniques "are being incorporated into social activist movements." She looks specifically at the "#feministselfie" campaign and the *RAISE Our Story* campaign for immigration reform. Catherine Connell, "Fashionable Resistance: Queer 'Fa(t)shion' Blogging as Counterdiscourse," in *WSQ: Women's Studies Quarterly* 41, nos. 1 & 2 (2013): 212; Minh-Ha T. Pham, "'I Click and Post and Breathe, Waiting for Others to See What I See': On #FeministSelfies, Outfit Photos, and Networked Vanity," in *Fashion Theory* 19, no. 2 (2015): 224.

61. Findlay, "Close-knit History," 169.

62. Ibid., 170.

63. Monica Titton, "Fashionable Personae: Self-identity and Enactments of Fashion Narratives in Fashion Blogs," in *Fashion Theory* 19, no. 2 (2015): 216–17.

64. Sophie Woodward, "The Myth of Street Style," in *Fashion Theory* 13, no. 1 (2009): 88–9.

65. Glam Editors, "Best Dressed at Governors Ball 2014" [www.mode.com, accessed May 15, 2015]; Link no longer connected to this site.

66. Anita Harris, *Future Girl: Young Women in the Twenty-First Century* (London and New York: Routledge, 2003).

67. Ibid., 6.

68. Ibid., 1.

69. Ibid.

70. Angela McRobbie, *The Aftermath of Feminism: Gender, Culture and Social Change* (Thousand Oaks, CA: Sage, 2009), 54.

71. Ibid.

72. Ibid., 62–3.

73. Ibid., 67–8.; Sandra Lee Bartky, *Femininity and Domination: Studies in the Phenomenology of Oppression* (London and New York: Routledge, 1990); Susan Bordo, *Unbearable Weight: Feminism, Western Culture, and the Body* (Berkeley, CA: University of California Press, 1993).

74. Minh-Ha T. Pham, "Susie Bubble is a Sign of the Times," in *Feminist Media Studies* 13, no. 2 (2013): 249.

75. Ibid., 245; emphasis in original.

76. Judith Butler, *Gender Trouble: Feminism and the Subversion of Identity*. 10th Anniversary Edition (London and New York: Routledge, 1999), 172.

77. "Fashion and beauty system" is a term Angela McRobbie uses in *Aftermath of Feminism* to refer to the institution of social regulation that has replaced patriarchy within contemporary culture, 63.

78. Emily Knecht (photographer), "The Best Street Style Looks from Coachella 2015," *Vogue*, April 13, 2015 [vogue.com; accessed May 13, 2019].

79. Polly Vernon, "What Polly Saw . . .: What Makes the Perfect Welly Leg?," *Grazia*, July 11, 2011: 47.

80. Anna-Marie Crowhurst, "Coachella: How to Get that Festival Look," *The Guardian*, April 18, 2013 [theguardian.com, accessed April 20, 2015].

81. Elizabeth Wissinger, "Modeling Consumption: Fashion Modeling Work in Contemporary Society," in *Journal of Consumer Culture* 9, no. 2 (2009): 284.

82. Marcel Mauss, "Techniques of the Body," in *Economy and Society* 2, no. 1 (1973).

83. Woodward, "The Myth of Street Style."

84. Ibid., 88.

85. Ibid., 92.

86. Ibid., 97.

87. Ibid., 98.

88. All interviews with young female participants in indie were conducted over the spring and summer of 2009. All names of respondents have been changed.

89. Ted Polhemus, "From Sidewalk to Catwalk," in *Textile View Magazine* 27 (1994); *Streetstyle: From Sidewalk to Catwalk* (London and New York: Thames and Hudson, 1994); *Stylesurfing: What to Wear in the 3rd Millennium* (London and New York: Thames and Hudson, 1996); "In the Supermarket of Style," in Steve Redhead *et al.* (eds) *The Clubcultures Reader: Readings in Popular Cultural Studies* (Oxford and Malden, MA: Blackwell Publishing, 1997).

90. Woodward, "The Myth of Street Style," 88–9.

91. Anon, *Grazia*, August 10, 2009: 56.

92. Anon, Topshop Autumn/Winter Style Guide, Summer 2009: 6–7 (insert) Like the Festival Guide from 2013, this guide was free to to pick up in store..

93. Woodward, "The Myth of Street Style," 92.

94. Caroline Evans and Lorraine Gamman, "The Gaze Revisited, or Reviewing Queer Viewing," in Paul Burston and Colin Richardson (eds) *A Queer Romance: Lesbians, Gay Men and Popular Culture* (London and New York: Routledge, 1995); Reina Lewis, "Looking Good: The Lesbian Gaze and Fashion Imagery," in Nicholas Mirzoeff (ed.) *The Visual Cultures Reader. 2nd Edition* (London and New York: Routledge, 2002).

95. Evans and Gamman, "The Gaze Revisited," 36.

96. Lewis, "Looking Good," 657.

97. Angela McRobbie, "Second-hand Dresses and the Role of the Ragmarket," in Angela McRobbie (ed.) *Zoot Suits and Second-hand Dresses: An Anthology of Fashion and Music* (Basingstoke: Macmillan, 1989), 29.

98. Fredric Jameson, *Postmodernism: or, The Cultural Logic of Late Capitalism* (Durham, NC: Duke University Press, 1991).

99. Anna König, "Glossy Words: An Analysis of Fashion Writing in British *Vogue*," in *Fashion Theory* 10, nos. 1 and 2 (2006).

100. Ane Lynge-Jorlén, *Between Edge and Elite: Niche Fashion Magazines, Producers and Readers* (London College of Fashion: PhD Thesis, 2009), 68.

101. Rocamora and O'Neill, "Fashioning the Street," 189.

102. On "subcultural capital," see Sarah Thornton, *Club Cultures: Music, Media and Subcultural Capital* (Middletown, CT: Wesleyan University Press, 1996). On "fashion capital," see Agnès Rocamora, "Fields of Fashion: Critical Insights into Bourdieu's Sociology of Culture," in *Journal of Consumer Culture* 2, no. 3 (2002). See also Joanne Entwistle and Agnès Rocamora, "The Field of Fashion Materialized: A Study of London Fashion Week," in *Sociology* 40, no. 4 (2006).

103. Entwistle and Rocamora, "The Field of Fashion Materialized," 742.

104. Ibid., 744; emphasis in original.

105 Ibid.

106. Ibid.

107. Michel Maffesoli, *The Time of the Tribes: The Decline of Individualism in Mass Society*, D. Smith (trans) (Thousand Oaks, CA: Sage, 1996).

108. Ibid., 76.

109. Ibid.

110. Ibid., 96; emphasis in original.

111. Evans and Gamman, "The Gaze Revisited," 16.

112. Efrat Tseëlon, *The Masque of Femininity: The Presentation of Woman in Everyday Life* (Thousand Oaks, CA: Sage, 1995).

113. See Erving Goffman, *The Presentation of Self in Everyday Life* (London: Anchor, 1959).

114. Michel Foucault, *Discipline and Punish* (London: Penguin, 1991 [1977]).

115. See Lorraine Gamman and Margaret Marshment (eds), *The Female Gaze: Women as Viewers of Popular Culture* (London: Real Comet Press, 1988).

116. Bartky, *Femininity and Domination*, 72..

117. The following comments are developed from observations of Oxford Street from June 25, 2014.

118. Alex Needham, "Coachella's Festival Fashion for Men: It's All about the Sexy Springbreak Cowboy," *The Guardian*, April 14, 2015 [theguardian.com, accessed April 20, 2015].

Notes

119. Joanne Entwistle, "From Catwalk to Catalog: Male Fashion Models, Masculinity, and Identity," in H. Thomas and J. Ahmed (eds), *Cultural Bodies: Ethnography and Theory* (Oxford: Blackwell Publishing, 2004), 61–2.

120. Ibid., 62.

121. Needham, "Coachella's Festival Fashion for Men."

122. Thornton, *Club Cultures*, 99–100.

123. Ibid., 101.

124. Needham, "Coachella's Festival Fashion for Men."

Chapter 4

1. James Spooner, *Afropunk: The Movie*, 2003 [www.youtube.com; accessed January 22, 2016].

2. "Pop bottles" is a reference to going out to the club and getting champagne table service—an oft-cited activity within mainstream hip-hop.

3. James Spooner, cited in Rawiya Kameir, "The True Story of How Afropunk Turned a Message Board into a Movement," *Fader*, August 21, 2015 [thefader.com; accessed February 22, 2016].

4. Mark Anthony Neal, *Looking for Leroy: Illegible Black Masculinities* (New York and London: New York University Press, 2013), 2.

5. Ibid., 3; he later uses the shorthand "playa, pump, hustler, thug, and nigga" (36).

6. Aisha Durham, "'Check on it': Beyoncé, Southern Booty, and Black Femininities in Music Video," in *Feminist Media Studies* 12, no. 1 (2012).

7. Neal, *Looking for Leroy*, 3–4.

8. Ibid., 4.

9. Black punk, cited in Spooner, *Afropunk: The Movie*, 40m2s–40m13s.

10. Simbarashe Cha, interview with author, November 9, 2016. All further quotations from Cha are sourced from this interview.

11. Stuart Hall, "What is this 'Black' in Black Popular Culture?," in *Social Justice* 20, nos. 1+2: 109–10.

12. Brian Josephs, "Is Afropunk Fest No Longer Punk?," *Vice*, August 17, 2015 [vice.com; accessed February 22, 2016].

13. Kameir, "The True Story."

14. Josephs, "Is Afropunk Fest No Longer Punk?"

15. Ibid.

16. Josephs, "Is Afropunk Fest No Longer Punk?," and Hannah Giorgis, "Gentrifying Afropunk," *The New Yorker*, August 26, 2015 [newyorker.com; accessed February 22, 2016].

17. Hannah Giorgis, "Gentrifying Afropunk."

18. Afropunk.com: accessed August 11, 2017.

19. Ian F. Blair, "A Weekend at Afropunk," *Pitchfork*, September 1, 2015 [pitchfork. com; accessed January 15, 2016].

20. Josephs, "Is Afropunk Fest No Longer Punk?"

21. On the first day of the 2015 festival, Afropunk posted to its Instagram account seventeen blank images to represent the "trans lives senselessly murdered this year" (see www.instagram.com/afropunk). Also, see Tamerra Griffin, for example, for a discussion of the relationship between Afropunk and the trans-movement: "Relationship Between AfroPunk And The Trans Justice Movement Is Imperfect, But Necessary," *Buzzfeed*, August 24, 2015 [buzzfeed.com; accessed January 22, 2016].

22. Afropunk.com; accessed August 11, 2017.

23. Dick Hebdige, *Subculture: The Meaning of Style* (London: Methuen, 1979), 94.

24. Rob Fields, "The Evolution of Afropunk," *Forbes*, September 1, 2016 [accessed November 9, 2018]; "Afropunk and Black Diversity, and What Marketers Need to Know," *Forbes*, August 21, 2014 [accessed November 9, 2018].

25. Jeffrey Bowman of Reframe: The Brand, cited in Fields, "The Evolution of Afropunk".

26. Jocelyn Cooper, cited in Fields, "The Evolution of Afropunk".

27. Nicholas Gazin, Noisey Staff, "The Afro-Punk Festival Happened this Weekend in Brooklyn," *Noisey*, August 27, 2012 [noisey.com; accessed March 22, 2016].

28. Celia L. Smith, "Street Style: Afropunk Festival," *Essence*, August 31, 2012 [essence.com; accessed February 22, 2016; Claire Sulmers, "Afropunk Festival 2012," *The Black Blog: Vogue Italia*, August 29, 2012 [vogue.it, accessed February 22, 2016].

29. Claire Sulmers, "Afropunk Festival 2012." Ashley Mears has also described *Vogue Italia* as "edgy" within a discussion of editorial versus commercial fashion; Mears, *Pricing Beauty: The Making of a Fashion Model* (Berkeley, CA: University of California Press, 2011), 177.

30. Stuart Brumfitt, "Afropunk is the Brooklyn Festival for Outsider Kids Interested in the Other Black Experience," *i-D*, August 1, 2014 [i-d.vice.com; accessed February 22, 2016].

31. Carol Tulloch, *The Birth of Cool: Style Narratives of the African Diaspora* (London and New York: Bloomsbury, 2016), 5.

32. Tamar-kali Brown, cited in Spooner, *Afropunk: The Movie*, 22m5s–23m6s.

33. Ibid., 42m17s–42m27s.

34. Kobena Mercer, *Welcome to the Jungle: New Positions in Black Cultural Studies* (London and New York: Routledge, 1994), 105.

35. Ibid., 108.

36. Ibid.; emphasis in original.

37. Ibid., 114–15.

38. Ibid., 115.

39. Ibid., 119.

40. Ibid., 119–20.

41. Monica Miller, *Slaves to Fashion: Black Dandyism and the Styling of Black Diasporic Identity* (Durham, NC: Duke University Press, 2009).

42. Ibid., 11.

43. Ibid., 178.

44. Ibid., 180–1.

45. Mercer, *Welcome to the Jungle*, 115.

46. Miller, *Slaves to Fashion*, 7.

47. Hall, "What is this 'Black,'" 110.

48. Mercer, *Welcome to the Jungle*, 100.

49. Ibid., 101; emphasis in original.

50. Ibid., 97.

51. Ibid., 100.

52. Noliwe M. Rooks, *Hair Raising: Beauty, Culture, and African American Women* (New Brunswick, NJ: Rutgers University Press, 1996).

53. Ibid., 5.

54. Ibid., 3.

55. Ibid., 4.

56. Ibid.

57. Ibid., 5–6.

58. Tanisha Ford, *Liberated Threads: Black Women, Style, and the Global Politics of Soul* (Durham, NC: The University of North Carolina Press; 2015), 3.

59. Ibid., 1.

60. Ibid., 2.

61. Ibid., 2–3.

62. Ibid., 2.

63. Marjon Carlos, "The Bold and the *Beautiful*: The Best Street Style at Afropunk," Photographs by Ben Rasmussen, *Vogue*, August 25, 2015 [vogue.com; accessed May 6, 2016].

64. Diane Allford (photographer), "15 Stunning Photos of Black Women Slaying AFROPUNK," *Coloures*, August 26, 2015 [www.mycoloures.com; accessed May 6, 2016; link no longer working].

65. Afropunk, Instagram posting, August 22, 2015 [instagram.com; accessed August 15, 2016]. Sandra Bland was an African-American woman who died in

July 2015, while in police custody in Texas. She had been arrested days earlier for a routine traffic violation. The case was - and continues to be - a focal point for the Black Lives Matter movement. As this book goes to press in summer 2019, a recently released video from Ms. Bland's phone, taken during the arrest and depicting the officer threatening to tase her, has prompted calls to reopen the case.

66. Driely S. kindly allowed me to follow her around at the 2016 festival.

67. Tiffany M. Gill, "#TEAMNATURAL: Black Hair and the Politics of Community in Digital Media," in Nka: *Journal of Contemporary African Art* 37 (2015): 72; emphasis in original.

68. Marjon Carlos, "Forces of Nature: 28 Afropunk Hair Portraits by Artist Awol Erizku," Photographs by Awol Erizku, *Vogue.com*, August 26, 2014 [vogue.com; accessed February 22, 2016].

69. Deena Campbell, "Hair Street Style: AFROPUNK Fest," Photographs by Hannan Selah, *Essence*, August 29, 2014 [essence.com; accessed September 9, 2017].

70. Andrea Arterbery, "12 Natural Hairstyles from AfroPunk Paris to Try Now," *Teen Vogue*, 2016 [teenvogue.com; accessed September 9, 2017].

71. Ibid.

72. Madame C.J. Walker, cited in Rooks, *Hair Raising*, 58; emphasis in original.

73. Rooks, Ibid.

74. Ibid., 52.

75. Ibid., 61.

76. Tiffany M. Gill, *Beauty Shop Politics: African American Women's Activism in the Beauty Industry* (Urbana, IL: University of Illinois Press, 2010).

77. Ibid., 18.

78. Ibid., 2.

79. Ibid., 95.

80. Ibid., 107.

82. Ibid., 108.

82. Maxine Leeds Craig, *Ain't I a Beauty Queen?: Black Women, Beauty, and the Politics of Race* (Oxford and New York: Oxford University Press, 2002).

83. Ibid., 78.

84. Ibid., 92.

85. Ibid.

86. Jeff Stilson (dir.), *Good Hair* (Chris Rock Entertainment 2009).

87. Gill, "#TeamNatural."

88. Ibid., 70–1.

89. Ibid., 76.

90. Ibid.

91. Ibid., Gill cites here a 2011 Mintel hair-care report: "natural is the new normal in Black haircare."

92. Photographer at Afropunk Fest, interview with author, August 23, 2015. With the exception of my interviews with Simbarashe Cha and Driely S., all interviews with photographers and attendees of Afropunk Fest were held over the course of the 2015 festival, August 22 and 23, 2015.

93. Observation taken on August 22, 2015.

94. Zipporah Gene, "Black America, Please Stop Appropriating African Clothing and Tribal Marks. Yes, that Means Everyone at Afropunk Too," *Those People*; September 3, 2015; accessed January 24, 2016.

95. Ibid.; emphasis in original.

96. Ibid.

97. Ford, *Liberated Threads*, 4.

98. Stuart Hall, "Through the Prism of an Intellectual Life," in B. Meeks (ed.), *Culture, Politics, Race and Diaspora: The Thought of Stuart Hall* (Kingston: Ian Randle, 2007), np, digital edition.

99. Gene, "Black America"; emphasis in original.

100. Hall, "Through the Prism."

101. Regarding popular interest in "cultural appropriation," see Minh-Ha T. Pham's article "Fashion's Cultural-Appropriation Debate: Pointless," *The Atlantic*, May 15, 2014 [theatlantic.com, accessed August 19, 2014].

102. There are numerous blogposts and media essays about cultural appropriation at festivals. See, for example, Adrienne Keene, "Headdresses and Music Festivals Go Together Like PB and ... Racism?," *Native Appropriations*, June 2, 2010 [nativeappropriations.com, accessed August 3, 2015]; Priya Elan, "What Does the Return of the Celebrity Bindi Mean?," *The Guardian*, April 15, 2014 [theguardian.com, accessed April 20, 2015]; Neha Chandrachud, "No Headdresses is a Start, But Music Festivals Need to Ban Bindis," *Noisey*, July 28, 2015 [noisey.com, accessed July 28, 2015]; Brooke Shunatona, "I Made the Mistake of Wearing a Native American Headdress; Please Don't Wear One to Your Music Festival; Or Anywhere, Really," *Cosmopolitan*, April 10, 2015 [cosmopolitan.com, accessed August 3, 2015]; Theresa Avila, "Here Are the Cultural Appropriating Outfits It's Time to Retire For Good," *Mic*, June 17, 2015 [mic.com, accessed August 3, 2015].

103. See, for example, on fashion and orientalism: Dorinne Kondo, *About Face: Performing Race in Fashion and Theater* (London and New York: Routledge, 1997); Sandra Niessen, Ann Marie Leshkowich and Carla Jones (eds), *Re-Orienting Fashion: The Globalization of Asian Dress* (Oxford: Berg, 2003); and Thuy Linh Nguyen Tu, *The Beautiful Generation: Asian Americans and the Cultural Economy of Fashion* (Durham, NC: Duke University Press, 2011).

104. Elizabeth Wilson, *Bohemians: The Glamorous Outcasts* (New Brunswick, NJ: Rutgers University Press, 2000), 140.

105. Ibid.

106. Michael Wadleigh (dir.), *Woodstock: Three Days of Peace and Music 40th Anniversary Edition*, Warner Brother, 2009: 1970.

107. Ibid., 1h09m–1h09m22s.

108. Murray Lerner (dir.), *Message to Love*, BBC and Castle Music Pictures, 1997: 1970.

109. Ibid., 3m49s–4m23s.

110. Mel Stuart (dir.), *Wattstax*, Stax Records, 1973.

111. Ibid., 4m55s–5m11s.

112. Danny Scott, "Festivals!," *The Face*, May 1993: 58.

113. Ibid.

114. On the significance of dance culture to the British youth scene in the 1990s, see Sarah Thornton, *Club Cultures: Music, Media and Subcultural Capital* (Middletown, CT: Wesleyan University Press, 1996).

115. Scott, "Festivals!," 59.

116. Ibid., 62.

117. Ibid.

118. Alex Needham, "Coachella's Festival Fashion for Men: It's All about the Sexy Springbreak Cowboy," *The Guardian*, April 14, 2015 [theguardian.com, accessed April 20, 2015].

119. Anon, "Jay-Z Uses Wonderwall to Diss Noel," *The Guardian*, August 7, 2008 [theguardian.com, accessed July 26, 2015].

120. Jon Caramanica, interviewed in Ben Ratliff (host), "Popcast: Pitchfork Post-Mortem," *The New York Times*, July 26, 2013 [nytimes.com; accessed October 27, 2018], 27m2s–27m38s.

121. Ford, *Liberated Threads*, 4.

122. Mercer, *Welcome to the Jungle*, 107.

123. Ibid.

124. Tracy Clayton and Heben Nigatu, "31 Ridiculously Gorgeous People at Afropunk," *Buzzfeed*, August 25, 2014 [buzzfeed.com, accessed February 22, 2016].

125. Deidre Schoo (photographer), "Vibrantly Original Style at Afropunk Fest," *New York Times*, August 25, 2015 [nytimes.com, accessed February 22, 2016].

126. I take my cue here from Minh-Ha T. Pham's analysis of fashion blogger Susanna Lau, a.k.a. Susie Bubble. She writes, "Sameness and difference are carefully calibrated to simultaneously articulate the aspirational digital subject to be at once distinctive and familiar, particular and universal. Lau's gender and ethnic difference is contained and made familiar by her English fluency, Euro-

Notes

American cultural references, her British citizenship, and her style personality"
(255); "Susie Bubble is a Sign of the Times in *Feminist Media Studies* 13, no. 2
(2013). 245–67.

127. Brent Luvaas, *Street Style: An Ethnography of Fashion Blogging* (London:
Bloomsbury, 2016), 18.

128. Ibid., 7.

129. Sarah Thornton, *Club Cultures: Music, Media and Subcultural Capital*
(Middletown, CT: Wesleyan University Press, 1996), 117. See also Stanley Cohen,
Folk Devils and Moral Panics: The Creation of the Mods and Rockers. 3rd Edition
(London and New York: Routledge, 2002 [1972]).

130. Thornton, *Club Cultures*, 136.

131. Ibid., 137.

132. Ibid., 151.

133. Ibid.

134. This conclusion was based on observation of the Afropunk Instagram account
and website in Summer 2017.

135. Thornton, *Club Cultures*, 151.

136. Agnès Rocamora makes a similar categorization of the fashion media in
2009. She writes, "I see the fashion press as comprising both fashion
magazines and the fashion pages of newspapers and periodicals," *Fashioning
the City: Paris, Fashion and the Media* (London and New York: I.B. Tauris,
2009), 60.

137. Elizabeth Wissinger, *This Year's Model: Fashion, Media and the Making
of Glamour* (New York and London: New York University Press, 2015),
222.

138. Ibid., 231.

139. Ashley Mears, *Pricing Beauty: The Making of a Fashion Model* (Berkeley, CA:
University of California Press, 2011), 196.

140. Ibid.

141. Ibid., 199.

142. Wissinger, *This Year's Model*, 240.

143. Ane Lynge-Jorlén, *Niche Fashion Magazines: Changing the Shape of Fashion*
(London and New York: I.B. Tauris, 2017), 25.

144. Paul Jobling, *Fashion Spreads: Word and Image in Fashion Photography Since
1980* (Oxford and New York: Berg, 1999), 35.

145. Lynge-Jorlén, *Niche Fashion Magazines*, 25.

146. Caroline Evans, "Dreams That Only Money Can Buy ... Or, The Shy Tribe In
Flight from Discourse," in *Fashion Theory* 1, no. 2 (1997): 176.

147. Rocamora, *Fashioning the City*, 61.

148. Lynge-Jorlen, *Niche Fashion Magazines*, 28.

149. Jobling, *Fashion Spreads*, 8.

150. Ibid.

151. Ibid., 113.

152. Anna König, "Glossy Words: An Analysis of Fashion Writing in British *Vogue*," in *Fashion Theory* 10, nos. 1 and 2 (2006).

153. Ibid., 205.

154. Ibid., 215.

155. Ibid., 220.

156. Pierre Bourdieu, *The Field of Cultural Production: Essays on Art and Literature* (London: Polity, 1993). See Lynge-Jorlén *Niche Fashion Magazines* on the application of Bourdieu's field theory within analysis of editorial voice and market position within the field of fashion media.

157. Kara Jesella and Marisa Meltzer, *How Sassy Changed My Life: A Love Letter to the Greatest Teen Magazine of All Time* (New York: Farrar, Straus and Giroux, 2007).

158. Ibid. In a discussion of writer Christina Kelly, Jesella and Meltzer explain that she was not "completely uninterested in the conventional trappings of womanliness. 'I have a pathological fear of cellulite and have stooped to purchasing all kinds of ridiculous products to rid myself of it,' she admitted in one arguably self-loathing 'We Try It'" (69).

159. Brooke Erin Duffy, *Remake, Remodel: Women's Magazines in the Digital Age* (Urbana, IL: University of Illinois Press, 2013).

160. Ibid., 76.

161. Ibid., 68.

162. See, for example, Marjon Carlos on Victory Jones and Tori Elizabeth (hosts), "Ep 11: Representation Matters ft. Marjon Carlos," The Colored Girl (podcast), April 16, 2019, 20m39s-22m38s; [listennotes.com; accessed July 8, 2019].

163. Hebdige, *Subculture*, 94.

164. Ibid., 98.

165. Marjon Carlos, "Why We Love the Showstopping Style of Afropunk's Leading Ladies," *Vogue*, August 21, 2015 [vogue.com; accessed January 15, 2016].

166. Ibid.; see also Mackenzie Wagoner, "5 Beauties Who Answer to Afropunk's Rebellions Call," *Vogue*, August 21, 2015 [vogue.com, accessed January 15, 2016].

167. Mackenzie Wagoner, "Exclusive! SZA Reveals Her New Copper Hair Color Transformation," *Vogue*, March 18, 2015 [vogue.com, accessed January 22, 2016].

168. Miller, *Slaves to Fashion*, 11.

169. Mercer, *Welcome to the Jungle*, 119.

170. Yomi Abiola, "This is Afropunk," Photography by Joanna Totolici, video by Marco Vacchi, Vogue Italia, August 26, 2015 [vogue.it; accessed January 20, 2016].

171. Melina Matsoukas (dir.), *Losing You*, performed by Solange Knowles, (Terrible Records, 2012).

172. Driely S., interviews with the author, August 2, 2016 and November 7, 2016. All further quotations from S. are sourced from these interviews.

173. Mikael Wood, "Beyoncé Came to Coachella, and Disrupted its Entire Culture," *Los Angeles Times*, April 15, 2018 [latimes.com, accessed October 17, 2018].

174. Marques Harper, "Less Boho Chic, More Streetwear Style on the Coachella Fashion Scene for 2018," *Los Angeles Times*, April 14, 2018 [latimes.com, accessed October 17, 2018].

175. See, for example, Jessica Andrews, "Pyer Moss Designer Kerby Jean-Raymond Hates Being Labeled Streetwear," *Elle*, February 12, 2016 [elle.com; accessed October 17, 2018].

Chapter 5

1. Pierre Bourdieu, *Distinction: A Social Critique of the Judgement of Taste* (London and New York: Routledge, 1984).

2. Angela McRobbie, "Second-hand Dresses and the Role of the Ragmarket," in A. McRobbie (ed.) *Zoot Suits and Second-hand Dresses: An Anthology of Fashion and Music* (Basingstoke: Macmillan, 1989).

3. Ibid., 24. In a later essay, she reflects on this critical contribution to subcultural theory, writing, "The assumption implicit in subcultural theory was that those who did this sort of thing were simply 'hustlers' who pushed their way into the subculture from outside, making a profit from something which in reality had no interest in or connection to commerce. As a result music and style and other related activities sprang onto the subcultural theory stage as though from nowhere," in "Shut Up and Dance: Youth Culture and Changing Modes of Femininity," in A. McRobbie, *Postmodernism and Popular Culture* (London: Routledge, 1994), 156.

4. Ibid.

5. Ibid., 27.

6. Ibid., 38.

7. Karen Tranberg Hansen, "Secondhand Clothing and Africa: Global Fashion Influences, Local Dress Agency, and Policy Issues," in S. Black *et al. The Handbook of Fashion Studies* (London: Bloomsbury, 2013), 412.

8. McRobbie, "Second-hand Dresses," 36.

9. Ibid.

10. Steven Bethell, interview with author, August 28, 2014. All further quotations from Bethell are sourced from this interview.

11. Jenna Rossi-Camus, interview with the author, June 16, 2009. All further quotations from Rossi-Camus are sourced from this interview.

12. Louise Crewe, Nicky Gregson, and Kate Brooks, "The Discursivities of Difference: Retro Retailers and the Ambiguities of 'the Alternative,'" in *Journal of Consumer Culture* 3, no. 1 (2003): 75.

13. Amber Butchart and Rob Flowers, interview with the author, June 16, 2014. All further quotations from Butchart are sourced from this interview.

14. Sean Nixon, *Hard Looks: Masculinities, Spectatorship & Contemporary Consumption* (New York: Palgrave Macmillan, 1996), 52.

15. Alexandra Palmer, "Vintage Whores and Vintage Virgins: Second Hand Fashion in the Twenty-first Century," in A. Palmer and H. Clark (eds) *Old Clothes, New Looks: Second Hand Fashion* (London and New York: Berg, 2005), 203.

16. Louise Crewe, Nicky Gregson, and Kate Brooks, "Alternative Retail Spaces," in Roger Lee *et al.* (eds) *Alternative Economic Spaces* (London: Sage, 2003), 98.

17. Nicky Gregson and Louise Crewe, *Second-hand Cultures* (Oxford and New York: Berg, 2003), 83.

18. Karen Tranberg Hansen, *Salaula: The World of Secondhand Clothing and Zambia* (Chicago, IL: University of Chicago Press, 2000); "Secondhand Clothing and Africa."

19. Hansen, "Secondhand Clothing and Africa," 416.

20. Ibid.

21. Heike Jenss, "Dressed in History: Retro Styles and the Construction of Authenticity in Youth Culture," in *Fashion Theory* 8, no. 4 (2004): 388.

22. Marilyn DeLong, Barbara Heinemann, and Kathryn Reiley, "Hooked on Vintage!," in *Fashion Theory* 9, no. 1 (2005): 39.

23. Palmer, "Vintage Whores and Vintage Virgins."

24. Ibid., 197.

25. McRobbie, "Second-hand Dresses," 29.

26. Charlotte Cotton, *Imperfect Beauty: The Making of Contemporary Fashion Photographs* (London: V&A Publications, 2000), 76 and 84.

27. Ibid., 76.

28. Crewe *et al.*, "Alternative Retail Spaces," 90–1.

29. Anon, British *Vogue*, September 2009: 208.

30. Anna König, "Glossy Words: An Analysis of Fashion Writing in British *Vogue*," in *Fashion Theory* 10, no. 1 (2006): 212.

Notes

31. Ibid.

32. Anon, British *Vogue*, September 2009: 239.

33. Crewe *et al.*, "Alternative Retail Spaces," 90.

34. Crewe *et al.*, "Discursivities of Difference," 71.

35. Ibid., 77.

36. Ibid., 77–8.

37. Ibid., 78–9.

38. Anon, "Cycle of Vintage," *Beyond Retro* [beyondretro.com; accessed December 4, 2015].

39. In the UK, in addition to the flagship Cheshire Street store, there are also Beyond Retro shops in Dalston (London), Soho (London), and Brighton. In Sweden, there are two shops in Göteborg, three in Stockholm, and one in Malmö.

40. Hansen, *Salaula*, 18.

41. Ibid., 104; see also Lucy Norris, "Trade and Transformations of Secondhand Clothing: Introduction," in *Textile: The Journal of Cloth and Culture* 10, no. 2 (2012).

42. Ibid.

43. Ibid., 113, 123, 254. A second controversy surrounding commercial firms has to do with impact on importing countries. As Olumide Abimbola and Andrew Brooks have explored separately, importers have little, if any, control over the bales they receive. Within an analysis of Mozambican vendors in Maputo, Brooks argues that "there is no direct coordination between retail and other upstream traders in the trading network beyond a price signal" (228), which has "led to vendors' frustrations with the seemingly random provision of high- and low-quality clothing bales" (235). Abimbola shows how, in order to overcome this impasse, Igbo importers in Benin send their apprentices to work for free in the British grading firms, from whom they import, so that they can see—and influence—what goes into the bales they import. Olumide Abimbola, "The International Trade in Secondhand Clothing: Managing Information Asymmetry between West African and British Traders," in *Textile: The Journal of Clothing and Culture* 10, no. 2 (2012); Andrew Brooks, "Riches from Rags or Persistent Poverty? The Working Lives of Secondhand Clothing Vendors in Maputo, Mozambique," in *Textile: The Journal of Cloth and Culture* 10, no. 2 (2012).

44. Ibid., 123.

45. Jana Hawley, "Digging for Diamonds: A Conceptual Framework for Understanding Reclaimed Textile Products," in *Clothing & Textiles* 24, no. 3 (2006): 264.

46. Ibid., 266.

47. Julie Botticello, "Between Classification, Objectification, and Perception: Processing Secondhand Clothing for Recycling and Reuse," in *Textile: The Journal of Cloth and Culture* 10, no. 2 (2012).

48. Ibid., 179.

49. Ibid., 168.

50. Observation on June 27, 2014.

51. Beyond Retro, "Festival Wear," *Beyond Retro*, August 4, 2017 [beyondretro.com; accessed October 7, 2017].

52. Dean Sidaway, interview with the author, August 14, 2014.

53. On upcycling and design, see Victoria Rovine, "Working the Edge: XULY.BET's Recycled Clothing," in A. Palmer and H. Clark (eds) *Old Clothes, New Looks*, op cit. There are many books that try to integrate a concern for production of textiles and garments, use of garments, and disposal/recycling of worn garments. Amongst others, these include Sandy Black, *Eco-Chic: The Fashion Paradox* (London: Black Dog, 2008); Black, *The Sustainable Fashion Handbook* (London: Thames & Hudson, 2012); Kate Fletcher, *Fashion and Sustainability Design for Change* (London: Laurence King, 2012); Fletcher, *Sustainable Fashion and Textiles: Design Journeys* (London and New York: Routledge, 2014); Alison Gwilt and Timo Rissanen (eds), *Shaping Sustainable Fashion: Changing The Way We Make and Use Clothes* (London and New York: Routledge, 2011); Janet Hethorn and Connie Ulaseqicz, *Sustainable Fashion: What's Next? A Conversation about Issues, Practices and Possibilities* (New York: Fairchild Books, 2015). There are also scholarly articles concerned to explore consumers' roles within waste reduction. These include: Kathryn Reiley and Marilyn DeLong, "A Consumer Vision for Sustainable Fashion Practice," in *Fashion Practice* 3, no. 1 (2011); Kristy A. Janigo and Juanjuan Wu, "Collaborative Redesign of Used Clothes as a Sustainable Fashion Solution and Potential Business Opportunity," in *Fashion Practice* 7, no. 1 (2015).

54. Hazel Clark, "SLOW + FASHION—an Oxymoron—or a Promise for the Future ...?," in *Fashion Theory* 12, no. 4 (2008).

55. Ibid., 434.

56. Ibid., 438.

57. Ibid., 440.

58. "SKU" is the abbreviation of "stock keeping unit." SKUs are used within the inventory of clothing or other products. A specific SKU refers to a specific item.

59. Beyond Retro, "Beyond Retro Label: The Story," *BeyondRetro.com*, April 24, 2015 [beyondretro.com; accessed October 7, 2017].

60. McRobbie, "Second-hand Dresses," 30.

61. Angela McRobbie, *British Fashion Design: Rag Trade or Image Industry?* (London: Routledge, 1998), 8.

62. Ibid., 9.

63. Adham Faramawy, interview with author, June 16, 2009..

64. Anon, "Wasteland Rental Policy," *Wasteland* [shopwasteland.com; accessed December 15, 2015].

Notes

65. Crewe *et al.*, "Alternative Retail Spaces," 102.

66. Angela McRobbie, *Be Creative: Making a Living in the New Culture Industries* (Cambridge and Malden, MA: Polity, 2016), 7–8.

67. Ibid., 8.

Conclusion

1. David Hesmondhalgh, "Indie: The Institutional Politics and Aesthetics of a Popular Music Genre," in *Cultural Studies* 13, no. 1 (1999): 34.

2. Stuart Hall, "What is this 'Black' in Black Popular Culture?" in *Social Justice* 20, nos. 1+2 (1993): 106–7.

3. Stuart Hall, "Through the Prism of an Intellectual Life," in B. Meeks (ed.) *Culture, Politics, Race and Diaspora: The Thought of Stuart Hall* (Kingston: Ian Randle, 2007), np, digital edition.

BIBLIOGRAPHY

List of interviewees

Adham Faramawy, Former employee Beyond Retro
Amber Butchart, Former employee Beyond Retro
Christian Joy, Costume designer
Dean Sidaway, Former employee Beyond Retro
Doug Brod, Editor-in-Chief at *Spin* magazine from 2006 to 2011
Driely S., Photographer
Jenna Rossi-Camus, Former employee Beyond Retro
Michelle Egiziano, Photo Editor at *Spin* magazine from 2006 to 2011
Rob Flowers, Former employee Beyond Retro
Simbarashe Cha, Photographer
Steven Bethell, Owner Beyond Retro

Magazines

Art & Music: Spring 2009
Dazed & Confused: Issue 14, 1995
Grazia: April 18, 2005; July 11, 2005
i-D: October 1986; December 1993; June 1994; October 1994; June 1995; September 2001
Melody Maker: September 12, 1992; December 21/28, 1996
New Musical Express (NME): May 22, 1993; November 6, 1993; November 20, 1993; January 7, 1995; February 18, 1995; August 1, 1998; June 30, 2001; December 22/29, 2001; May 18, 2002; November 29, 2003; January 31, 2004; November 18, 2006
Nylon Guys: September 2009
Sounds: July 5, 1986; August 30, 1986; December 20/27, 1986; December 24/31, 1988; October 27, 1990; December 15, 1990
The Face: March 1987; March 1993; May 1993; March 1994; April 1994; May 1994; May 1995; July 2001
Vogue (UK): April 1993; August 1994

Books and Articles

Abimbola, Olumide. "The International Trade in Secondhand Clothing: Managing Information Asymmetry between West African and British Traders." *Textile: The Journal of Clothing and Culture* 10, no. 2 (2012): 184–99.

Abiola, Yomi. "This is Afropunk." Joanna Totolici (photographer). Marco Vacchi (videographer). *Vogue Italia*, August 26, 2015.

Agosta, Michael and Marcy Medina. "Alternative Styling." *WWD*, September 8, 2005.

Allford, Diane (photographer). "15 Stunning Photos of Black Women Slaying AFROPUNK." *Coloures*, August 26, 2015.

Andrews, Jessica. "Pyer Moss Designer Kerby Jean-Raymond Hates Being Labeled Streetwear." *Elle*. February 12, 2016.

Arterbery, Andrea, "12 Natural Hairstyles From AfroPunk Paris To Try Now." *Teen Vogue*, June 9, 2016.

Avila, Theresa. "Here Are the Cultural Appropriating Outfits It's Time to Retire For Good." *Mic*, June 17, 2015.

Bannister, Matthew. *White Boys, White Noise: Masculinities and 1980s Indie Guitar Rock*. Hampshire and Burlington, VT: Ashgate, 2006.

Barnard, Malcolm (ed.). *Fashion Theory: A Reader*. London and New York: Routledge, 1997.

Bartky, Sandra L. *Femininity and Domination: Studies in the Phenomenology of Oppression*. London and New York: Routledge, 1990.

Berry, Jess. "Flâneurs of Fashion 2.0." *SCAN: Journal of Media Arts Culture* (2010).

Best, Tamara. "A Nigerian Artist Who Uses the Skin as His Canvas." *New York Times*, November 30, 2016.

Black, Sandy. *Eco-Chic: The Fashion Paradox*. London: Black Dog, 2008.

—— *The Sustainable Fashion Handbook*. London: Thames & Hudson, 2012.

Blair, Ian F. "A Weekend at Afropunk." *Pitchfork*, September 1, 2015.

Blanks, Tim. "Runway: Fall 2005 Menswear: Dior Homme." *Vogue*, January 30, 2005.

—— "Runway: Spring 2006 Menswear: Dior Homme." *Vogue*, July 7, 2005.

—— "Runway: Spring 2013 Ready-to-wear: Saint Laurent." *Vogue*, September 30, 2012.

Boltanski, Luc and Eve Chiapello. *The New Spirit of Capitalism*. London: Verso, 2005.

Bordo, Susan. *Unbearable Weight: Feminism, Western Culture, and the Body*. Berkeley, CA: University of California Press, 1993.

Borrelli-Perrson, Laird. "Festival Dressing Done Right: 16 Inspirational Looks from the *Vogue* Archive." *Vogue*, April 16, 2014.

Botticello, Julie. "Between Classification, Objectification, and Perception: Processing Secondhand Clothing for Recycling and Reuse." *Textile: The Journal of Cloth and Culture* 10, no. 2 (2012): 164–83.

Bourdieu, Pierre. *Distinction: A Social Critique of the Judgement of Taste*. R. Nice (trans), London and New York: Routledge, 1984.

—— *The Field of Cultural Production*. Ed. R. Johnson. Cambridge and Oxford: Polity, 1993.

Brooks, Andrew. "Riches from Rags or Persistent Poverty? The Working Lives of Secondhand Clothing Vendors in Maputo, Mozambique." *Textile: The Journal of Cloth and Culture* 10, no. 2 (2012): 222–37.

Brumfitt, Stuart. "Afropunk is the Brooklyn Festival for Outsider Kids Interested in the Other Black Experience." *i-D*, August 1, 2014.

Burchill, Julie and Tony Parsons. *"The Boy Looked At Johnny": The Obituary of Rock and Roll*. London: Faber & Faber, 1987.

Butler, Judith. *Gender Trouble: Feminism and the Subversion of Identity*. *10th Anniversary Edition*. London and New York: Routledge, 1999 [1990].

Buttolph, Angela. *Kate Moss Style: Inside the World's Most Famous Wardrobe*. London: Random House, 2009.

Campbell, Deena. "Hair Street Style: AFROPUNK Fest." Photographs by Hannan Selah, *Essence*, August 29, 2014.

Carlos, Marjon. "Forces of Nature: 28 Afropunk Hair Portraits by Artist Awol Erizku." Photographs by Awol Erizku, *Vogue.com*, August 26, 2014.

—— "Why We Love the Showstopping Style of Afropunk's Leading Ladies." *Vogue*, August 21, 2015.

—— "The Bold and the *Beautiful*: The Best Street Style at Afropunk." Photographs by Ben Rasmussen, *Vogue*, August 25, 2015.

Cartner-Morley, Jess. "Field Dressing for Festivals." *The Guardian*, May 7, 2009.

—— "What to Wear at the Music Festivals." *The Guardian*, April 20, 2010.

Cartner-Morley, Jess, Caterina Monzani, and Ekaterina Ochagavia. "Glastonbury 2014: How to Dress for Festivals—Video." *The Guardian*, June 25, 2014.

Cavanagh, David. *The Creation Records Story: My Magpie Eyes are Hungry for the Prize*. London: Virgin Publishing, 2001.

Chandrachud, Neha. "No Headdresses is a Start, But Music Festivals Need to Ban Bindis." *Noisey*, July 28, 2015.

Chauncey, George. *Gay New York: Gender, Urban Culture, and the Making of the Gay Male World 1890–1940*. New York: Basic Books, 1994.

Clark, Hazel. "SLOW + FASHION—an Oxymoron—or a Promise for the Future . . . ?" *Fashion Theory* 12, no. 4 (2008): 427–46.

Clarke, Gary. "Defending Ski-Jumpers: A Critique of Theories of Youth Sub-cultures." Birmingham: Centre for Contemporary Cultural Studies, University of Birmingham, 1982.

Clarke, John. "Style." In *Resistance Through Rituals: Youth Subcultures in Post-war Britain*, edited by Stuart Hall and Tony Jefferson, 175–91. London: Routledge, 1993 [1976].

Clarke, John, Stuart Hall, Tony Jefferson and Brian Roberts. "Subcultures, Cultures and Class." In *Resistance Through Rituals: Youth Subcultures in Post-war Britain*. 2nd Edition, edited by Stuart Hall and Tony Jefferson, 3–59. London and New York: Routledge, 2006.

Clayton, Tracy and Heben Nigatu. "31 Ridiculously Gorgeous People at Afropunk." *Buzzfeed*, August 25, 2014.

Cohen, Stanley. *Folk Devils and Moral Panics: The Creation of the Mods and Rockers*. *3rd Edition*. London and New York: Routledge, 2002 [1972].

Connell, Catherine. "Fashionable Resistance: Queer 'Fa(t)shion' Blogging as Counterdiscourse." *WSQ: Women's Studies Quarterly* 41, nos. 1 & 2 (2013): 209–24.

Corrigan, Susan. "Boys R Us." *i-D* (June 1995): 20–4, 26.

Cotton, Charlotte. *Imperfect Beauty: The Making of Contemporary Fashion Photographs*. London: V&A Publications, 2000.

Craig, Maxine Leeds. *Ain't I a Beauty Queen?: Black Women, Beauty, and the Politics of Race*. Oxford and New York: Oxford University Press, 2002.

Crewe, Ben. *Representing Men: Cultural Production and Producers in Men's Magazine Market*. Oxford and New York: Berg, 2003.

Crewe, Louise, Nicky Gregson, and Kate Brooks. "Alternative Retail Spaces." In *Alternative Economic Spaces*, edited by Roger Lee, Andrew Leyshon and Colin C. Williams, 74–106. London: Sage, 2003.

—— "The Discursivities of Difference: Retro Retailers and the Ambiguities of 'the Alternative.'" *Journal of Consumer Culture* 3, no. 1 (2003): 61–82.

Crowhurst, Anna-Marie. "Coachella: How to Get that Festival Look." *The Guardian*, April 18, 2013.

Daems, Jim (ed.). *The Makeup of RuPaul's Drag Race: Essays of the Queen of Reality Shows*. Jefferson, NC: McFarland & Company, 2014.

Davies, Helen. "All Rock and Roll is Homosocial: The Representation of Women in the British Rock Music Press." *Popular Music* 20, no. 3 (2001): 301–19.

DeLong, Marilyn, Barbara Heinemann, and Kathryn Reiley. "Hooked on Vintage!" *Fashion Theory* 9, no. 1 (2005): 23–42.

Duffy, Brooke Erin. *Remake, Remodel: Women's Magazines in the Digital Age*. Urbana, IL: University of Illinois Press, 2013.

Durham, Aisha. "'Check on it': Beyoncé, Southern Booty, and Black Femininities in Music Video." *Feminist Media Studies* 12, no. 1 (2012): 35–49.

Dyer, Richard. *The Matter of Images: Essays on Representation*. London and New York: Routledge, 1993.

Elan, Priya. "What Does the Return of the Celebrity Bindi Mean?" *The Guardian*, April 15, 2014.

Entwistle, Joanne. "From Catwalk to Catalog: Male Fashion Models, Masculinity, and Identity." In *Cultural Bodies: Ethnography and Theory*, edited by Helen Thomas and Jamilah Ahmed, 55–75. Oxford: Blackwell Publishing, 2004.

Entwistle, Joanne and Agnès Rocamora. "The Field of Fashion Materialized: A Study of London Fashion Week." *Sociology* 40, no. 4 (2006): 735–50.

Evans, Caroline. "Dreams That Only Money Can Buy ... or, The Shy Tribe In Flight from Discourse." *Fashion Theory* 1, no. 2 (1997): 169–88.

Evans, Caroline and Lorraine Gamman. "The Gaze Revisited, or Reviewing Queer Viewing." In *A Queer Romance: Lesbians, Gay Men and Popular Culture*, edited by Paul Burston and Colin Richardson, 13–56. London and New York: Routledge, 1995.

Fields, Rob. "Afropunk and Black Diversity, and What Marketers Need to Know." *Forbes*, August 21, 2014.

—— "The Evolution of Afropunk." *Forbes*, September 1, 2016.

Findlay, Rosie. "The Short, Passionate, and Close-knit History of Personal Style Blogs." *Fashion Theory* 19, no. 2 (2015): 157–78.

Fletcher, Kate. *Fashion and Sustainability Design for Change*. London: Laurence King, 2012.

—— *Sustainable Fashion and Textiles: Design Journeys*. London and New York: Routledge, 2014.

Flügel, J.C. "The Great Masculine Renunciation and its Causes." In *The Rise of Fashion*, edited by Daniel Purdy, 102–8. Minneapolis: University of Minnesota Press, 2004.

Foley, Bridget. *Marc Jacobs*. New York: Assouline Publishing, 2004.

Fonarow, Wendy. *Empire of Dirt: The Aesthetics and Rituals of British Indie Music*. Middletown, CT: Wesleyan University Press, 2006.

—— "Ask the Indie Professor: Why the Big Fuss over Coachella Festival?" *The Guardian*, April 13, 2011.

Ford, Tanisha. *Liberated Threads: Black Women, Style, and the Global Politics of Soul*. Durham, NC: The University of North Carolina Press, 2015.

Foucault, Michel. "Technologies of the Self." In *Technologies of the Self: A Seminar with Michel Foucault*, edited by Luther H. Martin, Huck Gutman and Patrick H. Hutton, 16-49. Amherst: University of Massachusetts Press, 1988.

—— *Discipline and Punish*. London: Penguin, 1991 [1977].

—— *The Use of Pleasure. The History of Sexuality Volume 2*. London: Penguin, 1985.

—— *Ethics: Subjectivity and Truth*. London: Penguin, 2000.

—— *Archaeology of Knowledge*. London and New York: Routledge Classics, 2002.

Freeman, Hadley. "The Right Notes." *The Guardian*, February 4, 2005.

—— "The World's Muddiest Catwalk." *The Guardian*, June 24, 2005.

—— "Are You a Pete or are You a Bill?" *The Guardian*, July 11, 2005.

—— "Dior Homme." *10 Men*, A/W 2005.

—— "Ask Hadley." *The Guardian*, June 20, 2010.

—— "Since When were Music Festivals Al Fresco Fashion Shows?" *The Guardian*, April 27, 2015.

Frith, Simon. "Afterthoughts." In *On Record: Rock, Pop & The Written Word*, edited by Simon Frith and Andrew Goodwin, 419-24. London and New York: Routledge, 1990.

—— "Fragments of a Sociology of Rock Criticism." In *Pop Music and the Press*, edited by Steve Jones, 235-46. Philadelphia: Temple University Press, 2002.

Frith, Simon and Howard Horne. *Art Into Pop*. London and New York: Methuen, 1987.

Frith, Simon and Angela McRobbie. "Rock and Sexuality." In *On Record: Rock, Pop & The Written Word*, edited by Simon Frith and Andrew Goodwin, 371-89. London and New York: Routledge, 1990.

Gamman, Lorraine and Margaret Marshment (eds). *The Female Gaze: Women as Viewers of Popular Culture*. London: Real Comet Press, 1988.

Gazin, Nicholas. "The Afro-Punk Festival Happened this Weekend in Brooklyn." *Noisey*, August 27, 2012.

Gene, Zipporah. "Black America, Please Stop Appropriating African Clothing and Tribal Marks. Yes, that Means Everyone at Afropunk Too." *Those People*, September 3, 2015.

Gill, Rosalind. "Power and the Production of Subjects: A Genealogy of the New Man and the New Lad." In *Masculinity and Men's Lifestyle Magazines*, edited by Bethan Benthwell, 34-56. Oxford and Malden, MA: Wiley Blackwell, 2003.

Gill, Tiffany M. *Beauty Shop Politics: African American Women's Activism in the Beauty Industry*. Urbana, IL: University of Illinois Press, 2010.

—— "#TEAMNATURAL: Black Hair and the Politics of Community in Digital Media." *Nka: Journal of Contemporary African Art* 37 (2015): 70-9.

Giorgis, Hannah. "Gentrifying Afropunk." *The New Yorker*, August 26, 2015.

Goffman, Erving. *The Presentation of Self in Everyday Life*. London: Anchor, 1959.

Golfar, Fiona. "Mr. Big Shot." British *Vogue*, September 2009.

Goodman, Lizzy. *Meet Me in the Bathroom: Rebirth and Rock and Roll in New York City 2001–2011*. New York: Dey Street Books, 2017.

Gregson, Nicky and Louise Crewe. *Second-hand Cultures*. Oxford and New York: Berg, 2003.

Griffin, Tamerra. "Relationship between AfroPunk And The Trans Justice Movement is Imperfect, But Necessary." *Buzzfeed*, August 24, 2015.

Grossberg, Lawrence. "The Media Economy of Rock Culture: Cinema, Post-modernity and Authenticity." In *Sound and Vision: The Music Video Reader*, edited by Simon Frith, Andrew Goodwin, and Lawrence Grossberg, 185–209. London and New York: Routledge, 1993.

Gudmundsson, Gester, Ulf Lindberg, Morten Michelsen, and Hans Weisethaunet. "Brit Crit: Turning Points in British Rock Criticism, 1960–1990." In *Pop Music and the Press*, edited by Steve Jones, 41–64. Philadelphia: Temple University Press, 2002.

Gwilt, Alison and Timo Rissanen (eds). *Shaping Sustainable Fashion: Changing The Way We Make and Use Clothes*. London and New York: Routledge, 2011.

Hall, Stuart. "What is This 'Black' in Black Popular Culture?" *Social Justice* 20, nos. 1 & 2 (Spring–Summer 1993): 104–14.

—— "Notes on Deconstructing 'the Popular.'" In *Cultural Theory and Popular Culture: A Reader, 3rd Edition*, edited by John Storey, 477–87. Harlow: Prentice Hall, 2006.

—— "Through the Prism of an Intellectual Life." In *Culture, Politics, Race and Diaspora: The Thought of Stuart Hall*, edited by Brian Meeks, np digital edition. Kingston: Ian Randle, 2007.

Hall, Stuart and Tony Jefferson (eds). *Resistance Through Rituals: Youth Subcultures in Post-war Britain*. London: Routledge, 1993 [1976].

Hansen, Karen Tranberg. *Salaula: The World of Secondhand Clothing and Zambia*. Chicago, IL: University of Chicago Press, 2000.

—— "Secondhand Clothing and Africa: Global Fashion Influences, Local Dress Agency, and Policy Issues." In *The Handbook of Fashion Studies*, edited by Sandy Black, Amy de la Haye, Joanne Entwistle, Agnès Rocamora, Regina A. Root, and Helen Thomas, 408–25. London: Bloomsbury, 2013.

Harper, Marques. "Less Boho Chic, More Streetwear Style on the Coachella Fashion Scene for 2018." *Los Angeles Times*, April 14, 2018.

Harris, Anita. *Future Girl: Young Women in the Twenty-First Century*. London and New York: Routledge, 2003.

Harris, John. *The Last Party: Britpop, Blair and the Demise of English Rock*. London and New York: Fourth Estate, 2003.

Hawley, Jana. "Digging for Diamonds: A Conceptual Framework for Understanding Reclaimed Textile Products." *Clothing & Textiles* 24, no. 3 (2006): 262–75.

Hebdige, Dick. *Subculture: The Meaning of Style*. London: Methuen, 1979.

Hesmondhalgh, David. "Indie: The Institutional Politics and Aesthetics of a Popular Music Genre." *Cultural Studies* 13, no. 1 (1999): 34–61.

Hethorn, Janet and Connie Ulaseqicz. *Sustainable Fashion: What's Next? A Conversation about Issues, Practices and Possibilities*. New York: Fairchild Books, 2015.

Hogan, Michael. "The 10 Best Kate Moss Moments." *The Guardian*, January 11, 2014.

Hornby, Nick. *High Fidelity*. New York: Riverhead Books, 1996.

Horyn, Cathy. "That Man From Saint Laurent." *New York Times*, August 10, 1999.

—— "Where the Boys Are Is Where the Girls Should Be." *New York Times*, February 1, 2005.

Huq, Rupa. *Beyond Subculture: Pop, Youth and Identity in a Postcolonial World*. London and New York: Routledge, 2006.

Hussein, Wandera. "Supreme's James Jebbia wins Menswear Designer of the Year at the 2018 CFDA Awards." *Fader*, June 5, 2018.

James, Alex. *Bit of a Blur*. London: Abacus, 2008.

Jameson, Fredric. *Postmodernism: or, The Cultural Logic of Late Capitalism*. Durham, NC: Duke University Press, 1991.

Janigo, Kristy A. and Juanjuan Wu. "Collaborative Redesign of Used Clothes as a Sustainable Fashion Solution and Potential Business Opportunity." *Fashion Practice 7*, no. 1 (2015): 75–97.

Jenss, Heike. "Dressed in History: Retro Styles and the Construction of Authenticity in Youth Culture." *Fashion Theory* 8, no. 4 (2004): 387–403.

Jesella, Kara and Marisa Meltzer. *How Sassy Changed My Life: A Love Letter to the Greatest Teen Magazine of All Time*. New York: Farrar, Straus and Giroux, 2007.

Jobling, Paul. *Fashion Spreads: Word and Image in Fashion Photography Since 1980*. Oxford and New York: Berg, 1999.

Jones, Cliff. "Looking for a New New England." *The Face*, May 1994: 40–6.

Jones, Steve and Kevin Featherly, "Re-viewing Rock Writing: Narratives of Popular Music Criticism." In *Pop Music and the Press*, edited by Steve Jones, 19–40. Philadelphia: Temple University Press, 2002.

Jones Victory, and Tori Elizabeth (hosts). "Ep 11: Representation Matters ft. Marjon Carlos." In *The Colored Girl* (podcast). Airdate: April 16, 2019. listennotes.com, 2019.

Josephs, Brian. "Is Afropunk Fest No Longer Punk?" *Vice*, August 17, 2015.

Kameir, Rawiya. "The True Story of How Afropunk Turned A Message Board Into A Movement." *Fader*, August 21, 2015.

Kearney, Mary Celeste. "The Missing Links: Riot Grrrl—Feminism—Lesbian Culture." In *Sexing the Groove: Popular Music and Gender*, edited by Sheila Whiteley, 207–29. London and New York: Routledge, 1997.

Keene, Adrienne. "Headdresses and Music Festivals Go Together Like PB and … Racism?" *Native Appropriations*, June 2, 2010.

Klosterman, Chuck. "Gang of Five." *Spin*, December 2003: 69–74.

Knecht, Emily (photographer). "The Best Streetstyle Looks from Coachella 2015." *Vogue*, April 13, 2015.

Knee, Sam. *A Scene In Between: Tripping through the Fashions of UK Indie Music 1980–1988*. London: Cicada Books, 2013.

—— *Untypical Girls: Styles and sounds of the transatlantic indie revolution*. London: Cicada Books, 2017.

Bibliography

Kondo, Dorinne. *About Face: Performing Race in Fashion and Theater*. London and New York: Routledge, 1997.

König, Anna. "Glossy Words: An Analysis of Fashion Writing in British *Vogue*." *Fashion Theory* 10, nos. 1 and 2 (2006): 205–24.

Laverne, Lauren. "Lauren Laverne on Fashion: What to Wear to a Festival." *The Guardian*, June 23, 2013.

Lerner, Murray (dir.). *Message to Love*. BBC and Castle Music Pictures, 1997: 1970.

Lewis, Reina. "Looking Good: The Lesbian Gaze and Fashion Imagery." In *The Visual Cultures Reader*. 2nd Edition, edited by Nicholas Mirzoeff, 654–69. London and New York: Routledge, 2002.

Luvaas, Brent. *Street Style: An Ethnography of Fashion Blogging*. London: Bloomsbury, 2016.

Lynge-Jorlén, Ane. *Between Edge and Elite: Niche Fashion Magazines, Producers and Readers*. London College of Fashion: PhD Thesis, 2009.

—— *Niche Fashion Magazines: Changing the Shape of Fashion*. London and New York: I.B. Tauris, 2017.

Mack, Kimberly. "'There's No Home for You Here': Jack White and the Unsolvable Problem of Blues Authenticity." *Popular Music and Society* 38, no. 2 (2015): 176–93.

Maffesoli, Michel. *The Time of the Tribes: The Decline of Individualism in Mass Society*. D. Smith (trans), Thousand Oaks, CA: Sage, 1996.

Martin, L., H. Gutman, and P.H. Hutton (eds). *Technologies of the Self: A Seminar with Michel Foucault*. Amherst: University of Massachusetts Press, 1988.

Matsoukas, Melina (dir.). *Losing You*, performed by Solange Knowles. Terrible Records, 2012.

Mauss, Marcel. "Techniques of the Body." *Economy and Society* 2, no. 1 (1973): 70–88.

McCauley Bowstead, Jay. "Hedi Slimane and the Reinvention of Menswear." *Critical Studies in Men's Fashion* 2, no. 1 (2015): 23–42.

McLaughlin, Noel. "Rock, Fashion and Performativity." In *Fashion Cultures: Theories, Explorations and Analysis*, edited by Stella Bruzzi and Pamela Church Gibson, 264–85. London: Routledge, 2000.

McLean, Craig. "To Dior for." *The Guardian*, September 25, 2005.

McRobbie, Angela. "Second-hand Dresses and the Role of the Ragmarket." In *Zoot Suits and Second-hand Dresses: An Anthology of Fashion and Music*, edited by Angela McRobbie, 23–49. Basingstoke: Macmillan, 1989.

—— *Postmodernism and Popular Culture*. London and New York: Routledge, 1994.

—— *British Fashion Design: Rag Trade or Image Industry*. London and New York: Routledge, 1998.

—— *The Aftermath of Feminism: Gender, Culture and Social Change*. Thousand Oaks, CA: Sage, 2009.

—— *Be Creative: Making a Living in the New Culture Industries*. Cambridge and Malden, MA: Polity, 2016.

McRobbie, Angela and Jenny Garber. "Girls and Subcultures." In *Resistance through Rituals: Youth Subcultures in Post-war Britain*, edited by Stuart Hall and Tony Jefferson, 209–22. London: Routledge, 1993 [1976].

Mears, Ashley. *Pricing Beauty: The Making of a Fashion Model.* Berkeley, CA: University of California Press, 2011.

Mercer, Kobena. *Welcome to the Jungle: New Positions in Black Cultural Studies.* London and New York: Routledge, 1994.

Miller, Janice. *Fashion and Music.* London: Berg, 2011.

Miller, Monica. *Slaves to Fashion: Black Dandyism and the Styling of Black Diasporic Identity.* Durham, NC: Duke University Press, 2009.

Mort, Frank. *Cultures of Consumption: Masculinities and Social Space in Late Twentieth-Century Britain.* London and New York: Routledge, 1996.

Mower, Sarah. "Runway: Spring 2016 Ready-to-wear: Saint Laurent." *Vogue,* October 5, 2015.

Neal, Mark Anthony. *Looking for Leroy: Illegible Black Masculinities.* New York and London: New York University Press, 2013.

Needham, Alex. "Coachella's Festival Fashion for Men: It's All about the Sexy Springbreak Cowboy." *The Guardian,* April 14, 2015.

Negus, Keith. *Producing Pop: Culture and Conflict in the Popular Music Industry.* London and New York: E. Arnold, 1992.

Niessen, Sandra, Ann Marie Leshkowich, and Carla Jones (eds). *Re-Orienting Fashion: The Globalization of Asian Dress.* Oxford: Berg, 2003.

Nixon, Sean. *Hard Looks: Masculinities, Spectatorship & Contemporary Consumption.* New York: St. Martin's Press, 1996.

—— "Exhibiting Masculinity." In *Representation: Cultural Representations and Signifying Practices,* edited by Stuart Hall, 291–336. London; Thousand Oaks, CA; New Delhi: Sage, 1997.

—— "Resignifying Masculinity: From 'New Man' to 'New Lad.'" In *British Cultural Studies: Geography, Nationality, and Identity,* edited by David Morley and Kevin Robins, 373–86. Oxford: Oxford University Press, 2001.

Norris, Lucy. "Trade and Transformations of Secondhand Clothing: Introduction." *Textile: The Journal of Cloth and Culture* 10, no. 2 (2012): 128–43.

On Call, performed by Kings of Leon. Director uncredited. RCA, 2007.

Palmer, Alexandra. "Vintage Wholes and Vintage Virgins: Second Hand Fashion in the Twenty-first Century." In *Old Clothes, New Looks: Second Hand Fashion,* edited by Alexandra Palmer and Hazel Clark, 197–214. London and New York: Berg, 2005.

Palmer, Alexandra and Hazel Clark (eds). *Old Clothes, New Looks: Second Hand Fashion.* London and New York: Berg, 2005.

Pham, Minh-Ha T. "Susie Bubble is a Sign of the Times." *Feminist Media Studies* 13, no. 2 (2013): 245–67.

—— "Fashion's Cultural-Appropriation Debate: Pointless." *The Atlantic,* May 15, 2014.

—— "'I Click and Post and Breathe, Waiting for Others to See What I See': On #FeministSelfies, Outfit Photos, and Networked Vanity." *Fashion Theory* 19, no. 2 (2015): 221–42.

Polhemus, Ted. "From Sidewalk to Catwalk." *Textile View Magazine* 27 (1994): 28–31.

—— *Streetstyle: From Sidewalk to Catwalk.* London and New York: Thames and Hudson, 1994.

—— *Stylesurfing: What to Wear in the 3rd Millennium*. London and New York: Thames and Hudson, 1996.

—— "In the Supermarket of Style." In *The Clubcultures Reader: Readings in Popular Cultural Studies*, edited by S. Redhead, D. Wynne, and J. O'Connor, 130–3. Oxford and Malden, MA: Blackwell Publishing, 1997.

Porter, Charlie. "Body Politic." *The Guardian*, June 30, 2001.

Purdy, Daniel (ed.). *The Rise of Fashion*. Minneapolis: University of Minnesota Press, 2004.

Rafaeli, JS. "The Definitive History of Landfill Indie in Seven Songs, Narrated by Johnny Borrell." *Noisey*, April 5, 2016.

Raiss, Liz. "28 Portraits that Prove Afropunk is the Most Stylish Festival on Earth." *Fader*, August 24, 2015.

Raphael, Amy. "Sex on a Stick?" *The Face* (March 1994): 68–71.

Ratliff, Ben (host). "Popcast: Pitchfork Post-Mortem." *New York Times*, July 26, 2013.

Rees-Roberts, Nick. "Boys Keep Swinging: The Fashion Iconography of Hedi Slimane." *Fashion Theory* 17, no. 1 (2013): 7–26.

Reiley, Kathryn and Marilyn DeLong. "A Consumer Vision for Sustainable Fashion Practice." *Fashion Practice* 3, no. 1 (2011): 63–83.

Reynolds, Simon. "Against Health and Efficiency: Independent Music in the 1980s." In *Zoot Suits and Second-Hand Dresses: An Anthology of Fashion and Music*, edited by Angela McRobbie, 245–55. Basingstoke: Macmillan, 1989.

—— *Rip it Up and Start Again: Post-punk 1978–84*. London: Faber and Faber, 2005.

Rhodes, Kate. "The Elegance of the Everyday: Nobodies in Contemporary Fashion Photography." In *Fashion as Photograph: Viewing and Reviewing Images of Fashion*, edited by Eugenie Shinkle, 200–13. London and New York: I.B. Tauris, 2008.

Rocamora, Agnès. "Fields of Fashion: Critical Insights into Bourdieu's Sociology of Culture." *Journal of Consumer Culture* 2, no. 3 (2002): 341–62.

—— *Fashioning the City: Paris, Fashion and the Media*. London and New York: I.B. Tauris, 2009.

—— "Personal Fashion Blogs: Screens and Mirrors in Digital Self-portraits." *Fashion Theory* 15, no. 4 (2011): 407–24.

—— "How New Are New Media? The Case of Fashion Blogs." In *Fashion Media: Past and Present*, edited by Djurdja Bartlett, Shaun Cole, and Agnès Rocamora, 155–64. London: Bloomsbury, 2013.

Rocamora, Agnès and Alistair O'Neill. "Fashioning the Street: Images of the Street in the Fashion Media." In *Fashion as Photograph: Viewing and Reviewing Images of Fashion*, edited by Eugenie Shinkle, 185–99. London and New York: I.B. Tauris, 2008.

Rooks, Noliwe. *Hair Raising: Beauty, Culture, and African American Women*. New Brunswick, NJ: Rutgers University Press, 1996.

Rosser, Esther. "Photographing Fashion: A Critical Look at the Sartorialist." *Image & Narrative* 11, no. 4 (2010): 158–70.

Rovine, Victoria. "Working the Edge: XULY.BET's Recycled Clothing." In *Old Clothes, New Looks: Second Hand Fashion*, edited by Alexandra Palmer and Hazel Clark, 215–28. London and New York: Berg, 2005.

Safronova, Valeriya. "Inside Dapper Dan and Gucci's Harlem Atelier." *New York Times*, March 20, 2018.

Schoo, Deidre (photographer). "Vibrantly Original Style at Afropunk Fest." *New York Times*, August 25, 2015.

Scott, Danny. "Festivals!" *The Face* (May 1993): 56–63.

Shunatona, Brooke. "I Made the Mistake of Wearing a Native American Headdress; Please Don't Wear One to Your Music Festival; Or Anywhere, Really." *Cosmopolitan*, April 10, 2015.

Simmel, Georg. "Fashion." In *The Rise of Fashion*, edited by Daniel Purdy, 289–309. Minneapolis, MN: University of Minnesota Press, 2004.

Slimane, H. *Berlin*. Göttingen: Edition 7L/Steidl, 2003.

—— *Stage*. Göttingen: Edition 7L, 2004.

—— *London: Birth of a Cult*. Göttingen: Steidl, 2005.

—— "As Tears Go By". January 7-February 18. Paris: Almine Rech Gallery, 2006.

—— *Rock Diary*. Zürich: JRP|Ringier, 2008.

—— *Anthology of a Decade*. Zürich: JRP|Ringier, 2011.

—— *Hedi Slimane*. Berlin: Stern, 2011.

—— "Sonic." September 18, 2014-January 11, 2015. Paris: Fondation Pierre Bergé-Yves Saint Laurent, 2014-15.

Smedley, Elliot. "Escaping to Reality: Fashion Photography in the 1990s." In *Fashion Cultures: Theories, Explorations and Analysis*, edited by Stella Bruzzi and Pamela Church Gibson, 143–56. London and New York: Routledge, 2000.

Smith, Celia L. "Street Style: Afropunk Festival." *Essence*, August 31, 2012.

Socha, Miles. "Hedi's New Book: For Pete's Sake." *WWD*, June 7, 2005.

Spitz, Marc. "The Rebirth of Cool." *Spin*, January 2003: 52–9.

—— "Gluttony, Envy, Wrath, Vanity, Avarice, Lust, and Sloth? We're Game." *Spin*, February 2005: 46–52.

Spooner, James. *Afropunk: The Movie*. 2003.

Street Porter, Janet. "Editor-at-large: At Last—a Fashion Designer Who Tells Men it's OK to Look Like a Wimp." *The Independent*, February 1, 2004.

Stuart, Mel (dir.). *Wattstax*. Stax Records, 1973.

Sulmers, Claire. "Afropunk Festival 2012." *The Black Blog: Vogue Italia*, August 29, 2012.

Swingle, Marcy (photographer). "Street Style at the Governors Ball." *New York Times*, June 8, 2015.

Testino, Mario (photographer). "Ragged Glory." *Vogue* (September 2013).

Thornton, Sarah. *Club Cultures: Music, Media and Subcultural Capital*. Middletown, CT: Wesleyan University Press, 1996.

Titton, Monica. "Fashionable Personae: Self-identity and Enactments of Fashion Narratives in Fashion Blogs." *Fashion Theory* 19, no. 2 (2015): 201–20.

Tseëlon, Efrat. *The Masque of Femininity: The Presentation of Woman in Everyday Life*. Thousand Oaks, CA: Sage, 1995.

Tu, Thuy Linh Nguyen. *The Beautiful Generation: Asian Americans and the Cultural Economy of Fashion*. Durham, NC: Duke University Press, 2011.

Tulloch, Carol. *The Birth of Cool: Style Narratives of the African Diaspora*. London and New York: Bloomsbury, 2016.

Veblen, Thorstein. "Dress as an Expression of a Pecuniary Culture." In *Fashion Theory: A Reader*, edited by Malcolm Barnard, 339–46. London and New York: Routledge, 1997.

Vernon, Polly. "What Polly Saw . . .: What Makes the Perfect Welly Leg?" *Grazia*, July 11, 2011.

Wadleigh, Michael (dir.). *Woodstock: Three Days of Peace and Music: 40th Anniversary Edition*. Warner Brothers, 2009: 1970.

Wagoner, McKenzie. "Exclusive! SZA Reveals Her New Copper Hair Color Transformation." *Vogue*, March 18, 2015.

—— "5 Beauties Who Answer to Afropunk's Rebellions Call." *Vogue*, August 21, 2015.

Wallace, Martin and Jarvis Cocker (dirs.). *Babies*, performed by Pulp. Gift, 1992.

Wener, Louise. *Just for One Day: Adventures in Britpop*. London: Ebury, 2010.

Whiteley, Sheila. *Women and Popular Music: Sexuality, Identity and Subjectivity*. London: Routledge, 2001.

Williams, Val. *Look at Me: Fashion and Photography in Britain 1960 to the Present*. London: The British Council Visual Arts Publications, 1998.

Wilson, Elizabeth. "Fashion and the Postmodern Body." In *Chic Thrills: A Fashion Reader*, edited by Juliet Ash and Elizabeth Wilson, 3–16. Berkeley and Los Angeles: University of California Press, 1992.

—— *Bohemians: The Glamorous Outcasts*. New Brunswick, NJ: Rutgers University Press, 2000.

Wintour, Anna. "Letter from the Editor." *Vogue* (September 2013).

Wissinger, Elizabeth. "Modeling Consumption: Fashion Modeling Work in Contemporary Society." *Journal of Consumer Culture* 9, no. 2 (2009): 273–96.

—— *This Year's Model: Fashion, Media and the Making of Glamour*. New York and London: New York University Press, 2015.

Wood, Mikael. "Beyoncé Came to Coachella, and Disrupted its Entire Culture." *Los Angeles Times*, April 15, 2018.

Woodward, Sophie. "The Myth of Street Style." *Fashion Theory* 13, no. 1 (2009): 83–101.

INDEX

Index

Index